WHAT IS POLITICAL ECONOMY?

Published under the Auspices of
the Center for International Affairs,
Harvard University

What Is Political Economy?

A Study of Social Theory and Underdevelopment

Martin Staniland

Yale University Press · New Haven and London

Designed by Nancy Ovedovitz and set in Baskerville type by Eastern Graphics. Printed in the United States of America by Vail-Ballou Press, Binghamton, New York.

Library of Congress Cataloging in Publication Data

Staniland, Martin.
What is political economy?
"Published under the auspices of the Center for International Affairs, Harvard University"—
Bibliography: p.
Includes index.
1. Economics. 2. Political science. I. Title.
HB73.S69 1985 338.9 84-13193
ISBN 0-300-03295-1

The paper in this book meets the guidelines for permanence and durability of the Committee on Production Guidelines for Book Longevity of the Council on Library Resources.

10 9 8 7 6 5 4 3 2 1

|| TO ALBERTA AND PAUL

CONTENTS

PREFACE

This book is an exploration of theories of "political economy." Such theories are the latest products of a long-standing intellectual enterprise concerned with understanding the relationship of politics and economics. Those involved in the enterprise have often wanted not just to describe how economics and politics are related but also to suggest how they should be related—to suggest how one should shape the other. In framing their theories, they have also involved themselves in academic arguments about the value and limitations of disciplines, as well as in essentially political arguments about the relationship of theory to action.

In recent times, the work of "theory building" has become more complicated because of the increasing involvement of governments in economic life, because of the growing complexity of international economic relations, and because of the pressures for development in Third World countries. These phenomena render existing theories redundant or at least suspect of oversimplification. But the effort to create theories that comprehend the complexity and variety of contemporary relationships presents great difficulties. One road leads to formulations that are abstract and abstruse, choked with jargon and cluttered with qualification; the other leads to asserting simple, universal verities that may not in fact be universal and indeed may well be oversimplified. In short, there is a tension between comprehensiveness and intelligibility, between the wish of the theorist to develop more sophisticated, more inclusive models and the need of the policymaker, the activist, and the ordinary citizen for analysis that is clear and readily usable for making choices, persuading potential followers, or simply understanding current events.

In writing this book, I have had to face these conflicting demands. I have tried hard to make the exposition of a complex web of ideas as unjargonized as possible and to resist the temptation to digress into the details of specialized professional debates. I have deliberately sacrificed sophistication to maintain an intelligible general argument. This strategy may annoy specialists, but I hope they will understand the reasons for the imperfect treatment of some issues and concepts.

The book consists of three general chapters and four chapters devoted to types of "political economy," especially in their application to Third World countries. Chapter 1 asks why political economy is fashionable, sets out a typology of political economy theory, and examines the basic question of whether general theories of this kind are possible or useful. The second chapter deals with the history of the political economy question, considering criticisms of economics and political science. The last four chapters concern attempts to define the relationship between politics and economics. Chapter 3 examines one solution, that of assimilating politics to economics by applying the assumptions and language of neoclassical economics to political behavior. Chapter 4 examines the opposite theme, that of the "primacy of politics" over economics. Chapter 5 is about "international political economy" in its liberal, mercantilist, and radical versions. The question here is how the problem of relating politics and economics is changed by introducing a dimension concerned with the relationship between "external" (international) and "internal" (domestic) forces. Does addition of this dimension produce better theory? Does it just add greater complication? Or is it simply an adornment of existing theories, transposed to a different plane? Chapter 6 deals with an important tradition of political economy—namely, Marxism. It looks at the problems for understanding politics that are generated by the fundamental assumptions of Marxism and at the particular problems of using a Marxist approach to understanding Third World politics. The concluding chapter raises issues concerning the need for theories and the uses and appeals of different kinds of theory.

Peter Berger remarks in the preface to his book *The Homeless Mind* that the work is "what German scholars call *unabgesichert*—that is, insufficiently protected from critical attacks." So is this one, but that is the price of trying to cover a broad topic and crossing disciplinary lines. Such defenses as it has are largely due to the helpful comments and tactful suggestions of other scholars. I owe a very special debt to Ronald Rogowski of the University of California, Los Angeles, whose friendship and support were crucial to making a book out of a working paper. Among the many others who gave time and thought to criticizing early drafts or otherwise contributed, I want especially to thank Ruth Berins Collier, Donald Emmerson, Dennis Encarnation, Zaki Ergas, Harvey Glickman, Isebill Gruhn, Michael Lipton, Michael Lofchie, Robert Mortimer, Douglas Rimmer, Richard Sklar, Tony Walters, and Joe Zasloff. Dudley Seers made searching and constructive criticisms of earlier drafts; his death was a great loss to all concerned with the moral and intellectual challenges of development to which he devoted his life. I also wish to acknowledge the valuable support extended to me by three institutions while preparing and writing the book: the Institute of International Studies at the University of California, Berkeley; the University Center for International Studies at the University of Pittsburgh; and the Africa Research Program of the Center for International Affairs at Harvard University. Barbara Sindriglis helped me enormously in the final preparation of the manuscript by typing up the draft impeccably and at short notice.

My greatest debt is to my wife and my son, who kept me sane while I drove them mad.

ONE
Fad, Theory, or Problem?

In the 1960s, authors bent on gaining professional recognition gave their books titles or subtitles beginning with the phrase "The politics of (urban renewal/waste disposal/gambling)." Then a change occurred. Subtly but inexorably, the fashionable symbol of earnestness became the prefix "The political economy of. . . ." A quick check of a university library catalog recently revealed some 117 books so titled, covering subjects as diverse as advertising, Appalachia, art, drug trafficking, East–West trade, human rights, independent Fiji, Turkish income distribution, Nasserism, the space program, indirect rule in Mysore, slavery, war, racism, and Pondoland (1860–1930).

Does this change signify anything more than academic faddishness? What, in fact, do writers mean when they refer to "a political economy approach?" Do they all mean the same thing? Why do they prefer such an approach to others?

The answer to the first question is clearly that although the term may be fashionable, it refers to a basic issue in social theory: the relationship between politics and economics. This issue has both explanatory and normative facets: it gives rise to statements about how the two processes are related and about how they should be related. Such statements can be found in the writings of social theorists as far back as Aristotle.

The answers to the other questions are less clear. Many of the books referred to above contain opening statements by their authors that the work in question takes "a" or "the" political economy approach. What this means is sometimes obscure. The "approach" is left undefined, its implications are not spelled out, and indeed often no more is heard about it until the last chapter, where the author announces that the approach has "yielded new insights" or whatever. Sometimes the term *political economy* seems to be a way of dressing up what the authors fear are dull subjects by attaching a title that promises grand theory. Even when the commitment is more substantial, the meanings given to the concept, and the attractions it holds, differ greatly from writer to writer.

For some writers, "political economy" seems to be a formal label applicable to any and all studies dealing with aspects of public policy. It has no particular methodological significance and is just a handy classificatory device, useful for drawing the attention of potential readers, finding books in a publisher's catalog, or rearranging volumes on a shelf. It may, however, signify that the study is concerned with measuring the costs and benefits entailed by particular policies or particular structures of decision-making. In other words, it is concerned with the economics of public policy but with the essentially political questions of who gains, who loses, and how. Closely related to this approach, but philosophically more aggressive, is the "new political economy" school, which wants to apply the assumptions, language, and logic of neoclassical economics to political behavior itself, and indeed to the entire range of public and private decision-making.

But to understand this school's missionary spirit (and why it is "new"), it is useful to appreciate other meanings attached to the term *political economy* and the different values and ambitions they represent. The most easily distinguishable alternative school is socialist political economy. Again, even a superficial glance over any bibliography of political economy reveals a pattern—namely, that at least half of the works using the term treat it as synonymous with Marxism. When the socialist and neoclassical schools are excluded, however, the methodological trail starts to grow faint. In some writing, the call for a political economy approach is less an advertisement for some identifiable methodology than a manifesto of intellectual discontent and even an invitation to the stoning of economists and political scientists. The immediate demand is one for a new agenda. It arises from the belief that a significant relationship exists which established disciplines have ignored or, indeed, are incapable of investigating. It asserts that politics and economics overlap and influence each other and that theoretical analysis should not just take account of this relationship but should be founded on it, should take it as an assumption, and should use concepts that illuminate the relationship.

The trouble is that much writing on political economy implicitly assumes that the term has unequivocal theoretical meaning, while other writing mistakes an agenda for a theory. Writers attached to the two main schools typically make the assumption of theoretical monopoly. This leaves a large number of other writers who content themselves with denouncing the sins of the existing social sciences and calling for (indeed, often claiming to have adopted) a political economy approach. Such an approach is said to be a "methodology" because it recognizes the connection between politics and economics and thus transcends the narrow assumptions of economics and political science.

But this position is like that of a man who thinks he knows how to win at poker because he has noticed a connection between playing cards and getting money. The existence of a connection is not problematic: the problem is to understand what the connection is and how it works. In this respect, political economy may be a victim both of its modishness and of its ideological appeal. Fashion has lent it the status of a theory when it deserves only that of a field—a rather broadly defined field, at that, and one over which control is disputed between opposing theoretical schools. The members of these schools, as well as all the others who favor some sort of "interdisciplinary approach," contribute to creating the impression that the desirability of a political economy approach makes its actual specification a technical detail. In this way, ambition is mistaken for achievement, and the identification of a problem is confused with its solution.

It is always easy to call for an interdisciplinary approach and to deplore the divisions within social science. The hard part is to prescribe "the terms on which a fusion of economics and politics might take place."[1] As Barry Jones has rightly pointed out in discussing the problems of international political economy, it is simplistic and pious merely to urge interdisciplinary cooperation without recognizing the genuine intellectual difficulties that such an enterprise faces.[2]

The fundamental difficulty lies in the radically incompatible perspectives of economics and political science, the first (in its non-Marxian versions) emphasizing markets, the second, power.[3] The assumptions and working logic of economics cannot easily accommodate, except as "externalities," the phenomenon of coercive power, since they rest on the axiom of a freely choosing individual. Equally, political science cannot easily accept the deductive procedures of economics, which seem to insist on exploring an imaginary world of unconstrained rationality instead of the empirically observable world of conflict, misunderstanding, and coercion.

Such intellectual difficulties are compounded by the extreme complexity and heterogeneity of political and economic relations in "the age of the finite world." It is hard enough to summarize in theoretical form the complex of political and economic relations obtaining within one nation-state. To devise a framework that will enable comprehensive yet comprehensible explanation of the maze of relationships within the global complex is an appalling challenge. Theorists working in this field surely deserve combat pay, and it is not surprising that, as Caporaso

1. Christopher Brown, "International Political Economy: Some Problems of an Inter-Disciplinary Enterprise," *International Affairs* 49, no. 1 (January 1973): 58. Brown continues: "Most ideas of the terms of fusion come down essentially to the proposition that one discipline should take over the defining characteristics of the other."

2. R. Barry Jones, "International Political Economy: Perspectives and Prospects—Part II," *Review of International Studies* 8, no. 1 (January 1982): 39. For similar comments on the dangers of forcing together "the intrinsically incompatible," see Michael Barratt Brown, *The Economics of Imperialism* (Harmondsworth: Penguin, 1974), 22, 23.

3. James A. Caporaso, "Pathways between Economics and Politics: Possible Foundations for the Study of Global Political Economy," paper presented at the annual meeting of the American Political Science Association, Chicago, 1–4 September 1983: 3, 26–27.

points out, they have failed to produce satisfactory theories. On the one hand, there are the grand overly abstract and oversimplified constructs of "world-systems theory." On the other, there are detailed case studies of international trade and other aspects of international relations, which offer little material for a general theory of global political economy.[4]

The difficulties of constructing a "global political economy" are not, however, purely analytic. Just as there is an ideological element in all social theory—at least in its starting assumptions—so the quest for a global political economy runs directly into the problem of cultural variety. What set of assumptions and values are truly global in scope? How, at an intellectual level, do we reconcile the undeniably great impact of "international forces" upon nation-states with the equally apparent individuality and heterogeneity of the societies they formally represent?

The point is that the creation, content, and impact of social theory is an ideological and cultural as well as an intellectual matter. The implication is that the work of examining a particular body of theory can take place at two levels. One level involves examining the concepts and logic of the theory and its debts to or conflicts with other theoretical models. The other level involves questions relating less to *content* than to *context*. Why is one kind of theory popular and "relevant" in one society but not in another? How is the usefulness of theory judged by nontheorists? How is the process of theorizing influenced by perceptions of the needs of particular constituencies or situations?

This book broaches both sets of questions, though the first much more than the second. At the level of content, it argues that there are several kinds of political economy theory. *The criterion for identifying such theory is whether or not it claims to depict a systematic relationship between economic and political processes.* Such a relationship may be conceived in different ways—as a causal re-

4. As Caporaso remarks, "the choices confronting the aspiring global political economist are not attractive. On the one hand, the concrete raw materials threaten to vaporize into the airy abstractions and historical meanderings of world systems theory and, on the other, to precipitate themselves into a multitude of micro-oriented, sectoral studies of industrial and commercial policies" (ibid., 5).

lationship between one process and another ("deterministic" theory), as a relationship of reciprocity ("interactive" theory), or as a behavioral continuity.[5] *Whether or not the theory in question is labeled "political economy" is secondary: the important issue is its claim to empirical explanation.*

But the empirical substance is interpreted by using concepts that are drawn from the working vocabularies of particular disciplines and are in fact most intelligible as products of a long process of argument between social theorists, the most recent phase of which dates from the publication of Adam Smith's *The Wealth of Nations*. The distinctions that became current during this process have had a fundamental semantic influence on the shaping of theories of political economy. This is not to deny the possibility of intellectual innovation, but merely to argue that the terms of contemporary arguments are to a great extent defined by the semantic legacy of earlier debates, the most important of which, for present purposes, is the one between liberals and their critics. This debate instituted basic distinctions—between the individual, society, and the state—which have formed a triangular framework shaping later theorizing.

It is, in fact, illuminating to imagine the operation of an intellectual dialectic of which theories of political economy are an outcome. This dialectic could be pursued as far back as the ancient Greeks, but we can reasonably break into it during the Enlightenment. A crude summary of its subsequent development might run as follows:

1. *Orthodox liberalism* regarded the individual (his behavior and interests) as analytically and normatively fundamental; society was seen as an aggregate or an outcome of the pursuit of individual interest; politics (and the state) was likewise just an agency through which individual interests were pursued.

2. *"Social" critiques of liberalism* attacked the liberal assumption that individuals exist and act in isolation and reacted by asserting that "society" shapes individual behavior. (Methodological col-

5. Under this last heading I have in mind "the new political economy" and the public-choice literature that asserts the relevance of a certain kind of rationality in decision-making irrespective of the sphere in which the decisions are made.

lectivism was thus ranged against "methodological individualism.") The former (the demand for social explanations) then divided on the lines of the received distinction between society and the state into:

3a. "*Economism,*" which asserted (as liberals had done) that political processes are an outcome of nonpolitical processes. But whereas liberals saw political processes as an outcome of interactions between individuals, economism saw them as an outcome of interaction between social forces. Such forces might (as in Marxism) be "classes" or (as in pluralist theory) "interest groups." But in both cases the possibility of states or other specifically political structures conceiving and acting to promote interests of their own was excluded.

3b. "*Politicism,*" which asserted that political structures can develop interests of their own and can impose these interests on specific economic interests. "Political rationality" can (to use another formulation) prevail over "economic rationality": "power" was seen as fundamental to the shaping of the economic system.

The plan of this book broadly follows this dialectic, tracing the expression of economistic and politicist approaches in a series of attempts to frame theories of political economy. This scheme embodies the view that political economy has developed as a fugue, with at least two closely related themes: how politics determines aspects of the economy, and how economic institutions determine political processes.[6] But, as noted earlier, deterministic models are only one kind of political economy. There are also interactive models, which conceive politics and economics as being functionally distinguishable but involved in exchange and reciprocal influence.

What kind of model we prefer depends on our own preconceptions about how society works. But it also depends on what we want in a theory. Both issues take us to the level of context. If we want a formula readily adaptable to action, whether by a social engineer (such as a planning administrator) or by a social revolutionary, then the deterministic model is the more attrac-

6. Joe A. Oppenheimer, "Small Steps Forward for Political Economy," *World Politics* 33, no. 1 (October 1980): 121.

tive.[7] It gives a firm view of instrumentality, indicating clearly what has to be changed (or seized) for change to occur elsewhere. It also lends itself well to the demands of political persuasion and rhetoric, enabling responsibility to be unequivocally fixed while sustaining optimism about the possibility of change. Categorical and causal simplicity fosters moral certainty and stimulates political impatience. From such a model we know who the enemy or what the obstacle is: it is definitely not a subtly intricate complex of contingently related variables. Simplicity is the strength, but also the weakness, of such models.

Interactive theories offer the strengths and weaknesses of complexity. They satisfy the intellectual urge to be comprehensive and to develop abstractions of social reality that capture as much as possible the complication and ambiguity of the world as it is (or as intellectuals find it). But the cost of making such seamless garments is to frustrate and annoy those who want ideas that can be quickly translated into policy or revolutionary praxis, who need something they can "get a handle on."[8]

The contrast between these types of model reflects a tension between demands made of social theory, specifically, between the demand for intellectual sophistication and the demand for usability and relevance. Such tension is expressed in arguments about professional legitimacy: what loyalties economists, for instance, should have; how conflicts of loyalty should be resolved; and what kinds of ideas and methods are implied by specific professional loyalties. The same problem exists outside the academic community among those who want to order or redirect societies. Such people are not dependent on academic theorists

7. As Henry Oliver remarks, "When policy interests govern the questions asked, the flow of causation is, of course, that dictated by the nature of the decision considered" ("Study of the Relationships between Economic and Political Systems," *Journal of Economic Issues* 7, no. 4 (December 1973): 509.

8. Joseph Schumpeter, in discussing the weaknesses of Marxist history, concluded with exasperation that many of the problems he had identified in Marxism could be solved by building in interaction between "the sphere of production and other spheres of social life. But [he noted] the glamour of fundamental truth that surrounds it depends precisely on the strictness and simplicity of the one-way relation which it asserts." Joseph A. Schumpeter, *Capitalism, Socialism and Democracy* (London: George Allen and Unwin, 1954), 13.

for the generation of ideas, and their criteria may be at odds with those which academics would apply.

The question of how the world of theory-building relates and should relate to the surrounding world of ideologies and action is taken up in the final chapter. I raise it here because much of what follows may seem entirely abstract to people concerned with pressing political and developmental issues. In fact, I sympathize strongly with those who feel that social theory has become excessively theoretical and self-absorbed. But there are dangers in an excessive, anti-intellectual reaction, and I think it is important to end by airing the larger issues and implications associated with theorizing about economic and political development, especially in the poorer countries of the world, and that occur to anybody with even a minimum of curiosity and compassion. Ideas not only have to work: they have to be seen to work. Political economy is not just a fad. It expresses a continuing effort to make a highly complex reality intelligible. For some theorists, it also represents the hope that, by being made intelligible, the reality can be made more manageable and better.

TWO
The Fall and Rise of Political Economy

In this and subsequent chapters, I explore the attempts of theorists to conceptualize the relationship between the world of public power and decision-making, politics, and the world of production and distribution, economics. Before looking at contemporary attempts, it is useful to consider the intellectual history of this enterprise.

Because we are dealing with a fundamental relationship, it is not surprising to find extensive (even overwhelming) discussion of the subject, as well as a profusion of definitions and approaches. Much of the argument converges on the term *political economy*, which carries a weight of historical associations as well as symbolizing, for many, the promise of intellectual progress in the field. What follows is necessarily schematic and involves a sacrifice of sophistication and detail for the sake of illuminating central issues and showing the deeper coherence underlying them.

POLITICAL ECONOMY AND ECONOMICS

Historically, the turning point in the development of ideas about the relationship of politics to economics clearly occurred in the eighteenth century. Previously, a *functional* division was accepted: it was agreed that *economics* and *politics* referred to distinct arenas of activity. But this analytic convention by no means meant that economics could be conducted practically or conceived theoretically as though it were self-sufficient in a moral, political, or intellectual sense. From the time of Aristotle until the late Middle Ages, the idea that economic processes could yield their own laws, generate their own imperatives, or provide the basis for a separate intellectual discipline was foreign to prevailing ethical and explanatory traditions. Economics was a means to realize specific moral ends or (in the mercantilist period of the sixteenth and seventeenth centuries) a means to sustain and increase political power (that of the state and the sovereign). In ancient Greece (or at least in Aristotle's *Politics*), economics was subsumed under the study of politics, itself part of a broad ethical and philosophical inquiry.[1] It was conceived initially as the art of domestic management, from which, by extension, the earliest meaning of *political economy* developed, referring to the art of managing a country's economy.[2] As the mercantilist James Steuart put it, *economy* was "the art of providing for all the wants of a family, with prudence and frugality. What oeconomy is in a family, political oeconomy is in a state."[3] Thus the role of the statesman was, "like the good father of a family, to provide everything necessary for supplying the wants

1. Gunnar Myrdal, *The Political Element in the Development of Economic Theory* (New York: Simon and Schuster, 1954), 56; D. M. Winch, "Political Economy and the Economic Polity," *Canadian Journal of Economics* 10, no. 4 (November 1977): 548; Joseph Cropsey, "On the Relation of Political Science and Economics," *American Political Science Review* 54 (March 1960): 8–11; Paresh Chattopadhyay, "Political Economy: What's in a Name?" *Monthly Review* 25 (April 1974): 23; William Anderson, "Political Science, Economics and Public Policy," *American Economic Association, Papers and Proceedings* 34, no. 1 (March 1944): 78.

2. In reference books, political economy is defined as "economic thought regarded as a branch of statecraft" (Alan Gilpin, *Dictionary of Economic Terms* [London: Butterworth's, 1966], 160); "the study of the most efficient and economical ways of operating a government" (John T. Zadrogny, *Dictionary of Social Science* [Washington, D.C.: Public Affairs Press, 1959], 254); and "an eighteenth-century branch of the art of government concerned with directing governmental policies toward the promotion of the wealth of the government and the community as a whole" (*Webster's Third New International Dictionary* [Springfield, Mass.: E. and C. Merriam and Co., 1976]), 1755. On the tradition of regarding the political community as a household, see Myrdal, *Political Element*, xi, 140–47.

3. *An Inquiry into the Principles of Political Economy* (1761) repr. 1967 (New York: Augustus M. Kelley), 1:2.

of the society and its members and to regulate the employment of the latter with a view to this end."[4]

Adam Smith and his successors opposed this doctrine as paternalistic. But they and many nineteenth-century economists held to its fundamental premise—the ultimate compatibility of individual and public interests—even while rejecting the authority and capacity of the state to create and manage economic development. Smith saw political economy as "a branch of the science of a statesman or legislator." But, compared to earlier writers, he enlarged the range of intended beneficiaries and restricted the role of government in satisfying them.[5] The aims of political economy, he argued, should be "first, to provide a plentiful revenue or subsistence for the people, or more properly to enable them to provide such a revenue or subsistence for themselves; and secondly, to supply the state or commonwealth with a revenue sufficient for the public services. It proposes to enrich both the people and the sovereign."[6] Smith's emphasis on "the people" and on their economic activity as a source of wealth contrasted sharply with the mercantilists' emphasis on the state as both source and beneficiary of economic growth. He explicitly wanted to remove from government "the duty of superseding the industry of private people and of directing it towards the employment most suitable to the interests of society."[7]

For the individual sovereign pursuing his interest, Smith sub-

4. "H. S.," "Political Economy: Scope," in *Palgrave's Dictionary of Political Economy,* ed. Henry Higgs (New York: August M. Kelley, 1894 [repr. 1963]), 129. The author claims that "originally the political economy was—as its name suggests—conceived to be the common portion of two arts, 'economy in general' and the art of government. 'Economy in general' was the art of regulating the employment of a family, or other group of human beings, so as to provide for all the wants of its members with prudence and frugality. 'Political economy,' accordingly, was conceived as the same art in its application to the group of human beings forming a political society or state. It was thus concerned with what was regarded as the chief *Domestic* business of a statesman" (italics in original).

5. *An Inquiry into the Nature and Causes of the Wealth of Nations,* ed. Edwin Cannan (New York: The Modern Library, 1937), bk. 4, p. 397.

6. Ibid., 397.

7. Ibid., 651.

stituted the sovereign individual pursuing his. Yet in his writing, Smith continued to see society as an organism: while transferring responsibility for its prosperity from the head to the members, he tacitly discounted the possibility of serious conflict and insuperable incompatibility of interests. If there was no likelihood of conflict, it should be possible to calculate what was in the public interest without threatening to infringe the right of each individual to determine and pursue his or her own "utility." The question of "how to make the multitude into a unified subject of valuations" was, then, essentially a technical question.[8]

This notion of a scientifically determinable general welfare accounts for certain paradoxes in the subsequent development of economics and, in some eyes, for the subsequent confusion of economists. Liberal political economy firmly believed in the reality and importance of collective phenomena, but its teaching firmly opposed intervention by public authorities in the basic economic processes of production and distribution. Its analysis rested on essentially normative terms, such as *value*, *welfare*, and *utility*, and drew heavily on the assumptions of natural law.[9] Yet economics saw itself as a skeptical science and, particularly with the advent of neoclassical economics, its practitioners portrayed it as a specialized, "positive" science, eschewing value judgments, public advocacy, and noneconomic factors. Increasingly, the science of economics gained over the science of legislation and

8. Myrdal, *Political Element*, 140. Economists since Smith have maintained either a highly individualistic or a highly organic view of society and have therefore been impatient of "politics." Indeed, in 1944 Frank Knight, in a discussion of possible interdisciplinary cooperation, complained, "Many political scientists teach their students to view politics as a struggle for power rather than a mechanism of cooperation" ("Economics, Political Science, and Education," *American Economic Association. Papers and Proceedings* 34, no. 1 [March 1944]: 75). In the late sixties, I was approached by a senior economist who had been invited by a West African government to head a large and expensive team of consultants. He needed an instant evaluation of the government itself. He asked, "Are they good chaps?" The political weaknesses of orthodox economists are considered later in this chapter.

9. Myrdal, *Political Element*, 14, 17–22; Cropsey, "Political Science and Economics," 13–14.

eventually the adjective *political* was dropped in favor of *economics* ("pure" or "positive").[10] Moreover, this science proceeded deductively, setting out from a limited number of abstract postulates and developing their implications—a procedure that enabled it to disregard, or to treat as manipulable, factors not covered by the original postulates. Yet, despite the self-conscious "academicization" of economics, economists continued to be vocal on policy matters, and politicians and the public saw economics as embodying laws and maxims that were "natural" and compelling rather than abstract and speculative.

POLITICAL SYSTEMS AND POLITICAL SCIENCE

Positive economics always had its critics and would-be successors, notably the institutionalists and the Marxists (both discussed later). Just as important, however, was the development of a liberal political science that shared the neoclassical economists' belief in separating politics and economics and treating each as constituting a self-sufficient realm of its own. However, theoretical development of this view came later in political science than in economics. Indeed, it really emerged only after World War II, with the advent of behavioralism and the concept of a political system.[11] But the previous orthodoxy in political science—which emphasized the study of institutional structure and constitutional law—rested, albeit implicitly, on the assumption of systemic separation. Moreover, political science was torn (perhaps even more than economics) by disputes between those who wanted an applied and "relevant" discipline committed to the reform of political life, and those who wanted to emulate the natural sciences—an ambition that fired the behavioral move-

10. Myrdal, *Political Element*, 7–13; Joel Jalladeau, " Restrained or Enlarged Scope of Political Economy? A Few Observations," *Journal of Economic Issues* 9, no. 1 (March 1975): 1; Brian Barry, *Sociologists, Economists and Democracy* (Chicago: University of Chicago Press, 1978), 11; Chattopadhyay, "Political Economy," 25.

11. See, for example, David B. Truman, "Disillusion and Regeneration: The Quest for a Discipline," *American Political Science Review* 59, no. 4 (December 1965): 865–73.

ment, with its disdain for moralizing and its emphasis on observation and measurement.

Just as positive economists such as Lionel Robbins argued that economics could and should rise above value judgments, so such political scientists as Gabriel Almond and Heinz Eulau argued that contemporary political science was distinguished by its dispassionate attitude toward its subject matter.[12] Almond, in his presidential address to the American Political Science Association in 1966, suggested that whereas theorists of the Enlightenment had been concerned with influencing and improving political life, contemporary theorists were interested in "how the Leviathan itself comes into existence."[13] Political scientists had managed, Almond believed, both to isolate their subject matter and to detach themselves from it. The first had been achieved by adopting the concept of a "political system":

> The principal advantage of the system concept is that it analytically differentiates the object of study from its environment. . . . [In] our efforts to establish the properties of political systems, compare them with each other, and classify them into types, we explicitly separate structure from function, structure from culture, social systems from political systems, empirical properties from their normative implications.[14]

In the same way, political science had liberated itself from tinkering with the ship of state. As Eulau remarked: "It is the function of science to understand and interpret the world, not to change it."[15] Political science differed from economics in that it tended to be more inductive. Rather than moving out from a set of postulates about individual psychology, it sought to test hy-

12. Robbins's view of "positive economics" is examined on pages 39–40; see also his article, "Economics and Political Economy," *American Economic Review. Papers and Proceedings* 71, no. 2 (May 1981): 1–10, and his earlier book, *An Essay on the Nature and Significance of Economic Science* (London: Macmillan, 1946 repr.).

13. Gabriel Almond, "Political Theory and Political Science," *American Political Science Review* 60, no. 4 (December 1966): 877.

14. Ibid., 876.

15. Heinz Eulau, *The Behavioral Persuasion in Politics* (New York: Random House, 1963), 9.

potheses linking particular variables (say, levels of education and levels of political participation), or it created large conceptual frameworks that would supposedly enable comparison of political systems themselves to be conducted. But the intellectual assumptions, professional ambitions, and political postures of orthodox political science closely resembled those of mainstream, neoclassical economics.

CRITIQUES OF UNIDISCIPLINARY SCIENCE

Grumbling about the inadequacies of both economics and political science took numerous forms and proposed different cures. Behind it lay several important changes in the non-academic world that undermined the working assumptions of the disciplines concerned.

The most important change was the increasing intervention by government in the economies of industrialized countries and the legitimacy given such intervention by the work of John Maynard Keynes. As Joe Oppenheimer has put it, "once Keynesian economics had given politicians a justified role in economics, economic theory could no longer be closed to political variables."[16] A sense of the consequent redundancy of disciplinary boundaries, and the unreality of the assumptions of economics, dominated discussions at a joint meeting of the American Economics Association (AEA) and the American Political Science Association (APSA) in 1944. One distinguished economist declared:

> Politics used to have a comfortable amount of the feeling that politics propose, but something called "economic law" disposes. Nowadays, they are forced to entertain an uncomfortable suspicion that economics proposes and politics disposes. Market forces operate on sufferance, and the "economic law" that decides what happens consists largely of things like the policies of the Triple-A and the decisions of the Federal Trade Commission.[17]

16. Joe A. Oppenheimer, "Small Steps Forward for Political Economy," *World Politics* 33, no. 1 (October 1980): 124.

17. J. M. Clark, "Educational Functions of Economics after the War," *American Economic Association. Papers and Proceedings* 34, no. 1 (March 1944): 59. For a later

Neoclassical economics, with its emphasis on the rational, maximizing individual and its assumption of perfect competition, could neither account for nor cope with a world in which economic life was dominated by large firms that could manipulate markets (and influence consumers' own perceptions of need).[18] Nor had it much to contribute to debates about "public goods," the level and character of which were heavily affected by nonmarket or at least noneconomic factors. Last, orthodox economics could contribute little to the evaluation of the purest political economies—those in socialist countries. Clearly, some theoretical redesigning was needed to deal with a world in which the polity had become "a process for economizing as well as a system of authority and power, while the economy [had] become a system of power as well as a process for economizing."[19]

Increasing government intervention in the industrialized economies was thus one factor creating uneasiness about the assumptions and concepts of liberal economics. Another was the belief that colonial powers—and even the industrialized world as a whole—had a duty to foster economic growth in the poorer tropical countries. Indeed, as early as 1944, at the AEA/APSA meeting referred to earlier, one speaker remarked that public intervention would be greatly stimulated by the "desire to push forward the progress of backward areas and peoples with a view to their ultimate independence."[20] By the late 1950s, the challenge of development to social scientists in general and economists in particular had intensified intellectually, politically, and

---

plea by Clark for interdisciplinary cooperation, see his book *Economic Institutions and Human Welfare* (New York: Alfred A. Knopf, 1957).

18. Winch, "Political Economy," 558ff.; John Kenneth Galbraith, "Power and the Useful Economist," *American Economic Review* 63, no. 1 (March 1973): 1–11; Allan Gruchy, "Law, Politics, and Institutional Economics," *Journal of Economic Issues* 7, no. 4 (December 1973): 625.

19. John E. Elliott, "Institutionalism as an Approach to Political Economy," *Journal of Economic Issues* 12, no. 1 (March 1978): 102–03.

20. William Anderson, "Political Science," 84. See also, A. W. Coats, "The Politics of Political Economists: Comment," *Quarterly Journal of Economics* 7, no. 4 (November 1960): 669, where it is suggested that concern with less-developed countries was exposing the "historical and institutional limitations of the competitive market economy on which so much theorizing has been based."

emotionally. Public opinion in industrialized countries became more aware of poverty in the Third World: academics and Third World politicians agreed that such poverty should be eliminated quickly and that planning and direct state intervention were essential to this purpose. Clearly, economic theory that denied a role to government was liable to be dismissed. But what was to replace it? Socialism was not acceptable to late colonial governments if it meant expropriation of private property and the creation of a large public sector. Also, the practicality and political wisdom of increasing the responsibilities and power of public officials were dubious in societies that offered temptations for the worst vices of bureaucracy. Yet, the indigenous private sector was typically weak, while foreign business continued to dominate external trade and sometimes domestic production and retail trading, even after independence.

So governments had to act, and social scientists were expected to help them. But the help they could provide was restricted by the cultural and conceptual limitations of the ideas and knowledge they had. Furthermore, the ideological battles of the 1960s stirred up fundamental issues of professional legitimacy, forcing social scientists to examine not only the intellectual and practical adequacy of their theories, but also the values underlying them and the political commitments they implied. Add to this the complaints of Third World intellectuals about the "cultural imperialism" of Western social science, and the welter of criticism directed at social science becomes overwhelming.

Criticism was broadly of three kinds: moral, political, and explanatory. These categories often overlapped and reinforced each other, but the conclusions critics drew from each often diverged.

The Moral Critique

By the moral critique, I mean the view that economists (and political scientists) had become "mere principleless technicians" and had betrayed the original reforming mission of political economy.[21] Economics in particular was attacked for its cultiva-

21. Frank D. Graham, "Discussion," *American Economic Association. Papers and Proceedings* 34, no. 1 (March 1944): 57. Economists, Graham remarked, "may be

tion of an approach that stressed "avoidance of explicit value judgments and dependence on relationships capable of rigorous expression, preferably mathematical notation."[22] As Duncan MacRae observed: "More than any other social science, economics has divested itself of controversial valuative concerns during the past half century, and has developed a self-contained, professional discourse. This discourse is seen as primarily that of positive science and as excluding valuative assertions."[23] One variation on this argument was to suggest, as Gunnar Myrdal did, that the value-freedom of economics is deceptive, that "basic concepts are frequently charged with normative implications":

> The linguistic forms which tradition offers to the economic theorist ensnare him at every turn in their old-accepted associations. They continually tempt him to propound variations and rules of conduct when he should only describe and explain disinterestedly. . . . From the point of view of its ideological origins, political economy is a grandiose attempt to state in scientific terms what ought to be.[24]

Unlike others (such as O. H. Taylor and Robert Heilbroner), Myrdal did not want to see economists return to moral and political commitment. Indeed, he argued (oddly like some positive economists) for a clear distinction between the roles of scientist and advocate: science could not indicate values or resolve conflicts of value. The economist could contribute to a "rational politics" by providing information and by clarifying the choices available.[25]

---

endowed with a vague good will but their *ad hoc* solutions of any posited problem are often quite alien to the spirit in which classical economics was conceived. The solutions have, inevitably, normative implications, but what they are is seldom asserted or even realized." For a similar protest against the profession's "exclusive respect for and cultivation of narrow, technical, purely economic—and scientific—methods," see O. H. Taylor, "Economic Science Only—Or Political Economy?" *Quarterly Journal of Economics* 71, no. 1 (February 1957): 1–18.

22. Robert Heilbroner, "On the Possibility of a Political Economics," *Journal of Economic Issues* 4, no. 4 (December 1970): 3.

23. Duncan MacRae, Jr., "Normative Assumptions in the Study of Public Choice," *Public Choice* 16 (Fall 1973): 28.

24. *Political Element*, 192, 195.

25. Ibid., 193–206.

Another variation was to claim that the amoral complexion of economics was not the fault of economists but was due to an abdication by political philosophy. Thus Joseph Cropsey claimed that attempts to reassemble political economy failed because they misconceived the proper basis of the relationship. Until the eighteenth century "nature" (and economics) had been regarded as subordinate. It was something to be mastered and shaped, property especially being a means, not an end—much less a basis—of political and moral theory. Unchecked acquisitiveness and mindless obedience to nature were thought to subvert civilization. From the time of John Locke, nature and "natural law" became the dominant frame of reference for political and economic theory, and the preservation (and enlargement) of property the rationale of government, at least in Western Europe and the United States.[26] An "essentially economic order of society" was established, converting nature from a means to an end, and reducing the job of the philosopher to that of elaborating the laws and injunctions of nature:

> In confining itself to making explicit what is implicit in man's primitive state, political philosophy caused itself to be supplanted primarily by economics, the discipline that systematically enlarges upon the self-preserving motive of pre-civil man. Political science inherited as its content the ministerial questions pertaining to the support of the essentially economic order of society. In this way, and in the indicated order of rank, economics and political science arose out of the self-limitation of political philosophy.[27]

The answer, in Cropsey's view, was to reestablish "the unalienable hegemony of political philosophy."

The Political Critique

By "political," writers such as Cropsey meant not just the way in which power was distributed and exercised, but also the choice and pursuit of values by a collectivity. There was the empirical fact of power, and there was the moral question of authority. Critics argued that, just as economics had abandoned

26. Cropsey, "Political Science and Economics," 8–13.
27. Ibid., 14.

normative commitments, so it had ignored the existence of power.[28] According to Donald Winch, this neglect stemmed from the deepest assumptions of liberal economics: "Perfect competition is the structure of a non-power society, a world in which everybody is a nobody. Once the logical edifice of the theoretical structure was complete the task appeared to reduce to keeping at bay the bogeyman of power."[29] Economics had concentrated on "bloodless 'man-to-nature' or 'man-to-himself' concepts," assuming that a harmonious equilibrium would be achieved through the pursuit of individual self-interest.[30] The intellectual and aesthetic appeal of developing the framework set up by Smith, Ricardo, and their associates had been so great as to crowd out inconvenient factors—power, nonpecuniary motives, group behavior, and the like.[31] Certainly, the emergence of monopolies disturbed neoclassical assumptions and indeed gave rise to institutional economics, which recognized the existence of organizations and collective interests and the reality of their power and of conflict between them. But mainstream economics managed to disregard the institutionalists (whose concern, indeed, sometimes seemed limited to devising conditions in which there might be really effective competition). Most importantly, monopoly was interpreted (conveniently but negatively) as the absence of competition rather than as an instance

28. Such complaints are legion, but see notably Heilbroner, "Political Economics," 10–11; K. W. Rothschild, ed., *Power in Economics* (Harmondsworth: Penguin, 1971), 7–14; Philip A. Klein, "Confronting Power in Economics: A Pragmatic Evaluation," *Journal of Economic Issues* 14, no. 4 (December 1980): 871–96; Michel de Vroey, "The Transition from Classical to Neoclassical Economics: A Scientific Revolution," *Journal of Economic Issues* 9, no. 3 (September 1975): 427, 435; Robert Solo, "The Need for a Theory of the State," *Journal of Economic Issues* 11, no. 2 (June 1977): 379–80; Michael Zweig, "New Left Critique of Economics," *Review of Radical Political Economics* 3, no. 2 (July 1971): 71; Gruchy, "Law, Politics," 627–28; Myrdal, *Political Element*, 193–98; and most recently, Paul Diesing, *Science and Ideology in the Social Sciences* (New York: Aldine Publishing Co., 1982), 40–41.

29. Winch, "Political Economy," 549–50.

30. Elliott, "Institutionalism," 103.

31. Rothschild, *Power in Economics*, 10–11. See also, Mark Blaug, "Kuhn versus Lakatos, or Paradigms versus Research Programmes in the History of Economics," *History of Political Economy* 7, no. 4 (Winter 1975): 399–433.

of the exercise of power. The question of power could thus still be ignored.[32]

This critique gave rise to a demand for analysis that acknowledged the existence of groups and organizations and encompassed the exercise of power. The radicals of the 1960s put this demand in a more specific form, calling for analysis that used the language of class conflict and urging a commitment by economists to help those who found themselves the subjects of power in capitalist societies. John Gurley, one of the "radical political economists" in the American Economics Association, compared the radical and conventional approaches thus:

> A political economist sees [the] power structures and puts them at the forefront of his analysis; a conventional economist—who sees only a society of free, self-interested economic men interacting as equals in the marketplace—does not. . . . The conventional economist not only fails to take account of relations of power and authority, and so fails to grasp the most socially relevant aspects of the problem, but, by being so blind to class interests and so caught up in his data and his techniques, he in effect supports a system that maltreats large numbers of people. . . . The political economist turned radical, on the other hand, not only studies economic problems within the historical context of ruler–subject relations, but he actively takes the side of the poor and the powerless, and he generally sees the system of capitalism as their oppressor.[33]

The charge against economists, then, was either that they suffered collectively from a "ritual power blindness," a *professional* disability born of a certain intellectual heritage, or that they were positively and politically conservative.[34]

32. Rothschild, *Power in Economics*, 11–12.

33. John Gurley, "The State of Political Economics," *American Economic Review* 61, no. 2 (May 1971): 55.

34. The phrase "ritual power blindness" occurs in H. Albert, "The Neglect of Sociology in Economic Science," in Rothschild, *Power in Economics*, 28. The charge of conservatism was made not only by Marxists, but also by radicals such as Heilbroner and even by liberals such as George Stigler: see Heilbroner, "Political Economics," 4–5; George J. Stigler, "The Politics of Political Economists," *Quarterly Journal of Economics* 73, no. 4 (November 1959): 522–32; and the exchange between John Weeks and Michael Zweig over the causes and cures of "reactionary" analysis in economics, in *Review of Radical Political Economics* 3, no. 2 (July 1971): 57–83.

The Explanatory Critique

The explanatory critique was really an extension of the criticism of "power blindness." But it was broader in scope and was particularly voiced by those concerned for the success of development planning. It argued that the perspective of economics, no matter how elegantly logical, was excessively narrow and excluded a great range of "noneconomic factors."[35] Such factors might be political, but they could include all beliefs and practices that did not conform to the rationality of neoclassical economics. Their exclusion made it difficult to explain behavior and implement policy, especially in societies with cultures and histories different from those of the societies in which classical political economy had developed its view of "economic man."

Essentially, this critique concentrated on psychology and values, and it suggested that conventional economics was shallow as well as narrow. It attacked economics for making a priori assumptions about consumer preferences, without considering "the mechanisms of want creation in a social system, the process by which preferences are formed, the distribution of power and its role in economic society, the interplay of social classes, the forces that tend to disrupt equilibrium, the conflicts, the contradictions, the structural changes. The examination of all these problems is abandoned to the other social sciences."[36] Economics was thus ahistorical as well as apolitical. And when it tried to account for change, it generally did so in a simple, unifactoral manner, choosing variables that were familiar, easily measurable, and congruent with its view of change in Western societies.

DEVELOPMENT AND THE "NONECONOMIC FACTOR"

Scholars and policymakers interested in the problems of Third World development were especially critical of the weak-

35. "Analytical elegance, economy of theoretical means, and generality obtained by even more 'heroic' assumptions have always meant more to economists than relevance and predictability" (Blaug, "Kuhn versus Lakatos," 410).

36. Jalladeau, "Restrained or Enlarged Scope," 4. For similar criticisms of the economic view of psychology, see, for example, Clark, "Educational Functions," 65, and particularly A. G. Papandreou, "Economics and the Social Sciences," *Economic Journal* 60 (December 1950): 715–23.

nesses of conventional economic analysis. Two examples will suffice, one from the work of the sociologist Everett Hagen, the other from a study of Trinidad made by Dudley Seers.

In a comparative article on development in Asia, Hagen pointed out that, according to the simpler models of development (which emphasized the spread of "modernity" and the accompanying opportunities for technological diffusion), Indonesia should be the most industrialized Asian country, followed by India and China, with Japan the least developed. Indonesia, after all, had had the longest contact with and exposure to Western institutions and ideas, while Japan had had the shortest. In fact, using all the conventional indicators of growth, the order came out as precisely the reverse. The moral, Hagen argued, was that "noneconomic factors [such as religious beliefs, attitudes to work and leisure, and the criteria of social status] must enter fully into the theoretical system as variables, with causal relationships flowing to as well as from them." The trouble was, he added, that although economists piously acknowledged the need "to take account of non-economic factors," they then "treated these factors much as Mark Twain accused everyone of treating the weather"—they talked about it but didn't *do* anything about it.[37]

Seers's account of the unemployment problem in Trinidad illustrates the inadequacies of orthodox economic analysis when brought to bear on questions of development strategy.[38] The dilemma here was that, although the island had a fairly high growth rate and (by Third World standards) was endowed with adequate physical resources, it had a steadily rising rate of unemployment. According to the canons of orthodox market economies, such a situation was as anomalous as the bumblebee in aerodynamics: with high unemployment, wages should have fallen, attracting capital for labor-intensive, import-substitution

37. Everett E. Hagen, "Turning Parameters into Variables in the Theory of Economic Growth," *American Economic Review. Papers and Proceedings* 50, no. 2 (May 1960): 623–25.

38. Dudley Seers, "A Step towards a Political Economy of Development: Illustrated by the Case of Trinidad/Tobago," *Social and Economic Studies* 18, no. 3 (September 1969): 217–53.

industries. In fact, wages had gone up (indeed, they had risen more steeply as unemployment mounted), import-substitution had failed, and the government had not devised any alternative.

Why? Seers concluded that it was "the non-economic factors which [made] a plausible economic solution hard to implement."[39] Such factors included high population growth (and the attitudes toward family, economic survival, and social mobility behind it), the educational system (which created a preference for white-collar jobs), the weaknesses of the civil service as an instrument of development policy, the political strength of labor unions, the power of foreign companies already installed in Trinidad, and the influence of foreign governments. Underlying the problem was "a set of tastes and attitudes, largely imported from abroad, which [meant] that a large section of the population would rather, in the last resort, face a continuation of chronic unemployment than a reduction in their consumption of imports."[40] Full employment depended on "apparently remote issues such as the syllabi of teacher-training college and how diplomats do their jobs." Just as importantly, successful policymaking depended on more relevant and realistic analysis. Economists had satisfied themselves with building models incorporating "exogenous" and "endogenous" variables and assuming that they had "analysed—or even solved—some problem, when they [had] merely used the variables in the model, usually the sort of variables to which economists [had] conventionally confined their attention."[41] There were, in short, two problems: the problem of developmental failure in Trinidad and the problem of how it was perceived by economists. Seers concluded, reasonably enough: "The unemployment problem looks insoluble in Trinidad and many other countries so long as one searches for optimal values of the manipulable 'variables.' The start of the road to a solution is to realize that these variables cannot be altered significantly until certain 'constants' have been manipulated."[42]

39. Ibid., 240.
40. Ibid.
41. Ibid., 251.
42. Ibid., 251–52.

THE "IRRELEVANCE" OF POLITICAL SCIENCE

In political science, very similar criticisms were made of behavioralism and its parallel orthodoxy, structural-functionalism. Political scientists were said to be overly concerned with imitating the physical sciences and, as a result, were "isolated from those they study, researching only those aspects of politics that receive methodological certification as defined by the paradigm."[43] Not only was their work irrelevant, but despite its supposed scientific objectivity it actually rested on normative assumptions "supportive of the *status quo* in the United States."[44] The concepts used for analyzing political development in Third World countries were said to be ethnocentric and biased toward liberal democratic values and institutions. Political science should identify itself with the struggle against inequality and oppression whether in the United States or in the countries subject to American imperialism. In order to do so, it needed a perspective that would take account of the nonpolitical forces bearing on the political system (those forces which, in the view of critics, made American pluralism as well as Third World nation-building, so ineffectual). Such a perspective would need to comprehend economic and political dimensions and in certain cases would need to have an international dimension.

The critiques reviewed in this section all pointed in the same direction. Most critics of economics would have endorsed Galbraith's verdict that the discipline's theoretical orthodoxy amounted to "an unrewarding combination of economics and archeology with wishful thinking."[45] Moreover, the "profound sense of dissatisfaction" which Heilbroner felt about economics was shared not just by radicals but also by development advisers and academics who wanted more sophisticated ways of under-

43. J. Peter Euben, "Political Science and Political Silence," in Philip Green and Sanford Levinson, eds., *Power and Community* (New York: Random House, 1969), 43.

44. Preface, to Green and Levinson, *Power and Community*, vii.

45. Galbraith, "Useful Economist," 4.

standing social processes—models that would provide a more reliable basis for prediction than those they had.

Similar criticisms were made of other social sciences. But proposals for reform usually focused on economics—an implicit tribute to the discipline's centrality and its reputation as the most scientifically sophisticated and publicly influential of the social sciences. The usual aim of reformers was (in Heilbroner's words) "to join the dimensions of political and sociological reality onto the flatland models through which conventional economics seeks to explicate the nature of the existing social order."[46] The outcome would be "an interdisciplinary general system, encompassing all aspects of the behavior of a society, and not merely its economic behavior."[47]

ECONOMICS: DEFENDING THE PARAMETER

Economists did not necessarily accept the criticisms of their discipline, least of all when they attacked its philosophical core. Their response to the demand for interdisciplinary cooperation typically took one of three forms (none of them acceptable to the critics). The first was to reassert the validity of the traditional assumptions and methodology of their discipline. The second was to try to accommodate the critics by a selective grafting of noneconomic variables onto essentially unchanged economic models. The third was to propose *wider* application of the methodology of liberal economics. The remainder of this chapter is concerned with the first two responses. The next chapter explores the third, expressed in the literature of "rational choice."

The Integrity of Economics

Against critics, the defenders of economics have argued that their discipline's cumulative intellectual achievements are standing proof of the validity—and superiority—of its methods. As the Scottish economist Duncan Black declared when arguing for

46. Heilbroner, "Political Economics," 1–2.
47. Hagen, "Parameters into Variables," 625.

the assimilation of political science by economics: "Economic science has been built up progressively and continuously over two centuries; it has worked its way through to a language which has laid an always firmer grasp on the concepts necessary for thought; the progress has been made by a succession of distinguished thinkers, each taking over and developing the work of his predecessors."[48] Political science, on the other hand, had been "little cultivated": "Its lists contain few names of a lustre similar to those of Economics; it has nothing to show of the same continuity of Development as Economics. In the one science the heritage of language is much richer, of greater pliancy and exactitude than in the other."[49] Even John Kenneth Galbraith, a persistent critic of the power blindness of his colleagues, balked at any suggestion that political economics implied a takeover by political scientists, "a prospect by which we would rightly be repelled." Political science, he thought, was a captive of its stereotypes, notably that of "citizen control of the state." So, he concluded, "politics does—and must—become a part of economics."[50] And at the 1944 AEA/APSA conference, William Anderson (a political scientist) said that interdisciplinary proposals were premature and rash. Economics and political science were, he said, doomed to coexistence, to an inescapably "intimate detachment," but there were insuperable differences of purpose and approach, among them the lack of quantitative rigor in political science.[51] Indeed, the political theorist Brian Barry has suggested that, given the impressive theoretical structure of economics, the relevant question was not whether its methods were valid, but rather why their application to other fields had been delayed for so long.[52]

48. Duncan Black, "The Unity of Political and Economic Science," *Economic Journal* 60 (September 1950): 507–08.

49. Ibid., 508.

50. Galbraith, "Useful Economist," 6.

51. The political scientist was not, Anderson admitted, usually able "to present demand and supply curves, tables of statistics, or mathematical formulae to prove his point. Hence [he concluded] his argument lacks some of the apparent accuracy of economic analysis" (Anderson, "Political Science," 81).

52. Brian Barry, *Sociologists, Economists and Democracy*, 10–11.

DEVELOPMENT ECONOMICS: COERCED COOPERATION

The economists' sense of intellectual superiority naturally tempted them to adopt what Kenneth Boulding has called a "haughty and superior attitude" toward their scientifically immature colleagues.[53] In the field of economic development, their impatience was compounded by a sense of the urgency of the Third World's needs, by confidence in the capacity of economic tools to deal with them, and by irritation at the amateurism and insouciance of their noneconomic colleagues. Development economics held to the faith that science could establish a "general welfare function"—a jargonized term for the old Benthamite notion of the greatest happiness of the greatest number. Government was there to realize this general welfare function; but politics stood in the way. The question—the essentially *technical* question—was how to overcome such obstacles, and it was the job of noneconomists who were technically informed about such things to help dispose of those obstacles.

The development economists' attachment to the idea of a scientifically determinable general utility made them especially antipolitical. They tended to distinguish (or to assume a distinction) between, on the one hand, government, a ubiquitous and undifferentiated enterprise concerned with social improvement and, on the other, politics, a form of social disease symptomized by irrationality in the individual and corruption and unruliness in society. Such a distinction made it possible for an anthropologist to complain in the mid-sixties that the Republic of Liberia had "refractory institutional arrangements," by which he meant "institutional arrangements unreceptive to development policies suggested by economists."[54]

Colleagues, as well as institutions, could be "refractory" when recruited for the interdisciplinary technocratic enterprise envis-

53. Kenneth Boulding, "The Legitimacy of Economics," in *The Political Economy of Development: Theoretical and Empirical Contributions*, ed. Norman T. Uphoff and Warren F. Ilchman (Berkeley: University of California Press, 1972), 30.

54. George Dalton, "History, Politics and Economic Development in Liberia," *Journal of Economic History* 25, no. 4 (December 1965): 571.

aged by economists. In particular, their lack of quantitative skills was a source of worry. For disciplines such as sociology and political science to be useful, it was necessary that they be able to feed measurements of noneconomic variables into the models devised by economists. Thus, the British economist Michael Lipton suggested that the lack of interdisciplinary studies (shortened to IDS) was due to "the resented position of economics as 'master' subject combined with the reluctance of other social scientists to approach IDS with quantitatively testable models and the consequent extreme weakness of political and sociological data in LDC [less developed countries]."[55] Lipton wanted to draft noneconomists into the planning process, arguing that research on development was "expert intensive, especially since [with interdisciplinary work] yet more time is needed for inter-expert communication." Noneconomists were useful, since "to predict the value of an economic variable in a region of a poor . . . and badly integrated country, it often helps us to know the current values of social and political variables within that region."[56] Historians, however, could not, in Lipton's view, contribute much, for "the data explosion" had made that discipline redundant. Economists had enough data to "test backward," and it was clear that "as social and political statistics develop, sociology and political science will proceed in essentially the same way."[57] As it was, however, economists were frustrated and "often bewildered" by the innumeracy of noneconomists and their lack of "quantitative and testable hypotheses." They were, it seemed, "simply not prepared to look at these questions in the hard, quantitative terms needed for development planning." The sad truth, Lipton concluded, was

> that economics, alone among social sciences, has a number of clearly specified models, with gaps for *real live data*, tested in several LDC environments: benefit/cost and linear programming among optimizing models, and input-output among descriptive models, come to mind. An economist who examines, in this context, the candidate models

55. Michael Lipton, "Interdisciplinary Studies in Less Developed Countries," *Journal of Development Studies* 7, no. 1 (October 1970): 5.
56. Ibid., 6.
57. Ibid., 10.

> of SDS [single disciplinary studies] is often bewildered: the alleged variables seem to be names, not tangible and measurable things; their connections are stated as relations of direction only; and, where there are clear hypotheses, the procedure for testing them is not suggested.[58]

What was necessary, therefore, was to "force the various SDS specialists out of their verbalizing shells, into the computer room."[59]

Interdisciplinary work, as conceived by Lipton and others, involved simply the drafting of specialists from other disciplines to increase the effectiveness of development projects and to help in stage-managing their implementation. No conceptual adaptation by economists was needed, but rather "a supplementation of economic thinking by bringing in fragmentary theses from the other social sciences."[60] As an exercise in intellectual integration, it represented a one-way version of bussing (and an exceptionally clumsy one at that).

"POSITIVE" VERSUS "POLITICAL" ECONOMICS

The alternative to keeping politics in its place might well be a politically oriented economics. But one thing upon which the

58. Ibid., 12 (emphasis added).

59. Ibid., 15.

60. Papandreou, for example, suggested that what was needed was "a careful inventorying of all the tentatively valid propositions of psychology, anthropology and sociology in an effort to equip economics with the tools necessary to impose restrictions upon the relations among economic variables in order that operationally meaningful hypotheses may be formulated" (A. G. Papandreou, "Economics and the Social Sciences," 722). In the same vein, a prominent development economist, Hollis Chenery, noted that sociologists and political scientists "utilize a number of the economic magnitudes analyzed by economists, and in turn study some of the variables taken as given in models of economic development. The greater use of quantitative methods in these fields should make interdisciplinary collaboration increasingly feasible and rewarding." ("Economic Development," in *Economics*, ed. Nancy D. Ruggles (Englewood Cliffs, N.J.: Prentice-Hall, 1970), 153). For comments on this approach to interdisciplinary cooperation, see James A. Caporaso, "Pathways between Economics and Politics: Possible Foundations for the Study of Global Political Economy," paper presented at the annual meeting of the American Political Science Association, Chicago, 1–4 September 1983: 9–10.

more conservative defenders of economics were completely agreed was that, pace critics like Heilbroner, the discipline had been advanced, not crippled, by a detachment from moral and political commitment. As Lionel Robbins put it: "Economics deals with ascertainable facts; ethics with valuations and obligations. Propositions involving the verb 'ought' are different in kind from propositions involving the verb 'is.'"[61] "Positive," properly scientific economics dealt with only the latter kind of propositions, which could, contrary to Myrdal's view, be normatively neutral and should be made so.[62] Indeed, as long as economic theory produced falsifiable predictions, economists need not be concerned about the validity of their initial assumptions.[63] Nor, where these assumptions referred to the beliefs and values of individuals, need they be concerned about how such beliefs were generated.[64] To argue that values underlay economics, James Buchanan protested, was to remove "all scientific content from the discipline and [reduce] discussion to a babel of voices making noise." The economist must hold to "the faith that there does exist an independent body of truth in his

61. Lionel Robbins, *An Essay on the Nature and Significance of Economic Science* (repr. London: Macmillan, 1946), 148–49.

62. Lionel Robbins, "Economics and Political Economy," *American Economic Review. Papers and Proceedings* 71, no. 2 (May 1981): 4. "It is important to recognize that the propositions of economics . . . are positive rather than normative. They deal *inter alia* with values; but they deal with them as individual or social *facts*. The generalizations which emerge are statements of existence or possibility. . . . There can be events or institutions having an economic aspect which we ourselves regard as ethically acceptable or unacceptable. But, insofar as the explanations to their causes or consequences are scientific, they are neutral in this respect." As for Myrdal, Robbins commented: "I don't think that the proposition that, if the market is free and demand exceeds supply, prices will tend to rise, has any ethical content whatever. Nor do I concede that recognition of the consequences on investment of disparity between rates of interest and rates of return depends in the least on the political presuppositions of the economist who perceives it" (ibid., 4).

63. Milton Friedman, "The Methodology of Positive Economics," in Friedman, *Essays in Positive Economics* (Chicago: University of Chicago Press, 1953).

64. "While we assume that different goods have different values at different margins, we do not regard it as part of our problem to explain why these valuations exist" (Robbins, *Economic Science*, 94–95).

discipline, truth that can be discerned independently of value judgments."[65] Lionel Robbins acknowledged that the logical basis of welfare economics was flawed, that it was impossible to arrive at a scientific definition of the general good from an examination of individual preferences. But governments had to make judgments about such matters, and values were inescapably involved in such judgments. Therefore Robbins proposed dividing the field into "political economy," which dealt with such important but essentially unscientific matters, and "economic science," which would continue the central, normatively neutral tasks of analyzing the facts of economic behavior.[66]

"LIBERAL" VERSUS "WELFARE" ECONOMICS

Robbins's proposal, and indeed the entire preceding discussion, reveals an apparent divergence of opinion concerning the basis and purpose of economics. On the one hand, we have the developmentalists (and the welfare economists) who clearly believe in the scientific authority of economics and who see their duty as one of helping government to maximize the utility of citizens. Some call themselves "political economists," claiming that political economy can help governments to make rational choices involving the most efficient use of scarce resources for the benefit of the largest number of citizens. On the other hand, we have liberals or conservatives, such as Buchanan and Friedman, who are both political and methodological individualists. Buchanan, for example, argues that

> it is wholly beyond his task for the economist to define goals or objectives of the economy and then to propose measures designed to implement these goals . . . he verges dangerously on irresponsible action when he allows his zeal for social progress . . . to take precedence over

65. James M. Buchanan, "Economics and Its Scientific Neighbors," in Buchanan, *What Should Economists Do?* (Indianapolis: Liberty Press, 1979), 136.

66. Robbins, "Economics and Political Economy," 5–8. Political economy would cover "that part of our sphere of interest which essentially involves judgments of value. Political Economy, thus conceived, is quite unashamedly concerned with the assumptions of policy and the results flowing from them" (ibid., 8).

> his search for and respect of scientific truth, as determined by the consensus of his peers.[67]

Like Mancur Olson, Buchanan argues that what distinguishes economics is its "theory of behavior, not any 'theory of material goods.'"[68] Because it has such an intellectual identity, it is shallow simply to call for a union of economics and political science just because of the observation that economic and political processes overlap with and affect each other. Such a demand stops short of the central philosophical issue—namely, what is to become of the premises and methodology on which economics has traditionally depended. Both are rooted in individual behavior, and economics is thus fundamentally microeconomics. Its scientific mission, then, is to illuminate the rationality of *individual* choice. So far as it is concerned with politics, it would treat politics as "the complex set of institutional interactions among individual persons which is generated as a result of their attempts to accomplish mutually desired goals effectively."[69] Buchanan (and others of his school) insist that government is not "some supraindividual decision-making agency . . . separate and apart from the individual persons for whom choices are being made." Economists who do see it in this way become, he says, accomplices in a type of "benevolent despotism" which is both apolitical and antipolitical.[70] True liberals, on the contrary, are dedicated to enlarging individual self-determination: government is merely a means, an agency, through which individuals achieve their ends. This view, Buchanan claims, is opposed to

67. James M. Buchanan, "An Economist's Approach to 'Scientific Politics,'" in Buchanan, *What Should Economists Do?*, 146–47.

68. Buchanan, "Economics," 119–20; Mancur Olson, Jr., "The Relationship between Economics and the Other Social Sciences: The Province of a 'Social Report,'" in Seymour Martin Lipset, ed., *Politics and the Social Sciences* (New York: Oxford University Press, 1969), 141–42.

69. Buchanan, "Economist's Approach," 14–16.

70. Ibid., 144–45. Buchanan argues that welfare economics involves a usurpation of democracy by science which has the effect of rendering politics illicit: "Politics, the behavior of ordinary men in this process, becomes tainted activity, albeit necessary in a begrudgingly admitted way. But politics should be allowed to interfere as little as possible with the proper business of government" (ibid., 14–15).

the collectivism of many welfare economists and the majority of political scientists, who attribute interests, and even values, to institutions and "systems."

It does seem that there is a deep philosophical division here between fundamental liberals, such as Buchanan, and the social welfare utilitarians. Both claim to be true to the scientific inheritance of economics, and indeed both are. Their division arises not from any misrepresentation, but rather from the ambiguity of classical economics (noted earlier) about the possibility of deriving a "social welfare function" from individual preferences. One interpretation points toward a political economy that treats government itself as a rational actor trying to realize that function (perhaps through planning and with the help of rational-choice "theorists"). The other points toward the maximizing of individual choice, free-market economics, and minimal government. But they have important premises in common: a belief in the natural harmony of interests and a distaste for collective entities, which are seen as undermining the realization of *either* individual *or* general welfare. They also have (as a consequence of these premises) important defects in common: an inability to conceptualize power, to explain conflict, and sometimes to make even political participation comprehensible.

The tension betwen these two interpretations of classical economic philosophy has marked the efforts of economists and others to develop a "new political economy." This movement expresses the belief that the approach to rational individual choice traditionally used in economics can usefully be extended to the study of social processes conventionally monopolized by other disciplines, notably political science. It is the response of the philosophical loyalists in economics—and their sympathizers elsewhere—to the onslaughts of critics. The next chapter examines the assumptions and methodology of this school and reviews work that applies them to political and social relations in the Third World.

THREE
"The New Political Economy"

The approaches variously described as "the new political economy," "rational choice," and "public choice" represent a vigorous counterattack by the supporters of economics against critics of the types described in the previous chapter. They claim to offer an understanding of politics and other forms of social behavior that is not provided by the conflict-oriented, cultural, and pluralist approaches characteristic of political sociology and political science.

The framework is based (and must be based) on the individual actor and his or her pursuit of perceived interests. Thus, it adopts the fundamental philosophical principles of liberal economics. It assumes that man is "an egoistic, rational, utility maximizer" and applies itself to understanding his "endeavor to relate means to ends as efficiently as possible."[1] In this view, "the actor is assumed to have certain specified properties including a set of tastes or preference orderings and a capacity for rational decisions or the ability to choose the most efficient resolution of his choice dilemmas."[2] This approach can, in principle, be applied to any situation—to a voter in a polling booth, to a

1. Dennis C. Mueller, *Public Choice* (Cambridge: Cambridge University Press, 1979), 1; Ronald Rogowski, "Rationalist Theories of Politics: A Midterm Report," *World Politics* 30, no. 2 (January 1978): 299.

2. William C. Mitchell, "The New Political Economy," *Social Research* 35, no. 1 (Spring 1968): 82. See also Mitchell's article, "The Shape of Political Theory To Come: From Political Sociology to Political Economy," *The American Behavioral Scientist* II, no. 2 (November–December 1967): 8–20.

consumer buying yogurt in a supermarket, to a policymaker deciding on new weapons systems, or to peasants trying to decide what cash crops to grow or whether to join a guerrilla movement. Political economy in this form is interested in all these dilemmas but applies the same assumptions and concepts an economist would apply to the second to all the others.

One justification for the approach is that economics has to come to terms with "nonmarket decision-making," meaning mainly the activities of governments. The increasing intervention by governments in economic markets implies that economists must expand their agenda to include examination of the processes by which public goods are produced and distributed, as well as of the impact of government on the market. Such an expansion involves, at least in the perspective of the new political economy, seeing the political system itself as analogous to a market. In the words of William C. Mitchell, political systems should be regarded

> not only as choice mechanisms for making economic decisions having an impact on the private economy, but also as economies in their own right making decisions on budgets or the production and distribution of public goods and services. As price theory is a prime focus of private economic choice, so are political institutions the focus of concern for the new political economist. Comparisons of markets and political institutions (usually in terms of efficiency) are, therefore, typical activities.[3]

Mitchell goes on to provide a specific comparison of questions and topics as defined by an economist with the questions and topics a political economist would explore:

> *Economist*: To what uses are productive resources put? Or, what goods are produced? In what quantities?
>
> *Political economist*: Composition of the public budget. Which goods are produced? In what quantities?
>
> *Economist*: How are goods produced? Problem of economic organization of production.
>
> *Political economist*: How are budgetary choices made?

3. Mitchell, "New Political Economy," 77–78.

Economist: How are goods distributed? Problem of the distribution of income.

Political economist: Who gets how much of the benefits produced and/or distributed?[4]

Rational choice may, then, apply to the government as actor (within the framework of welfare economics) or to an individual voter. The criteria applied are the same and the opportunities are assumed to be comparable.

> The political economist typically views a political situation, at least in democracies, as affording *exchange* possibilities among citizens, political parties, governments, and bureaucracies. On the one hand, voters are treated as "buyers" of collective goods while governments and political parties are considered as alternative "suppliers" competing to produce public policies (goods and services) or promises thereof, having utility or providing satisfaction in return for the contingent support of voters at elections. . . . The basic conceptual schema for the economist is a "political market" roughly analogous to the regular marketplace.[5]

"Public choice," for its part, is concerned with exploring the properties of social welfare or social choice functions: "It focuses on the problems of aggregating individual preferences to *maximize* a social welfare function, or to satisfy some set of normative criteria, i.e., on the problem of which social state *ought* to be chosen, given the preferences of the individual voters."[6] The basic feature of the approach, then, is an emphasis on assessing and illuminating the rationality of decisions, whether by individuals or by government. It does not deny the possibility of collective interests (or collective actions), but (as in Smith's view) it sees them as resulting from the pursuit of individual interests. It does not deny the existence of politics, but it assumes that political behavior and institutions can be analyzed as analogous to economic behavior and market institutions.

Such an approach has both analytic and prescriptive applications. It can be used to show how behavior otherwise interpreted

4. Ibid., 77.
5. Ibid., 82–83 (emphasis in original).
6. Mueller, *Public Choice*, 2 (emphasis in original).

according to ideological or cultural categories can be as well or better explained as expressing an individual's perception of self-interest. It can be used to illuminate the conditions for successful collective action and to show why some interests may be more successfully "aggregated" than others. It can also be used to clarify the choices facing a decision-maker (individual or institutional) and to help him, her, or it to decide how best to achieve specific goals "as efficiently as possible."

This list of applications also suggests both the biases and limits of the approach. Critics have argued that the characteristics which provide its elegance and intellectual appeal also limit the questions with which it can deal. Even in Western democracies, "rational choice" theories often make their intellectual mileage by adopting assumptions that strain credibility and by avoiding questions which seem to many students of politics rather fundamental. In particular, as Richard Sklar has pointed out, such political economy "is predicated upon a conception of politics that retains very little power content."[7] Power and domination are excluded definitionally. Common sense suggests that a political economy which assumes that all actors are equally informed and equally placed to state and realize their preferences has not been exposed much to the rougher realities of political life. Further, a political economy which assumes that governments, for their part, are always preoccupied with the further embellishment of welfare economics, and are engaged (and have to engage) with citizens as equals, seems already to have found the best of all possible worlds—before the rest of us.

To many political scientists, the rational choice approach seems simplistic as well as naïve. It misses the "institutional richness" of political life, preferring highly abstracted analysis resting on assumptions which are narrow and completely a priori.[8] Moreover, it is, in their view, question-begging in several respects. Not only does it lack any broader theoretical basis that

7. Richard L. Sklar, "On the Concept of Power in Political Economy," in *Toward a Humanistic Science of Politics. Essays in Honor of Francis Dunham Wormuth*, ed. Dalmas H. Nelson and Richard L. Sklar (Lanham, Md.: University Press of America, 1983), 179.

8. This criticism is noted in Mueller, *Public Choice*, 5.

might explain the variability of political institutions, but its very notion of "self-interest" is culture-bound, or is simply oblivious to culture. As Keohane has remarked, "the assumption that individuals are self-interested and rational . . . is ambiguous, since 'self-interest' is defined culturally rather than as an objective given."[9] Because the rational choice approach abstracts individual decision-making from any "irrational" social influences and takes "society" and "culture" as given, it cannot account for the creation of tastes, for changes in preferencs, or for apparently irrational decisions by individuals.

To this, the rational choice theorists reply that they never claimed to be able to do such things. They are less concerned with the plausibility of their initial assumptions than with the logical soundness of their approach and its capacity to predict outcomes. Because the approach is deductive, it has to be judged rather differently from an inductive approach. If it "works"—if it can give an intelligible interpretation of an actor's behavior and decisions and if its predictions come true—then it is a sound procedure, no matter how arbitrary, abstract, or narrow the initial assumptions are and no matter how many other factors are consigned to the outer darkness of ceteris paribus.

If we ask how such a framework solves the problem of the relationship between politics and economics (and between political science and economics), the answer is clearly that it dissolves it, by a piece of semantic chemistry. Rather than providing a new synthesis, perhaps a theory that would help us understand the mutual impact and overlapping of the processes in question, it simply applies the language of economics to institutions and behavior usually called political. This is a solution by relabeling, not a solution derived from fresh analysis. It makes politics into a colony of economics instead of illuminating the dynamics governing relations between these spheres.

Again, such an objection would leave the advocates of rational choice unmoved. They happily admit that their approach is

9. Robert O. Keohane, review of Mancur Olson, *The Rise and Decline of Nations: Economic Growth, Stagflation, and Social Rigidities* (New Haven: Yale University Press, 1982), in *Journal of Economic Literature* 21 (June 1983): 559.

"simply the application of economics to political science" (more exactly, the application of a basic assumption of economics to political science).[10] Such colonization is, in their view, justified, not to say overdue, given the scientific backwardness of political science compared to economics. In Mitchell's words: "Unlike political science, economics has long employed a rather sharply defined and widely accepted conceptual framework within which to analyze behavior and produce empirical and theoretical propositions. The new political economist has simply extended this framework to include political behavior."[11] As before, rational choice theorists would argue that the significant test is whether or not the approach gives superior explanatory and predictive results. Preserving disciplinary jurisdictions is irrelevant unless it can be shown that such jurisdictions signify genuine philosophical and methodological differences, and even then they need not be respected if one discipline's approach has shown itself to be scientifically better than another's. Sovereignty is as sovereignty does.

Indeed, much intellectually elegant and useful work has been done using this method in the United States and in Western Europe, especially on such questions as voting behavior, the formation of coalitions, certain aspects of conflict and collective action, and—more recently—on comparative economic history.[12] The

10. Mueller, *Public Choice*, 1.

11. Mitchell, "New Political Economy," 82.

12. Some of the better-known works include Anthony Downs, *An Economic Theory of Democracy* (New York: Harper & Row, 1957); Mancur Olson, *The Logic of Collective Action: Public Goods and the Theory of Groups* (Cambridge, Mass.: Harvard University Press, 1965); Thomas Schelling, *The Strategy of Conflict* (Cambridge, Mass.: Harvard University Press, 1960); James Buchanan and Gordon Tullock, *The Calculus of Consent: Logical Foundations of Constitutional Democracy* (Ann Arbor: University of Michigan Press, 1962); and Ronald Rogowski, *Rational Legitimacy: A Theory of Political Support* (Princeton, N.J.: Princeton University Press, 1974). Three recent works in the rational choice tradition dealing with questions of economic growth and decline are: Robert Gilpin, *War and Change in International Politics* (Cambridge: Cambridge University Press, 1981); Douglass C. North, *Structure and Change in Economic History* (New York: W. W. Norton, 1981); and Mancur Olson, Jr., *The Rise and Decline of Nations: Economic Growth, Stagflation, and Social Rigidities* (New Haven: Yale University Press, 1982). For a useful review of these works, see Ronald Rogowski, "Structure Growth, and

question, however, is how useful such an approach can be when adopted for the analysis of societies outside the traditional perimeter of Anglo-Saxon liberal democracy. To answer it, and to clarify some of the strengths and weaknesses of this style of "political economy," we shall examine in detail three works organized around the principles of rational choice. Two—Popkin's *The Rational Peasant* and Bates's *Markets and States in Tropical Africa*—are attempts to construe the rationality of peasant behavior in both its economic and its political aspects; the third—Rothchild and Curry's *Scarcity, Choice, and Public Policy in Middle Africa*—is an essay in the application of rational choice to "policy analysis."

POPKIN'S *The Rational Peasant*

One of the better-known applications of the new political economy to Third World societies is Samuel L. Popkin's *The Rational Peasant: The Political Economy of Rural Society in Vietnam.*[13] In this work, Popkin questions the assumptions, analyses, and conclusions of a group of scholars he collectively dubs the "moral economy" school. In particular, he takes issue with James C. Scott's *The Moral Economy of the Peasant*—appropriately enough, since Scott's study is also concerned with Indochina and indeed draws on several of the same written sources as Popkin's work.[14]

According to Popkin, the moral economy school errs both in its depiction of precolonial peasant societies and in its analysis of peasant responses to capitalism. By extension, it misconceives the nature of peasant revolutions and misleads policymakers.

The "Moral Economy" Perspective

What is the moral economy view of peasant society? In Popkin's collective summary, it holds that peasants are distin-

Power: Three Rationalist Accounts," *International Organization* 37, no. 4 (Autumn 1983): 713–38.

13. Samuel L. Popkin, *The Rational Peasant: The Political Economy of Rural Soceity in Vietnam* (Berkeley: University of California Press, 1979).

14. James C. Scott, *The Moral Economy of the Peasant: Rebellion and Subsistence in Southeast Asia* (New Haven: Yale University Press, 1976).

guished by a preoccupation with safeguarding subsistence which makes them extremely wary of innovation and risk.[15] This preoccupation, this "safety-first" attitude, may lead them to prefer, for example, a progressive system of taxation to a flat-rate system. As Moore points out, writing about Japan, a flat and fixed rate, if it is suitably low, is attractive to farmers intent on increasing production and profit: the more they produce, the smaller the proportion of their income will go for taxes and the higher their profits will be.[16] "Risk-averse" peasants, however, see mainly the potential *danger* of such a tax—namely, that it would be invariable in bad years as well as in good.

This concern with subsistence is reflected (moral economists argue) in the values and social relations prevailing within peasant villages, as well as in attitudes toward involvement with the outside world. In their pristine form, villages are "corporate" in the sense of accepting a significant level of mutual dependence and obligation between members and in asserting, through various rules of allocation, a communal obligation to assure all villagers a basic subsistence.[17] The village possesses a "moral economy" not because its members (or peasants in general) are better people than the rest of us, but because the rules of village life produce moral outcomes.[18] In particular, these rules impose an obligation to protect the subsistence needs of the community's poorer and more unfortunate members. They also allocate burdens according to means and, by consensual processes of decision-making, protect the community against the greater evils of inequality.

The village is not, therefore, just an association of producers. It is "a ritual and cultural unit" possessing a strong sense of identity and prescribing an all-inclusive moral code.[19] Inequality may exist, but its effects are feared. It is accepted because the wealthy and powerful themselves accept the norms of noblesse oblige. The legitimacy of the patron (landlord or "big man") is

15. Popkin, *Rational Peasant*, 2–15.

16. Barrington Moore, Jr., *Social Origins of Dictatorship and Democracy: Lord and Peasant in the Making of the Modern World* (Boston: Beacon Press, 1966), 259.

17. Popkin, *Rational Peasant*, 10–11.

18. Ibid., 3.

19. Ibid., 15.

predicated on his generosity toward men of lesser means, his willingness to contribute to their subsistence in bad times, and his restraint in not threatening "the subsistence reserves of the poor."[20]

As regards the outside world, peasants are held (in the moral economy view) to be suspicious and fearful of market relationships. They are wary of (or indifferent to) commercial agriculture and only grow cash-crops as a last resort—and then only to achieve a "target income" determined by the requirements of custom and status within the village.[21]

The moral economy view of peasant revolution is consistent with its emphasis on peasant conservatism. Peasants revolt to stem the advances of capitalism, to defend the social and moral integrity of their communities against the corrosive inroads of individualism and acquisitiveness which capitalism brings, and to restore the institutions and relationships of precapitalist society. Revolts only occur when outside forces (capitalist and/or colonial) have produced a general and immediate threat to peasant subsistence, when both the survival of the peasants and the survival of the communal structures of welfare and reciprocity which are their safety nets are in imminent danger.

The "Political Economy" Interpretation

Popkins's response to the moral economy orthodoxy is much in the spirit of Will Rogers's remark, "Things ain't as good as they used to be—but then they never were." He argues that colonialism and capitalism have been less destructive than moral economists claim, largely because there was less to destroy than they believe: a realistic portrayal of precapitalist village societies reveals greater individualism and much less communal support than is suggested by moral economists.[22]

Popkin, indeed, proposes a complete reevaluation of Vietnamese rural history from the precapitalist period through the years of French colonialism down to 1945. The framework for

20. Ibid., 14.
21. Ibid., 9.
22. Ibid., 23, 25–26, 39–49.

his reevaluation is a political economy view of peasant behavior, which entails "a focus on individual decision-making" in place of the holistic and organic approach of moral economy, with its emphasis on "culture" and "values."[23] Popkin claims that

> by applying theories of individual decision-making to villages, we can begin to develop a deductive understanding of peasant institutions and move the analysis back one step to the level of the individual. By using the concepts of individual choice and decision-making, we can discuss how and why groups of individuals decide to adopt some sets of norms while rejecting others.[24]

His method, then, is to ask what kind of behavior could be expected if peasants were "rational maximizers," to find out whether such behavior in fact occurred, and to refine his terms and his logic to exclude alternative explanations. This procedure, he suggests, enables us to determine the rationale behind values and rules instead of taking them as given. It enables us to conceive explanations for changes in norms and procedures. It allows us to identify points of tension between individual and collective interests. And, lastly, it allows us to compare values and rules in communities with broadly similar environments.

Popkin's major premise is that the peasant is "a rational problem-solver, with a sense both of his own interests and of the need to bargain with others to achieve mutually acceptable outcomes." He is, as Ronald J. Herring has put it, *homo economicus rusticus*, calculating costs and benefits, evaluating "the possible outcomes associated with [his] choices in accordance with [his] preferences and values." So far from villages being naturally harmonious communities, there may be "conflicts between group and individual interest." "What is rational for an individual may be very different from what is rational for an entire village or collective."[25] While Popkin is careful to stress that individuals are not "solely concerned with material commodities or money incomes," he does argue that they apply a "unifying investment

23. Ibid., 17.
24. Ibid., 18.
25. Ronald J. Herring, review, *American Political Science Review* 74, no. 2 (June 1980): 566; Popkin, *Rational Peasant*, 30–31.

logic" to all choices that confront them, from decisions about having children or selecting crops to decisions about involvement in political and religious movements.[26]

In the economic sphere, Popkin accepts that peasants are (and must be) individually concerned about threats to their subsistence. But he questions the assumption that this concern inhibits risk-taking and the seeking of profit once a suitable and reliable surplus is on hand. Also, he denies that the preoccupation with subsistence is so general as to impose a communal and cultural veto on individual entrepreneurship. Indeed, the norms prevailing in a village, far from being repressive and inflexible, are themselves "malleable, renegotiated, and shifting in accord with considerations of power and strategic interaction among individuals."[27] Such strategic interaction has, moreover, worked generally to limit communal restraints, obligations, and cooperation. Pace "moral economy," the precolonial village was not "egalitarian, leveling, welfare-oriented, or necessarily harmonious." It was not "a kind of New Deal society, in which an ideology of the survival of the weakest prevailed."[28] Collective action of any kind was hard to achieve and difficult to sustain. To the extent that the community's institutions allocated burdens and protected subsistence, they did so in ways that preserved rather than reduced inequality. Distribution of the community's tax levy was rarely, if ever, on progressive lines; mutual aid was organized on strictly reciprocal and explicit lines; and access to emergency help from the community (in reality, the patron and wealthier peasants) was granted in a consistently grudging spirit and in the most restrictive ways.[29] Moreover, Popkin argues, moral economists have exaggerated the beneficial aspects of patron–client relationships. "Big men" manipulated such relationships so as to thwart collective demands on their wealth and to prevent changes (such as the extension of literacy or improve-

26. Ibid., 31, 244.

27. Ibid., 22.

28. Jonathan Lieberson, "The Silent Majority," *New York Review of Books* 22 (October 1981): 34.

29. Popkin, *Rational Peasant*, 39–43, 46–56.

ments in agricultural techniques) that might reduce their power and the dependence of peasants upon them.[30]

The corollary of this disenchanted version of village life is a less cataclysmic view of the impact of capitalism. Popkin suggests, indeed, that, rather than capitalism aggressively "penetrating" hostile or indifferent rural societies, it was often members of villages themselves who took the initiative in establishing relations with outsiders. Frequently they embraced opportunities for developing cash-crops. Indeed, the overall effects of capitalism (and the accompanying encroachments of the state) might well be liberating and progressive, especially for those without land.[31]

Revolutions and other forms of peasant protest were not, therefore, intended to restore the institutions of a precapitalist golden age. Rather, they aimed at "taming" capitalism and, indeed, at destroying feudal customs and impositions which villagers had come to see as exploitative and obstructive. Revolutionary movements were inspired by a sense that progress was possible, by a wish to improve living standards—not by a fearful, nostalgic impulse to crawl back into the protective womb of the "corporate" village.

Such a summary inadequately conveys the vigor of Popkin's exposition, the breadth of his scholarship, and the sophistication with which he analyzes and compares material about Vietnam and many other societies, both contemporary and historical. The book raises important questions and is fearlessly ambitious in its theoretical claims. How well does it deal with these questions, and how far are its claims justified?

Criticisms of Popkin

The issues prompted by *The Rational Peasant* readily sort themselves into three categories. The first concern his view of moral economy. Is his description of the school accurate? Are his criticisms of it fair and relevant? The second concern his own

30. Ibid., 72–78.
31. Ibid., 63ff.

political economy approach. Is it coherent, is it useful? What are its strengths and weaknesses? The third concern the application of this approach to Vietnamese peasant society. How convincing an interpretation of individual behavior and of relations within villages does it provide? How persuasive is its account of relations between villagers and outsiders, whether capitalist traders or revolutionary organizers?

"Moral" Versus "Political" Economy Several commentators have claimed that Popkin has perpetrated a caricature in his collective portrait of the "moral economy" school, and that in particular he has seriously oversimplified Scott's position.[32] The moral economy school is said to be reduced to "an amalgam of Durkheim, Rousseau, and the Good Samaritan."[33] Popkin is especially criticized for misrepresenting his rivals' view of morality in the precapitalist village. They did not claim that village life was impeccably noble, or that individual behavior was never calculating or selfish. They did not even claim that "outcomes" were generally moral. All they claimed—all anybody could ever claim of a morality—was the existence and common acknowledgment of a set of rules. Such rules were important, not because they were invariably observed (what rules are?), but because they expressed "a distinctive economic rationality" and because they were widespread in rural communities.[34]

It is actually unclear what Popkin is dismissing in his dismissal of moral economy. As is apparent later in the book, it is not the existence of "values" as significant factors in behavior. (Indeed, as we shall see presently, his idea of rationality is incomplete without reference to and identification of "values.") If he were simply protesting against romanticization of village life, his point would be clear. But it would not be one made at the expense of Scott, since he does not really romanticize village life.

32. See, for example, Herring, review, *American Political Science Review* 74, no. 2 (June 1980), 565; Lieberson, "Silent Majority," 37; and Clive S. Kessler, review, *American Historical Review* 85, no. 3 (June 1980): 702.

33. Herring, review, *American Political Science Review* 74, no. 2 (June 1980): 565.

34. Kessler, review, *American Historical Review* 85, no. 3 (June 1980): 702; and Lieberson, "Silent Majority," 37.

The problem is that Popkin seems intent on establishing the ubiquity of "rational individualism" as a basis for behavior. This assertion has the rhetorical merit of setting his model clearly apart from others. The trouble is that it cannot work on its own for the purposes of explaining the phenomena he wants to explain. This inadequacy has nothing to do with Popkin's research or his specific analyses of Vietnamese history, all of which seem to a layman quite scholarly and empirically sound. It arises directly from his utilitarianism and the logical chains it drags behind it.

Historically, utilitarianism has been more useful as a tool for logical criticism—sorting out plausible from implausible theories—than as a basis for broader interpretations of behavior. To ask how an individual's interest is served by a given action, involvement in an organization, or whatever, is a useful corrective to overabstraction and loose generalization and an affirmation of the need to ground theory in social reality—a kind of memento mori for theory-builders. But calculations of individual interest are not made in isolation, and rationality itself is contingent on a selection of values and preferences. To say that peasants "evaluate the possible outcomes associated with their choices in accordance with their preferences and values" is to give a strategic answer to questions that are essentially philosophical or cultural. Why do peasants have some preferences rather than others, and how is their range of values shaped in the first place? Such questions require an explanatory framework that is "social" or "cultural" in scope. To say that individuals "pursue their interests" or "maximize their utility" sounds tough-mindedly realistic, but only until we start asking why "reality" is seen differently by people who are presumably equally rational.

Popkin concedes as much. He does so in his definition of *rationality*, in the very terminology he employs, and in his analyses of social movements. A consistently individualistic approach would stress (as Popkin does) the extreme difficulty of cooperative action, but it would also avoid (as Popkin does not) such terms as *group* or *collective interest*. By definition, there can be no such thing as "group interest," except as a shorthand term for a passing coincidence of individual interests. It seems even more illogical to talk about "conflicts between group or individual interest" or to conclude that "what is rational for an individual may be very different from what is rational for an entire village or collective."[35] Such a contrast is predicated on the existence of a supraindividual entity which lies outside the premises of liberal political economy.

This problem, indeed, raises the larger question of how political economy understands and explains politics. Quite logically, Popkin argues that "the individual interests of the villagers shape and determine the nature and scope of village-level cooperation."[36] His peasants are political without being civic-minded; they have a sharp sense of power but little sense of community. They are chronically wary of "free riders" benefiting from cooperative arrangements and forever trying to maximize returns while minimizing costs. The peasant is not crudely materialistic, but he is "primarily concerned with the welfare and security of self and family."[37]

This approach is useful insofar as it helps to expose and explore conflicts and inequalities within villages, but it prompts two questions. The first relates to Popkin's critique of moral economy; the second, to his analysis of religious and revolutionary movements.

How different, in reality, is Popkin's self-regarding calculator from Scott's "safety-first" guardian of minimum subsistence? Scott's peasant is averse to all risks: Popkin's to large risks. But both are cautious about anything that threatens their subsistence reserves. Scott's peasant accepts that "all are entitled to a *living* out of the resources within the village." Popkin's peasant becomes "cautious about contributing to insurance and welfare schemes" once there is a general threat to subsistence.[38] Scott's subscribes to a "subsistence ethic," partly for fear of the damages

35. Popkin, *Rational Peasant*, 31; see also, ibid., 245.
36. Ibid., 132.
37. Ibid., 31.
38. Scott, *Moral Economy of the Peasant*, 5 (emphasis in original); Popkin, *Rational Peasant*, 23.

to life and property that the "abandoned poor" would represent: Popkin's applies "investment logic" to all situations.[39]

Yet this concept of investment logic is never clearly defined, and in some of the examples cited it seems simply to mean emphasis on long-term security rather than short-term security. To say that people "invest" in children as a form of old-age insurance is surely to use *invest* in a metaphorical rather than an orthodox economic sense. They are hoping for a "return," just as a farmer who plants seed is hoping for a return, but there is no evidence (and apparently no intention of implying) that any sense of profit or element of exploitation is present.[40] Would any moral economist (or any peasant, for that matter) quarrel with such assertions as that peasants "place a high priority on investment for old age" and that "children are viewed as a source of future income"? Popkin's claim here is that, in pursuit of security, peasants consciously decide between "public" and "private," short-term and long-term "investments." But did anybody ever argue that peasants do not make decisions or that they are less aware of the long-term implications of such decisions than non-peasants?

Closer examination of such examples reveals at work the irritating tendency of this school of political economy to mistake changing of labels for distinctions of substance. What new insight is actually gained, for instance, by using such terms as *family firm* (for *family*) and *tradeoffs* (for *choices*), without first showing that the assumptions and implications usually associated with such terms are in fact valid for the institutions or processes in question?[41] When Popkin writes (for example) that "as a family firm . . . peasant couples will make tradeoffs between children and property which have a long-run focus,"[42] the reader may

39. Scott, *Moral Economy of the Peasant*, 5.

40. See Popkin, *Rational Peasant*, 19, for examples of "investment logic."

41. Cf. Brian Barry's remark that "the constant danger of 'economic' theories is that they can come to 'explain' everything merely by redescribing it. They then fail to be of any use in predicting that one thing will happen rather than another." *Sociologists, Economists and Democracy* (Chicago: University of Chicago Press, 1978), 33.

42. Popkin, *Rational Peasant*, 19–20.

wonder what is new except the wrapping. When he cites, in support of his argument, Robert Bates's observation that "in Zambia, the family is a mutual support system within which those who possess resources can reasonably be expected to distribute them to those who do not, and children are viewed as a source of future income,"[43] the reader may wonder whether the "new" political economy even knows how to distinguish its products from those of its rivals.

Political Economy and Political Participation The school's propensity to overload language and beg questions shows itself most clearly in Popkin's analysis of four religious and revolutionary movements (the Cao Dai, Hoa Hao, and Roman Catholic religions, and the Communists). All four represented a challenge to feudalism, Popkin argues, and participation in them involved significant long-term gambles on the efficacy, equity, and honesty of mass movements and their leaders. How do we explain their success, given the self-regarding, suspicious nature of Popkin's peasants? Why were people who could take years to agree on village irrigation schemes, who were perennially on guard for "free riders" and embezzling leaders, willing to join movements that offered only long-term and uncertain returns for short-term and undeniable risks? Why were they prepared to trust the leaders of such movements when they were reluctant to give any credit to fellow villagers whom they knew well and saw every day?

This conundrum is not really solved by arguing, as Popkin does, that these movements offered peasants not a return to some precapitalist golden age, but rather the promise of higher incomes and expanded opportunities, through the actual destruction of feudal ties.[44] For his "rational maximizing" model requires that in joining such a movement each peasant can assure himself that he will thereby receive "selective incentives" denied to nonparticipants. Clearly, the larger the movement or the more uncertain its eventual success, the weaker is its credibility in offering "selective incentives."[45]

43. Ibid., 19.
44. Ibid., 245.
45. For Popkin's discussion of "selective incentives," see ibid., 253–59.

A further problem is raised by Popkin's observation that the appeal of radical movements varied in different parts of Vietnam. Revolutionary organizers succeeded earlier and more easily in the more affluent, southern region of Cochinchina than in the less developed regions of Tonkin and Annam.[46] This contrast confirms his argument that peasants do not rebel only when faced with an immediate threat to their subsistence. He argues, indeed, that it supports the theory that rebellion is seen as a way to raise living standards rather than as a desperate act of self-defense. The peasants in the north were harder to win over but, once won over, were more loyal and enthusiastic than those in the south, as the Vietminh provided them with tangible rewards for participation that they had an interest in defending.[47]

But this interpretation, if anything, makes it harder to understand the "rationality" of the southern peasants who, after all, had more to lose. Was it more rational for them to invest in a mass movement in the hope of greater benefits, or to invest in individual security to protect the surplus they already had? They supposedly had more to lose and, under colonial governments, a good chance of suffering in the process. Also, why were relatively affluent peasants attracted to radical movements that might ultimately discriminate against them? Why were generally down-to-earth maximizers so drawn to syncretistic religions that offered the most unworldly and remote rewards to "investors?"

Popkin deals with these matters in a suitably paradoxical way. The problem of regional variation is explained by emphasizing the role of organization, the credibility of leaders, and the peasants' estimation of their "political efficacy."[48] Such an emphasis, of course, involves a tacit admission that the simple utilitarian framework is inadequate. In a curious way, it also revives the re-

46. Ibid., 258. The summary on this page needs to be taken in light of a more nuanced picture presented on pp. 229–42, where the problems of "individualism" for revolutionary organizers are clearly set out. For comments by another scholar of Vietnamese revolutionary movements, see William J. Duiker, review, *Pacific Affairs* 53, no. 4 (Winter 1980–81): 795.

47. Ibid., 263.

48. See especially, ibid., 259–66 (and 252): also on p. 262: "Credibility, moral codes, and visions of the future . . . all affect a peasant's estimate that his investment will either contribute directly to a collective goal or will bring an acceptable return of individual benefits."

jected assumption of "moral economy" that outside initiative is vital to the launching of peasant revolt. The difference is that whereas the moral economists point to the penetration of capitalism as crucial, Popkin points to revolutionary leaders and improvements in "communication and coordination."[49]

Yet we still have the problem of why organization succeeds and why leaders are followed. On this issue, Popkin virtually embraces cultural and moral explanations. The success of movements depended on their manipulation of "cultural themes," on "visions of the future," and on appeals to nationalism. Consider the following passage in the light of the premises of political economy:

> The greater success of religious movements *vis-à-vis* the Communists before the latter began to utilize cultural themes underscores, even more than the failed appeals of Westernized organizers, the cultural bases of competence and credibility estimates made by the peasants. So long as the Communists argued only in terms of material incentives and neglected to add an ethnic, Vietnamese content to their discussions of the future, they were unable to present a credible vision of the future to the peasants; hence, their early failure at organization. The religious movements, on the other hand, brought visions of the future consonant with peasant beliefs, and peasants were able to relate these visions to their contemporary actions.[50]

This contrast is quite persuasive, but it reintroduces concepts that are closer to moral economy. Once Popkin begins to invoke such concepts, he dilutes his original belief in self-interest. In order to save "investment logic" and "rational individualism," we have to stretch them to include almost every form of human behavior, including (especially in this context) actions that seem incomprehensible within the conventional meanings of "rational self-interest." An obvious case is that of the Buddhists who burnt themselves to death. Did such actions reflect investment logic? Relative to what? The monks' reputations for spirituality? Their prospects in the afterlife? The truth is that, as with so much else

49. Ibid., 248. Duiker (*Pacific Affairs* 53, no. 4 [Winter 1980–81]: 796) shares this view of the crucial role of organization leadership.

50. Ibid., 261; cf. 223.

"reinterpreted" by the advocates of this approach, cases of this kind involve stretching the meaning of concepts to the point that, in explaining everything in general, they cease to explain anything in particular.

Moreover, an emphasis on leaders and organizations, apart from introducing a deus ex machina, only prompts another question. What motivates the leaders? Why is it in their interest, above all, to take the most extreme risks, and make the most complete "investment?" If they are as self-interested as the peasants, why should the latter follow them (given their ingrained suspicion of leaders)? If they appear to be different, how can the peasants understand them? Popkin argues that early Communist organizers failed because they came round the villages mouthing abstractions incomprehensible to the peasants.[51] Yet in explaining the success of later organizers he seems to argue that it was just such a cultural difference that made them credible:

> a major factor in the credibility of both the Communist and religious movements over the century, in contrast to the failed bourgeois organizations, was the self-abnegation of the leadership. The self-denial of Communist organizers, the celibacy of missionary priests, the scorn of conspicuous consumption by Hoa Hao organizers, were striking demonstrations to peasants that these men were less interested in self-aggrandizement than were the visibly less self-denying organizers from other groups.[52]

In short, to paraphrase Groucho Marx, the only clubs peasants would join were those led by people unlike themselves!

Ironically, "good leadership" turns out to be, in Popkin's eyes, the key to successful cooperative action, whether in villages or in mass radical movements. Not only the leaders but also many followers are thought to participate "for reasons of ethic, conscience, or altruism."[53] Again, the conclusion may be accurate

51. Ibid., 260, 262.

52. Ibid., 261.

53. Ibid., 254. On p. 223 Popkin remarks: "The Vietminh mobilization is a clear case of the importance of contributions, some of which were not stimulated by any expectation of future selective payoff. It emphasizes how important internalized feelings of duty or ethic can be."

enough, but it is hardly compatible with the "logic of collective action" as developed by Popkin on the basis of Mancur Olson's work.[54] Such logic normally requires a manifest and preferably exclusive reward for the individual in the conventional sense, and it implicitly depends on a clear distinction between "self" and "other." It is hard to see how the notions of "self-interest" and "rational individualism" can be expanded to include "ethic, conscience, or altruism" without effectively destroying this distinction.

These comments on Popkin's work are not intended to criticize the substance of his study but to illustrate the problems of applying this model of political economy. In fact, a careful reading of his chapter "Up from Feudalism" shows a pattern of religions, including complex political rivalries, which he handles in the manner of an orthodox political historian, showing the many local variations and maneuverings. The imposition of a political economy model seems gratuitously to create as many problems as it solves. It serves well to explain the occurrence of conflict, the difficulties of collaboration, and generally to correct the more mechanically "sociological" interpretations of behavior.[55] It does less well in accounting for the generation of values, the existence of authority, and the contribution of support to organizations. For all these purposes, it is necessary to transcend "rational individualism," to devise a framework that comprehends both rational individualism and "rational collectivism" and enables us to understand how the boundary between self-regarding and other-regarding behavior is conceived and shaped. In this respect, political economy tends to overreact, denying significant influence to the environment in which individuals make decisions. In doing so, it also fails to provide a satisfactory framework for understanding the collective, "social" institutions and beliefs that make up the sphere of politics. "Political economy" as conceived by Popkin may help clarify the choices of individuals. But the limitations of such an approach become clear

54. Specifically, *The Logic of Collective Action* (Cambridge, Mass.: Harvard University Press, 1965).

55. Cf. Barry, *Sociologists, Economists and Democracy*, 6–10.

when we start treating social behavior as merely the aggregated product of individual decisions made in isolation, in effect denying explanatory value to concepts which are intrinsically "social" in character.

BATES'S *MARKETS AND STATES IN TROPICAL AFRICA*

A rather more successful attempt to relate peasant rationality to politics is made by Robert Bates in his study of the failures of agricultural policies in postcolonial Africa.[56] His general argument is that the crisis of food production in Africa is due to policies that, though helpful to the short-term political interests of those in power, reduce the incentives to smaller producers of both food crops and the exported cash-crops on which the economies and exchequers of many African states depend. Specifically, governments keep food prices artificially low, use marketing boards to extract large surpluses from cash-crop farmers, systematically favor urban and industrial interests (and some larger farmers), and use agricultural extension services and subsidies as political weapons.

Peasants are at a great disadvantage as far as finding ways to organize themselves politically to change such practices, both because of the intrinsic difficulty of mobilizing hundreds of thousands of smallholders scattered across the countryside and because of the repressive attitude of African governments toward rural opposition. Peasants therefore "use the market against the state"—that is, they give up growing unprofitable crops; they look for better outlets for their produce (including outlets in neighboring countries); or they give up farming and migrate to the towns.[57] For all this Bates gives ample and convincing evidence drawn from a wide range of countries.

His assumptions and methodology are like Popkin's in several respects, although both are more implicit than in *The Rational Peasant.* Bates is equally skeptical of moral economy explanations. For example, he challenges Goran Hyden's view that the

56. Robert H. Bates, *Markets and States in Tropical Africa: The Political Basis of Agricultural Policies* (Berkeley: University of California Press, 1981).

57. Bates, *Markets and States,* 82ff.

decline in food production in Tanzania in the 1970s reflected a rejection of capitalism by an "uncaptured peasantry." Rather, he suggests, the appearance of declining production was due in large part to a reduction in sales by producers to state marketing agencies (which issued the statistics). This decline actually reflected dissatisfaction with the prices these agencies were offering. In short, there was "a flight from the government-controlled market, and a massive diversion of produce into private channels of trade." Drought did cause a decline in production, but in the long term it was the policies of the Tanzanian government that had a more serious effect on food supply.[58]

Further, Bates shares Popkin's view of the importance of studying the rationality of individual action (and, by extension, the importance of providing incentives for individual initiative). Against those who stress the primacy of "international forces" and those attached to "statist" philosophies of development, he suggests that "scholars should pay more attention to the capacity for autonomous choice on the part of local actors, both public and private, and give greater weight to the importance of these choices in shaping the impact of external environments upon the structure of local societies."[59] Like Popkin, Bates is aware of the tenuousness of all forms of collective action and emphasizes the factors that inhibit or facilitate such action on the part of different groups.

Bates, however, is more successful than Popkin in depicting political conflict. One reason may be that he is less insistent on asserting the universal triumph of self-interest over collective interest, or at least on making the two mutually exclusive. He prefers to concentrate on the ways in which the pursuit of self-interest leads to conflicting collective interests. Bates implicitly accepts that there may be different kinds of self-interest, political as well as economic, and he recognizes not only that the pursuit of individual interest may lead to conflict but that also that an elite's pursuit of its immediate political interest may undermine its longer-term economic and even political interests. He

58. Ibid., 85. Hyden's interpretation is given in its fullest form in his study, *Beyond Ujamaa: Underdevelopment and an Uncaptured Peasantry* (Berkeley: University of California Press, 1980).

59. Bates, *Markets and States*, 8.

shows quite clearly that while African governments may be able to keep power by favoring urban interests over those of peasant farmers, in the long run their policies will create scarcities, force up prices, require food imports, and lead to shortages of foreign exchange—all of which will obviously threaten their popularity among the very groups from whom they curry favor.[60]

This approach distinguishes Bates from both the purest liberals (who expect harmony to result from the general pursuit of self-interest) and the simpler welfare economists (who assume the possibility of identifying and realizing a "general welfare function"). He begins by posing the question, "Why should reasonable men adopt public policies that have harmful consequences for the societies they govern?"[61] But he goes on to recognize that politics constitutes a sphere distinct from the market: it is not merely the resultant of individual actions or an "irrational" force obstructing the operation of economic forces. (Indeed, Bates specifically criticizes the political economy interpretations of economists such as Michael Lipton and Keith Griffin who treat politics in a cursory fashion.) There is political rationality just as there is economic rationality, and each has its own arena. Thus "people turn to political action to secure special advantages they are unable to secure by competing in the marketplace."[62]

Politicians, for their part, choose policies both to secure social objectives and to protect and tighten their hold on power. Indeed, they treat the market as "an instrument of political control." Their intervention generally leads to scarcities of some kind, and such scarcities provide the resources for political patronage and corruption—they create "policy-generated rents" which can be selectively allocated to reward friends and punish enemies. Thus, in writing of policies favoring urban industrial development, Bates remarks:

> These policies create economic environments which generate rents. The rents are both economically valuable and politically useful, and from them are forged bonds of self-interest that tie African govern-

60. See, for example, ibid., 129–30.
61. Ibid., 3.
62. Ibid., 4.

ments to their miniscule industrial base. Thus policy choices, made to serve a new vision of the public good, have created a network of self-interest which has proved more enduring than the faith which that vision initially inspired.[63]

Peasant farmers are poorly placed to participate effectively in the political arena. In terms of the "logic of collective action," each has too small a stake and too small a chance to affect the outcome to make joining political movements attractive—apart from the sheer organizational problems of mobilizing a dispersed constituency and the "free rider" problems that its size and the prospective balance of costs and benefits would create. Peasants therefore resort to the market: "The marketplace offers only private 'solutions' to the collective problem confronting farmers, alternatives that can be chosen by individual farm families."[64]

But the government's intervention in the market, its deployment of patronage, and its threat of repression have restricted, shaped, and indeed given a rational ordering to the choices open to farmers. The sad result is that it is

> in the interests of individual rural dwellers to seek limited objectives. Political energies, rather than focusing on the collective standing of the peasantry, focus instead on the securing of particular improvements. . . . Rather than appeals for collective changes, appeals instead focus on incremental benefits . . . individual rural dwellers come, as a matter of personal self-interest, to abide by public policies that are harmful to agrarian interests as a whole.[65]

Bates's analysis, in fact, goes a long way toward meeting the demands of political critics of economics. It preserves the emphasis on the rational, individual maximizer characteristic of the rational choice school, but it avoids several problems to which this approach is prone. One is a tendency to equate self-interest with antisocial and apolitical behavior rather than with a habit of rational calculation. Another is a related tendency to trivialize or discount altogether the dimensions of power and inequality by

63. Ibid., 105. The general argument is outlined on pp. 97–99.
64. Ibid., 87.
65. Ibid., 117–18.

disregarding the institutional and organizational structures through which they are expressed and reinforced. For purposes of exploring the rationality of individual decisions, it is reasonable to take such structures as given. But it is unreasonable and unrealistic to conceive a whole *political system* as an arena in which perfect competition and perfect information obtain and which will normally produce a harmonious and equitable accommodation of interests.

Bates avoids these problems by recognizing (if not approving) the reality of political institutions that provide the basis for a distinctive rationality and can affect the pursuit of individual economic interest in the market, as well as the chances each individual has of realizing his or her interest. Indeed, Bates seems to stand halfway between the rational choice school and the institutionalist school of economics, with its emphasis on the power of entrenched interests. His "political economy" is economic in its values, but explicitly political in its methodology.

ROTHCHILD AND CURRY'S *SCARCITY, CHOICE, AND PUBLIC POLICY IN MIDDLE AFRICA*

Another way of dealing with the problem of relating "individual" to "public" interest (within the framework of the new political economy) is to impute interests and goals to collective organizations—to treat them *as if* they were rational, maximizing actors. Such a solution is, of course, directly contrary to the most basic assumptions of liberal conservatives such as Buchanan, but it provides, implicitly and explicitly, the philosophical basis for much writing on "public choice." Such writing is meant to clarify the choices open to public officials by helping them to assess the costs and benefits of particular courses of action and thereby helping them to choose the most "rational" policy.

In view of the poverty of Third World countries, any effort to show how resources can be used more effectively or can be increased without excessive cost deserves attention. *Scarcity, Choice, and Public Policy in Middle Africa*[66] is such an attempt, and the

66. Donald Rothchild and Robert L. Curry, Jr., *Scarcity, Choice, and Public Policy in Middle Africa* (Berkeley: University of California Press, 1978).

substantive chapters of the book give a well-informed and reasonable analysis of the problems facing African governments that try to increase living standards while preserving the greatest possible degree of independence.

The book also illustrates, however, some of the problems and dangers arising from the application of the new political economy and from the deductive method it uses.

The first problem is to know what the authors mean by "a political economy approach." In their introduction, they claim that through "policy analysis" social scientists can both remain true to their disciplines and "identify with the needs and aspirations of the governments and peoples of Africa."[67] They then suggest that "a political economy framework" provides "an appropriate analytical tool to deal with the dynamics of social change that require the formulation and ranking of priorities and the developing and implementing of policy alternatives . . . political economy offers a useful means of inquiring into the interaction between social, political, and economic organization and process."[68] It quickly turns out that prescription and analysis are to proceed in tandem. The analysis proposed is to be within the framework of the new political economy (the philosophical basis and tenets of which are never, however, spelled out). This approach is said to provide a junction between both economics and political science and between "pure" and "applied" social science. It can help establish

> what rational courses of action are open to decision-makers in light of availing [*sic*] societal demands and constraints. . . . Decision-makers in the less developed countries are immersed in the problems of development administration. They appear to be seeking a comprehensive framework for making rational choices on questions of public concern. Combining analytic and prescriptive insights, a political economy approach seems appropriate as a conceptual framework.[69]

The Logic of Deductive Optimism

This statement begins to expose the dangers dogging an approach adopted because it can allegedly perform "both analytic

67. Ibid., 3.
68. Ibid., 4.
69. Ibid., 9, 25–26.

and prescriptive functions." The main danger is that statements of preference will get confused with analytic statements: writers will see what they want to see. It is not, for example, clear what grounds Rothchild and Curry have for their assertion that Third World politicians are "immersed in the problems of development administration," much less for their claim that these politicians are avid for the conceptual wonders of rational choice methodology. From a developmental (or from a development economist's) point of view, it would obviously be encouraging if both statements were true. Indeed, the authors regard optimism as an essential ingredient of policy analysis. They go so far as to criticize Colin Leys's work on neocolonialism in Kenya on the ground that its conclusions "do not offer the kind of optimism required for generating public interest policies."[70] Having a happy face is thus a major qualification for entering this field.

From such a point of view, desirability determines what is practicable, and whatever is desirable and rational is possible. Following these imaginative principles, Rothchild and Curry lay out a formal model of "an African community's decision-making." This model is entirely hypothetical and rests on three suitably congenial assumptions. The first is that "a significant number of the community's population have similar patterns of taste and, consequently, preferences for benefit patterns as they relate to community output"; the second, that some citizens deviate from the community's preferences, either moderately or radically; and the third, that "the community's institutions, rules, and processes are broadly responsive to majority demands."[71]

Because of their deductive procedure ("Let us assume a boat, Let us assume a sail"), the authors do not try to show that these assumptions are credible, although they do admit that the ways in which preferences are determined in African states may be different from those which obtain elsewhere. They plunge on enthusiastically, developing an elaborate decision-making model that involves seven graphs indicating "indifference curves," "production possibilities curves," and "money price-ratio lines."

70. Ibid., 23.
71. Ibid., 28.

They claim that such a model is "usable in the sense that it provides a conceptual basis for analyzing institutional structures and processes that a community might develop in order to decide on what to produce, how to produce, and for whom to produce."[72]

All this is some way from the authors' original claim for "political economy"—namely, that it is able "to combine the subjective of politics and society with the objective goals of economic growth."[73] If this claim means anything, it presumably means showing what is possible, given the present social and political character of African states. Instead, Rothchild and Curry set down postulates which *they* see as necessary and desirable for purposes of development and then derive from them certain logical implications for "the subjective of politics and society." The empirical reality of the latter, the actual distribution of power and status in actual societies, is not regarded as setting limits, any more than original sin sets limits to the potentialities of divine grace. Rather, it is part of the decision-maker's environment which needs management and manipulation. So we are back in the creative wonderland of economic analysis, where all assumptions are hypothetically valid and where the only necessities are logical necessities.

Rationality versus Politics

This approach leads inexorably into a dissociation between the realm of "rational" decision-making and the realm of "politics" that is familiar to students of economics.[74] Consider, for instance, the following (which introduces a descriptive chapter on "Changing Institutional Resources"):

> *Although* policy choice in middle Africa is the central subject of this work, we think that a look at the main institutions affecting the process of choice is essential to a full understanding of the environment in which these priorities are established. After all, priorities cannot be

72. Ibid., 33–34.

73. Ibid., 10.

74. It also produces the stream of disembodied jargon such model-building usually seems to create, with references to "inadequate input bases," "acculturated mutants," and "mixed scanning approaches."

> determined unless structures are there to organize the interactions among actors, and they cannot become realized objectives unless institutional resources exist to put them into effect.[75]

At this point, the creatures have clearly taken over the laboratory and driven the humans out. For what these sentences seem to say is that the determination of priorities and policies occurs (or can occur) outside the world of politics or is somehow a given around which that world has to organize itself. However, politics (it is implied) does have some influence, so it is useful to know how it works, especially since the institutions of politics are going to have to organize people so that policies can be implemented.

This dissociation of politics, down there, from the capsule in which rationality, objectivity, and statesmanship orbit around the world leads to a consistently rosy view of what "statesmen" (apparently the good guys who actually run governments) are doing and a corresponding tendency to discount the credentials of "politicians" and others who may disagree with or oppose "statesmen." Thus, in considering the centralization of power in African countries after independence, the authors give an interpretation which, behind the jargon, resembles that favored by the "nation-building" school in the 1960s. This interpretation takes as a datum-line for analysis the justifications given by politicians—surely the most willful act of self-mystification any observer of politics can commit. Indeed, Rothchild and Curry say in their conclusions: "We regard current trends toward executive leadership, single-party or no-party dominance, or administrative centralization with understanding and considerable sympathy."[76] With considerable sympathy, certainly. For earlier they claim that the dismantling of laws and institutions protecting the rights of oppositions and minorities and safeguarding civil liberties was justified by and attributable to the wish of African politicians to reduce "decision costs":

> Such structures impeded effective decisional capacity and control and raised doubts about the credibility of the economic and political system. . . . By diffusing and limiting the exercise of central authority,

75. Ibid., 37 (emphasis added).
76. Ibid., 303.

> these structural arrangements raised decision costs, thereby compelling leaders to invest greater resources in the decision-making process than they were wont to do. . . . The transformation of African political structures has largely been in response to the ruling elite's determination to utilize institutions as resources for coping with such problems as national integration and economic development.[77]

This certainly *is* an example of obligatory optimism. There are plenty of less optimistic explanations of this "transformation" that the authors do not consider and have the merit of not depending exclusively on the images of themselves that politicians want to project. By taking a rather narrow, politically self-denying approach, however, Rothchild and Curry make themselves hostages of whoever utters the rhetoric of "development" and "nation-building."

The analysis of "System Goals, Decision-making Rules, and Collective Choices" proceeeds in the same innocently apolitical fashion. The authors assert that there are five factors conditioning governmental decision-making: "information, values, beliefs, analytic capacity, and bureaucratic organization."[78] From this, we are apparently to conclude that African politics is quite different from American politics, in which influence is exercised, power is applied, politicians organize coalitions, and voters and lobbyists campaign, complain, shove and compete. African politics, it seems, is entirely more sedate, with politicians having to pay little heed to the irrational brethren outside their offices and free to determine the greatest good of the greatest number solely according to the quality of their information, their own preferences and intellectual abilities, and the skills of their devoted civil servants.[79] If this image seems incongruous to anyone who has seen at first hand what seems to be confusion, corruption, incompetence, and instability in bureaucracies from Dakar to Dar-es-Salaam, then the lesson is obviously that they have approached these sights with the wrong assumptions in mind.

77. Ibid., 89, 70, 87.

78. Ibid., 91, 99.

79. The authors do in fact say that "the community's leadership has a wider scope for initiative in determining preferences under modern African circumstances" (ibid., 28).

In fact, the authors' own perception seems to be split. They describe the state as "an action agency geared to coping with tasks which the people pose for it through the vehicle of a leadership elite."[80] But they also claim that the system has "goals" which are "paramount"—"ensuring systemic survival," "establishing a national identity," "integrating societies," "creating an acceptable authority system," "mobilizing and distributing resources efficiently," and "securing freedom from external control." We might ask how systems can have goals. But in any case these are the goals which "decision-makers" as well are said to pursue, applying to them their own "preferences and predispositions."[81]

As a statement of what is abstractly and in general necessary for a nation-state to survive and be stable, all of this is unexceptionable enough. But there is no reason to believe that it actually describes the goals which African (or any) politicians actually pursue. Since they are, for better or worse, the real decision-makers, it would be useful to try to find out what their real priorities are, as indicated by their actions as well as by their speeches. Moreover, even if the goals Rothchild and Curry describe were in fact those which politicians espouse, why should they assume that they correspond to the "tasks which the people pose"? The fact is that, again, Rothchild and Curry are postulating, quite arbitrarily, certain "system goals" and "needs" which *they* consider desirable and necessary (their "prescriptive" function) and asking readers to believe that their statements describe reality.

Completely lacking from this analysis is any conception of the actual distribution of power and status, any recognition of political conflict and competition as a reality any more enduring than the "obstacles to development" so often confronted by the older generation of development economists. Indeed, not just "politics," but competing values seem to be the foes of "rational choice." The result is paradoxical-seeming statements such as that "by channeling actions along certain lines, socially-shared values can act to inhibit rational choice-making."[82] Elsewhere,

80. Ibid., 92.
81. Ibid., 97, 98.
82. Ibid., 100.

the authors claim that "optimal policy-making is constrained by the bureaucratic environment in which analysts must operate. They are not free to determine lines of action as they wish, that is, to set rational policies in terms of the most efficient calculation of costs and benefits availing."[83] In both cases, we are left with the impression of a higher realm of rationality that has to impose itself, whether on the bureaucracy or against commonly held values (presumably what "the people" want). This higher order is commanded by "analysts"; but who they are and where they are to be found remains a mystery.

The new political economy, as used here, works by postulating end-states to be achieved, by postulating conditions needed to achieve them, by sketching out some general features of the environment in which these ends are to be pursued, and then by defining what the choices would be and what would therefore be "rational" *if* these ends were adopted, *if* these conditions were obtained, and *if* the environment were open to appropriate manipulation. None of this is illogical or worthless. But it would help us to be shown that it is actually relevant—that the postulates are, in this case, credible in light of what we know of government and politics in Africa. Rothchild and Curry do not seriously try to persuade readers, and they seem to believe that a commitment to development is an alternative to treating power and conflict seriously. And since power and conflict are central to politics, it is hard to see how their political economy model can be a serious attempt to fuse political science and economics.

The three books discussed in this chapter represent three variants of political economy as conceived by the rational choice school. They also reflect the tension between individualist and welfare economics, the one effectively denying explanatory significance to collective and social phenomena, the other attempting to treat "the general welfare" as an objective function, with government as the appointed maximizing, rational actor.

If we imagine a continuum between these positions, Popkin would be at the individualist extreme, and Rothchild and Curry

83. Ibid., 103–04.

at the welfare maximizing extreme. These extremes touch, however, in the sense that both focus on the rationality of individual choices, without regard to influences impinging on the individual. Popkin insists (perhaps overinsists) on the self-sufficiency of individual decision-making, whereas Rothchild and Curry treat government as a potentially self-sufficient agent of general welfare.

Such insistence has costs in both cases. In Popkin's, it involves a cumulative inconsistency as the author progressively reintroduces ideas of culture and morality to explain behavior that is incompatible with his isolationist view of self-interest. Rothchild and Curry's approach involves the abstraction of politics from the process of "rational" decision-making.

The virtue of Bates's approach, by contrast, is that it posits a working relationship between the pursuit of individual interest and the establishment of political "coalitions"—between the market choices of individuals and the political strategies of groups (or the lack of them). It thus acknowledges the impact of institutions and organizations upon the individual actor, whether a person or a government, and incorporates politics into political economy. Bates even refers at one point to "the overriding importance of political considerations" in the formulation of agricultural policy. But he does not embrace a formal politicist theory, preferring to conceive economic and political rationality as distinguishing features of two spheres, the market and the state. In the next chapter, we examine frameworks which *are* fully "politicist" in an explanatory or prescriptive sense.

FOUR
The Primacy of Politics

In 1670, Colbert, minister to Louis XIV of France, wrote enthusiastically to his master about the king's "monetary war against all European states," noting especially his "campaign" against the Dutch: "Your Majesty has founded companies which attack them everywhere like armies. The manufacturers, the shipping canal between the seas, and so many other new establishments which Your Majesty sets up are so many reserve corps which Your Majesty creates from nothing in order that they may fulfil their duty in this war."[1] Colbert's military images capture the spirit of mercantilism and exemplify the approach to economics with which this chapter deals. Mercantilists believed that conflict, not harmony, was intrinsic to economic life, certainly to international economic life. The duty of the ruler therefore was to ensure the wealth and security of his state, which would necessarily be done at some cost to the wealth and security of his neighbors. All other considerations and interests had to be subordinated to the overriding priority of consolidating the power of the state which was a basic condition for such prosperity as the subject might enjoy. Even Adam Smith accepted that governments had a right and a duty to bend or suspend the general rules of free trade in the more fundamental interests of survival: "defence [Smith wrote] is of much more importance than opulence."[2]

1. Quoted in Eli F. Heckscher, *Mercantilism,* 2d ed. (London: George Allen and Unwin, 1955), 2:18.

2. Heckscher, *Mercantilism,* 2:16.

However, where Smith and the mercantilists parted company was over long-term objectives. While Smith regarded deference to *raison d'état* as exceptional (if necessary) and as a means to the broader end of advancing economic growth, the mercantilists generally regarded the enlargement of state power as an end in itself. As Heckscher says, "mercantilism as a system of power was . . . primarily a system for forcing economic policy into the service of power as an end in itself."[3]

POLITICISM

Economics "in the service of power" or as "reflection of power relationships" is the theme of this chapter. The writers and models examined here have in common the view that politics or power is, can be, or should be dominant over economic processes. This view leads to or develops from the criticism of economics as failing to take account of power.

But such a view does not just represent a corrective reaction to the more apolitical flights of liberal thought. It arises also from a radically different tradition which, indeed, has a longer lineage than liberalism, particularly outside the Protestant, Anglo-Saxon world. As noted in chapter 2, the belief that economics should be subordinate to the dictates of morality goes back as far as the Greeks. Associated with it is the philosophical tradition that sees society as an organism, the interests of which are necessarily higher than those of individual citizens: indeed, it usually portrays the citizens as deriving their identity and moral purpose from the larger organism, which inevitably becomes synonymous with "the state." This organic, statist tradition can be traced from Plato through Roman law into medieval social thought and thence into romantic conservative and nationalist thought in the nineteenth century. Mercantilism had roots in this tradition: more recently, it has been associated with doctrines, such as corporatism, that are usually regarded as right-wing.[4]

3. Ibid., 17.

4. On the philosophical lineage of corporatism, see Alfred Stepan, *The State and Society: Peru in Comparative Perspective* (Princeton; N.J.: Princeton University

"Politicism" (to use a term coined by the Argentinian political scientist Guillermo O'Donnell) is not, however, limited to societies in which the organic, statist tradition is dominant.[5] If we consider those writers who have demanded greater consideration for "power" and "politics" in analysis of economic issues, it quickly becomes clear that many do not belong to this tradition, and indeed are hostile to it. For example, it makes no sense to treat American "institutionalists," such as Commons or Galbraith, as "politicists" in the same sense as the nationalists of the German historical school in the nineteenth century.

We have, indeed, to make a broad distinction between lines of development in respect of politicism. This distinction applies to the interpretations advanced, the concepts used, and the overall character and context of theorizing. The theories examined in previous chapters essentially belong to one line. They were developed mainly in the early industrializing, Anglo-Saxon societies of North America and Western Europe—in liberal democracies where the values and political power of a property-owning middle class were firmly established by the mid-nineteenth century. Beyond this perimeter lay not only the areas now designated as the Third World, but also those continental European countries which had a different political and philosophical legacy and typically a different experience of domestic development in the nineteenth and twentieth centuries. Among the characteristics common to such countries were a more lasting acquaintance with absolutism, a legal and philosophical tradition that emphasized the reality and the rights of "the state" or the ruler, a weak commercial and industrial middle class (dependent on a domestic oligarchy or aristocracy or on outside political and economic support), and a correspondingly frail tradition of liberalism.

Not all continental states fit this description. France, notably,

---

Press, 1976), 26–40. In such theory, Stepan remarks, "the state is conceived of as playing a relatively autonomous, architectural role in the polity" (ibid., 31).

5. Guillermo O'Donnell, "Corporatism and the Question of the State," in *Authoritarianism and Corporatism in Latin America,* ed. James M. Malloy (Pittsburgh: University of Pittsburgh Press, 1977), 52–55.

was a model of étatisme, but the strength of its middle classes and of their radical and republican traditions set it apart from those cases in which centralization and the lack of a propertied, independent, and assertive middle class contributed to the prevalence of authoritarian, "statist" regimes and philosophies. Further, this last category is clearly developmental rather than geographical in character. Thus several writers have pointed out the similarity between forms of authoritarianism in "late-developing" Europe (mainly in Germany, Italy, the Iberian countries, and parts of Eastern Europe) and those in Latin American and other Third World countries. These latter countries have had to respond—ideologically, developmentally, and diplomatically—to the problems posed by the existence and influence of a core of powerful, more industrially developed states.

What the older "liberal" industrialized societies and the later developing and/or "absolutist" states do have in common is the experience of radical social and economic change accompanying industrialization. They also have in common a pattern of challenge to the principles of liberalism, whether pressed from within or imposed from outside, whether strongly or weakly established. In all, closer and more persistent ties have formed between the economic and political spheres, and both institutions and theory have had to adapt to this change.

But the political outcomes and the ways in which theorists depict them differ sharply according to which group we are studying. The difference can be illustrated by considering two issues: one is the application of the term *corporatism* to industrializing and industrialized societies; the other is the character and context of theory.

CORPORATISM: "SOCIETAL" AND "STATIST"

The term *corporatist* has been widely applied to regimes in which governmental and private sector institutions interlock. Such interlocking is sometimes formalized in constitutional provisions: sometimes it subverts formal allocations of authority. Typically, "corporatist" regimes have adopted procedures for consultation with the larger business, financial, and labor organizations, and such procedures have the effect of excluding from real political influence individuals and groups unfortunate enough not to have been coopted.

One of the problems about corporatism as a category is that it seems to be found in societies which are very different in their histories, cultures, and institutions. It is applied to the bicycle monarchies of the Low Countries and Scandinavia, to the fascist states of the 1930s, and to the "bureaucratic authoritarian" states in Latin America, such as Argentina, Brazil, and Mexico.[6] Now, to find Argentina and the Netherlands in the same category immediately raises questions about the value of the classification being used. Obviously, some other fairly basic distinctions have to be introduced if the category of corporatism is not to become strained.

Philippe Schmitter has, in fact, suggested one such broad distinction that enables us to salvage the concept of corporatism while recognizing the profound differences in historical experience and regime type that blanket application of the term may conceal. Schmitter distinguishes between what he terms "societal corporatism"—in which the intersection of public and private sectors is a partial and reciprocal matter—and "state corporatism"—in which the initiative and the locus of control is heavily on the side of the state.[7] The first, more genteel, negotiated form is found in advanced industrial states such as the Scandinavian countries, the Netherlands, and the United Kingdom. Here corporatism has evolved through the dynamics of liberal economic and political institutions, through the gradual accumulation and concentration of economic power in the hands of large firms, financial institutions, and labor unions, and through the inexorable if incremental involvement of government in the management and stabilization of increasingly complex economies. These processes have quietly but irretrievably undermined the conditions that made liberalism credible as an explanatory and normative theory applied to industrial democratic societies.

6. See Philippe Schmitter, "Still the Center of Corporatism?" *Review of Politics* 36, no. 1 (January 1974): 102–03.

7. Ibid., 102–11.

The reality has diverged from the vision: individual choice is in practice limited, the market is dominated by powerful organizations, and the political system is controlled by the administrative and party bureaucracies. But a large degree of power remains in the hands of organizations outside the formal public sector, and the working arrangements of corporatism are the result as much of initiative and interest on the part of business and labor as of any intervention or imposition by government. As Schmitter puts it: "Societal corporatism appears to be the concomitant, if not ineluctable component of the postliberal, advanced capitalist organized democratic welfare state . . . [its origins] lie in the slow, almost imperceptible decay of advanced pluralism."[8] Indeed, as Alan Cawson has pointed out, the group theories of liberal pluralism, which are usually seen as proclaiming the relative *openness* of Western societies, actually represent a crucial regression from classical liberal thought and prepare the way for societal corporatism.[9]

Yet the political practice of regimes under societal corporatism remains radically different from that under state corporatism. Indeed, the two outcomes represent two fairly easily distinguishable historical routes. State corporatism is characteristic of those societies referred to earlier which have experienced "delayed capitalist development," in which the state has taken a dominant, autonomous role in shaping both the distribution of power within society and the direction of economic development. In such societies, corporatism signifies not the decay of pluralism, but its abortion: it represents an attempt to satisfy rising popular demands for economic improvement while controlling the political process through which such demands are expressed.[10] In domestic politics, state corporatist regimes are authoritarian, but not necessarily totalitarian: they presume to organize political expression, not to determine its content in any detailed and pervasive way.[11] In foreign policy, they tend to be

8. Ibid., 105, 106.

9. Alan Cawson, "Pluralism, Corporatism and the Role of the State," *Government and Opposition* 13, no. 2 (Spring 1978): 180.

10. Schmitter, "Century of Corporatism?" 106, 108.

11. Robert A. Monson, "Perspectives on Corporatist Approaches to Political

nationalistic and mercantilistic, reflecting an acute sensitivity to the vulnerability which late development involves.

"INTERACTIVE" AND "DETERMINISTIC" THEORY

This distinction between types of corporatism corresponds to a distinction between forms of politicism in the realm of theory. In both advanced and late-developing capitalist societies, the independent influence of politics and the existence of power in the economic system have been themes invoked by critics of liberalism (and Marxism). But in the advanced capitalist societies the prevalent idea seems to be that of power *within* the economic system, while in the late-developing group the emphasis is upon the determining imposition of the political order (the state) upon the economic order.[12] In the first case, debate proceeds by incremental reformulations of pluralism, by observation of the growing differentiation of resources and opportunities *within* the market, by argument between supporters of market economics and advocates of redistributive and regulative government intervention. "Government" continues to be seen as a utility for solving problems generated by "society," rather than as an organic entity pursuing a distinct, higher, and immanent mission concerned with "national destiny." (Politicians and civil servants in advanced industrialized societies do, of course, talk about "the national interest," but reference to this idea always prompts a barrage of skeptical, debunking comment from the spokesmen of pluralist orthodoxy, who tend to see the very idea

---

Change in Latin America," *Plural Societies* 10, nos. 3–4 (Autumn and Winter 1974): 22, citing Juan Linz, "An Authoritarian Regime: Spain," in *Mass Politics: Studies in Political Sociology,* ed. Erik Allardt and Stein Rokkan (New York: Free Press, 1970), 329.

12. This emphasis is noted by Simon Schwartzman when he writes: "in corporatist regimes, the state is stronger than civil society. . . . To say that the state is 'stronger than society' is to say that the group which controls the state is able to impose its will upon other, private sectors of society, thanks to its control of extractive resources, military manpower, or communication networks" (Simon Schwartzman, "Back to Weber: Corporatism and Patrimonialism in the Seventies," in *Authoritarianism and Corporatism,* ed. Malloy, 92).

as a rhetorical facade for whatever coalition of special interests happens to be on top for the time being.)

In the late-developing countries, theory tends to be more deterministic, postulating either the determination of the political order by the economic or (as in this case) determination of the economic order by the political. Since political power is so centralized and since the middle class does not constitute a significant independent concentration of economic power, politics tends to be seen as a zero-sum game, and the most persuasive theories are those which emphasize conflict, domination, exploitation, and exclusion. Theories that stress the overriding need to maintain order and authority vie with theories that, equally absolutely, stress the need to seize power and wreak vengeance.

Social and political theory thus takes on the lean and hungry look of political life itself. Its uncompromising simplification and its insistence on the subordination of one variable to another reflect the polarization and the preoccupation with secure possession of power that mark the political sphere itself. Theories depicting separation between economics and politics, a diffusion of power, or an exchanging, bargaining, interactive relationship between the two spheres are (understandably) seen as irrelevant.

Thus, just as pluralism as a theory and "societal corporatism" are related chronologically, so the bolder forms of determinism are related dialectically. The extremes touch and react to each other: the more starkly "economistic" forms of Marxism and the more "statist" versions of corporatism not only coexist but nurture each other.

In the following sections, I want to fill out this rather summary and abstract typology by referring to particular writers, schools, and societies.

"SOCIETAL CORPORATISM" AND ECONOMIC POWER

The criticism of orthodox economics as "power-blind" was noted in chapter 2 and does not need much elaboration here. Essentially, it argued that because of its concern with individuals and its assumption of harmony as the natural outcome of individual choice in a free market, liberal economics had floated away into a kind of intellectual Disneyland inhabited by a multitude of industrious dwarfs, happily hammering away at their anvils and humming over their money bags, apparently untaxed, unexploited—and untempted by lust, avarice, or power. Every story automatically had a happy ending, as it usually had only one character.

Against the caricature of individualism, the institutionalists and others argued that it was imperative to emphasize "the broader *political* character of economic life," to redefine economics as "the study of the shaping and sharing of power," and in these ways to reestablish a truly political "political economy."[13] Institutionalists from Commons and Veblen down to John Kenneth Galbraith have emphasized the centrality of conflict in economic life and have indeed depicted it in evolutionary terms. Their analysis tends to concentrate upon the very factors treated as "noneconomic" in orthodox theory (and especially upon the role of technology). They see capitalism as evolving under the influence both of market dynamics and of the conflicting organized interests and priorities to which it gives rise. Continuing growth may be prevented by "institutional obstructions" and "vested interests," the existence of which provide a justification for types of government intervention, whether in the form of antitrust laws or in that of actual planning and injection of resources.

Just as government becomes involved in management of the economy, so the major institutions of the private sector acquire the rationality of bureaucracies, constituting (in Galbraith's words) a "planning system" of their own. The larger corporations lose the propensity for risk-taking and profit-maximization characteristic of the entrepreneur and become preoccupied with security and controlling their environment. These changes lead

13. John E. Elliott, "Institutionalism as an Approach to Political Economy," *Journal of Economic Issues* 12, no. 1 (March 1978): 91; Allan G. Gruchy, "Law, Politics, and Institutional Economics," *Journal of Economic Issues* 7, no. 4 (December 1973): 626. In the following section I have drawn heavily on these two excellent accounts of institutionalist thought.

to the acceptance of closer relations with government and to attempts to limit the normal uncertainties of the market.

Consequently, institutionalists look to political action to contain the threats to consumer choice (and in some cases democratic accounability) created by such concentration of corporate power. Some (such as Veblen) actually wanted "a socialist regime of workmanship," but others have sought a remedy in the reinvigoration of political institutions, such as Congress, and in the establishment of countervailing organizations representing consumers and other excluded interests.[14] While most claim to be concerned with preserving the most important values of market economics, they also envisage permanent structures of public regulation, encircling the market and preventing the iniquities and casualties that occurred in the free-booting days of capitalism: they refer to "workable capitalism" and "limited capitalism." Thus institutionalists neither deny the existence of power in the economic sphere nor seek to appropriate all such power to the state. Rather, they seek to legislate and entrench its redistribution, much in the spirit of the populist movement.

The outcome of such proposals would be a form of mixed economy, an institutionalized pluralism that would ensure the representation of all major interests (little consumers as well as big business and big labor). Thus Lord Keynes, whose analysis and prescription resembled those of the North American institutionalists (though in a very different political context) advocated arrangements effectively foreshadowing the types of societal corporatism that later appeared in Western Europe. He anticipated "the growth and recognition of semi-autonomous bodies . . . bodies which in their ordinary course of affairs [would be] mainly autonomous within their prescribed limitations, but [would be] subject in the last resort to the sovereignty of democracy expressed through parliament."[15] In Britain, proposals for societal corporatism of this kind were, in fact,

14. Gruchy, "Law, Politics," 632.

15. John Maynard Keynes, "The End of Laissez-Faire" in Keynes, *Essays in Persuasion* (London: Rupert Hart-Davis, 1952), 313–14 (cited in Schmitter, "Century of Corporatism?" 110).

aired long before the "social contract" and the prices-and-incomes policies of the sixties and seventies. Most, like Keynes's plan, did not imply the supplanting of parliamentary government, but rather the establishment of consultative and planning bodies linking specific ministries with organized interests in the private sector.[16]

Compared to some theorists, institutionalists and neoinstitutionalists do not have either a universal theoretical model or a grand design for the reorganization of society. Their theory arises from close observation of the problems of economies already well advanced in industrialization. Their prescriptions are typically intended to domesticate capitalism, to preserve the principles and institutions that made it dynamic while protecting people who have been hurt by its operational excesses. Intellectually, they seek to reconstruct economics by "making room for the analysis of the role of power in economic affairs."[17] In typically pluralist fashion, they treat power specifically and pragmatically. It is conceived not as the generalized property of collective institutions such as the state, but as inhering in particular relationships, reforms for which they advocate.

Indeed, the very notion of "the state" was virtually absent from the literature of institutionalism and pluralism. Galbraith writes of "the New Industrial State," but in this literature the state is usually merely a synomym for "the general area of central government in contradistinction to society."[18] In the political theory of industrializing Anglo-Saxon societies, as we noted earlier, politics is essentially an arena within which social interests resolve their conflicts.[19] In this sense, liberalism either en-

16. Trevor Smith, "Trends and Tendencies in Re-Ordering the Representation of Interests," paper presented to the annual conference of the Political Studies Association, Nottingham, England, 22–24 March 1976.

17. Gruchy, "Law, Politics," 625.

18. J. P. Nettl, "The State as a Conceptual Variable," *World Politics* 20, no. 4 (July 1968): 591.

19. As Robert Gilpin remarks, for liberals "the state represents an aggregation of private interests: public policy is but the outcome of a pluralistic class struggle among interest groups" (Robert Gilpin, *U.S. Power and the Multinational Corporation: The Political Economy of Foreign Direct Investment* (New York: Basic Books, 1975), 28.

tirely ignored politics or treated the political process rather deterministically—as a dependent variable of social and economic processes, as a black box that received inputs, digested them, and disgorged outputs. It did not seriously contemplate the possibility that the collection of executive, legislative, judicial, and administrative institutions known on the European continent as "the state" might have or might develop autonomous authority or interests.[20] This notion was regarded as the metaphysical burden of less happy lands, a symptom of the unfortunate legacy of absolutism, romanticism, and nationalism. Arthur Bentley, one of the founding theorists of "the group approach" to politics, dismissed interest in the state as "among the intellectual amusements of the past."[21] The institutionalists stopped short of considering the state as an independent force for the good reason that the societies with which they were familiar (Great Britain and the United States) were relatively "stateless," at least in their domestic politics.[22]

"INSTITUTION-BUILDING" AND POLITICAL DEVELOPMENT

The tendency to treat politics as a dependent variable of social and economic processes (which liberalism shared with Marxism) carried over into the social science literature on "modernization" and "political development." This literature commonly identified social and economic prerequisites for political development

20. See Nettl, "State as Conceptual Variable," 561–62, 591; Stepan, *The State and Society,* 4–16. O'Donnell notes that both liberals and Marxists "deny or ignore the specificity of the state as a societal factor endowed with varying, but rarely insignificant, capabilities for autonomous impulse or initiative. By denying or ignoring such specificity, they make of the state a dependent or instrumental variable of civil society" (O'Donnell, "Corporatism," 52).

21. Arthur F. Bentley, *The Process of Government,* ed. Peter H. Odegard (Cambridge, Mass.: The Belknap Press of Harvard University Press, 1967), 263 (cited in Stepan, *The State and Society,* 11).

22. Nettl, "State as Conceptual Variable," 561–62. See, for example, the earlier work of Gabriel Almond (and the critique of "modernization" by C. S. Whitaker, Jr., in his article, "A Dysrhythmic Process of Political Change," *World Politics* 19, no. 2 (January 1967): 183–214.

and assumed that the dynamics of modernization in one sector would be accompanied by modernization in others.[23]

During the 1960s, Samuel P. Huntington developed a critique of such writing from what was essentially a politicist (though not corporatist) point of view.[24] In criticizing the logical superficiality of students of political development, Huntington suggested that one of their main errors was to equate "development" with "modernization." The latter could create enormous pressures for improvements in standaards of living that might break down the rather fragile political institutions of new states. Thus, in characteristically politicist manner, Huntington argued that the strengthening of political institutions was a priority in developing countries, and one that should be respected even at the cost of slowing down modernization and limiting popular participation in politics.[25] For, "without strong political institutions, society lacks the means of defining and realizing its common interests": and the reality of many developing countries was not political development, but political instability and institutional decay.[26]

In the climate of the 1960s, this thesis elicited violent criticism, much of which interpreted it as a specious defense of authoritar-

23. A poignant example of this tendency is the writing on the effects of industrialism in South Africa. Liberals assumed that "the logical imperatives of industrialization" would break down the "irrationalities" of apartheid. This view has been attacked since the 1960s by radicals and others who argue either that industrialism sustains segregation and the South African state or that it is neutral with respect to apartheid. See, in this connection, Herbert Blumer, "Industrialization and Race Relations," in *Industrialization and Race Relations: A Symposium,* ed. Guy Hunter (London: Institute of Race Relations/Oxford University Press, 1965), 220–53; Frederick A. Johnstone, "White Prosperity and White Supremacy in South Africa," *African Affairs* 69, no. 274 (April 1970): 124–40; David Yudelman, "Industrialization, Race Relations and Change in South Africa," *African Affairs* 74, no. 294 (January 1975): 82–96; and Martin Legassick and Duncan Innes, "Capital Restructuring and Apartheid: A Critique of Constructive Engagement," *African Affairs* 72, no. 305 (October 1977): 437–82.

24. See especially his article, "Political Development and Political Decay," *World Politics* 17, no. 3 (April 1965): 386–430, and his book, *Political Order in Changing Societies* (New Haven: Yale University Press, 1968).

25. "Political Development and Political Decay," 405–07.

26. Ibid., 411.

ianism. Such criticism was shallow insofar as Huntington's analysis of institutions stressed the importance of adaptability and legitimacy. Indeed, the direction of criticism said more about the romantic anarchism of many critics than it did about Huntington's own ideas. Moreover, when it was the Left that was reviling Huntington, the choice of target was quite ironic, since one of the most pervasive features of his work was an admiration for the Leninist model of party control![27]

Such excesses and irrelevance aside, however, Huntington's position was unapologetically conservative and politicist relative to those of the liberal and democratic socialists, in that it placed a higher value on order than on material progress and popular participation (or at least claimed that achievement of the first was a condition for achieving the others). It thus attracted the criticism of seeming to approve of the accumulation of power for its own sake, regardless of the means by which the accumulation was engineered or of the uses to which it was put.

"STATE CORPORATISM": THE GERMAN PROBLEM

The statist tradition bypassed or challenged liberalism even in the early nineteenth century. In Germany especially, romantics and nationalists such as Fichte, Müller, and List followed Hegel in believing that the individual realizes himself and his freedom through the state. They criticized what they saw as the individualism and materialism of Adam Smith and the English utilitarians, and stressed the need to ground economic theory and policy in national interest.

This emphasis on the primacy of the state reflected a sense of Germany's vulnerability, of the humiliations to which she was liable as long as the fragmentation from which she suffered in the early nineteenth century persisted. It led to the advocacy of mercantilist policies and even to the suggestion that paper currencies were preferable to metallic currencies, since they tied the citizen's material interest to the fortunes of the state. Similar anxieties ran through the writings of the German historical

27. See, for example, "Political Development and Political Decay," 428.

school, which insisted that there could be no universal economic laws and that the needs of Germany were different (notably) from those of Great Britain. They appear later in the writings of Max Weber, and even Engels wrote in a rather sympathetic way about the humiliations to which Germans were subject abroad.

Engels, in fact, was involved in a famous dispute with a minor member of the German historical school, E. K. Dühring, whose "force theory" is a good example of politicism. Dühring declared that his analysis was based on "the principle that the political conditions are the determining cause of the economic order."[28] He continued:

> The formation of *political* relationships is, historically, the *fundamental fact,* and the economic facts dependent on this are only an *effect* or a particular case, and are consequently always *facts of the second order.* Some of the newer socialist systems take as their guiding principle, the superficial idea of a completely reverse relationship, in that they make the political phenomena subordinate, and, as it were, grow out of the economic conditions.[29]

Such economism was, indeed, embraced by both Engels and Marx. Engels argued (in the "Anti-Dühring" and an unfinished supplementary manuscript) that it was the mode of production which shaped the political system and determined its survival or destruction. Specifically, he claimed that "whenever, in the past, political force had come into conflict with economic development, the conflict had always ended with the overthrow of political force: economic development had broken through inexorably."[30]

Engels applied this generalization to contemporary German politics, holding that the imperatives of economic development (and the material interests of the German bourgeoisie) were the

28. Quoted in Friedrich Engels, *Herr Eugen Dühring's Revolution in Science* ("Anti-Dühring") (New York: International Publishers, 1939), 176.

29. Engels, "Anti-Dühring," 176 (emphasis in original).

30. *The Role of Force in History: A Study of Bismarck's Policy of Blood and Iron,* ed. Ernst Wangermann (New York: International Publishers, 1968), p. 13. (This volume is a translation, with introductory commentary, of an unfinished manuscript by Engels, intended to extend the argument presented in the sections entitled "The Force Theory" in the "Anti-Dühring").

vital factors in the customs union and the movement toward unification. Political factors (in this case, the geopolitical ambitions of Prussia) might exist, but they were of secondary importance. The decisive issue was "the incompatibility between modern industry and commerce and Germany's feudal-bureaucratic system," which would have to be resolved by the replacement of the archaic Junkers by a bourgeois-dominated regime. The contradictions of the capitalist mode of production would then accelerate and a dictatorship of the proletariat would eventually be established.[31]

Unfortunately, though Engels's prediction of a united Germany came true, his expectations of the German bourgeoisie were disappointed. Bismarck successfully defied its parliamentary representatives in 1862 and established a state designed to domesticate both the middle classes and the proletariat. Yet Engels continued to believe that ultimately "the German bourgeois" would be "compelled to do his political duty, to oppose the present system."[32] Even after Bismarck's dismissal in 1890, the middle classes continued to be subservient and, indeed, became a source of enthusiastic support for the imperialism and naval expansion of Kaiser Wilhelm.

Such a failure of interpretation—along with the equally embarrassing failure of the German Left to create an effective opposition—was bound to attract critical attention to the theoretical framework of Marxism itself. It is surely question-begging to argue, as Wangermann does, that late nineteenth-century German history provides "an example, not indeed of political force determining economic conditions, but of an outworn, reactionary regime securing its survival by combining military conquest with some adjustment to the requirements of industrial and commercial expansion. It is an example of a reactionary regime successfully drawing the political sting out of economic expansion."[33] The obvious question is why was the regime able to do so. Eventually, of course, it did collapse, but neither a revolu-

31. *The Role of Force*, 13.
32. Ibid., 20.
33. Ibid., 27–28.

tionary proletarian state nor a stable middle-class republic succeeded it. A "state corporatist" regime, even a totalitarian state, came to power under the Nazis, crushing both the Left and the constitutional democrats.

From the pre–World War I experience of Germany, Max Weber drew both some of the main themes of his work and some theoretical conclusions that directly challenged basic propositions of Marxist thought. Like earlier German writers, Weber was concerned about the vulnerability of Germany as a late-developing economy and saw the state as essential to the growth and self-preservation of German society.[34] His analysis of recent German history also led Weber to emphasize the significance of the state as an actor in its own right and to criticize the analysis of politics developed by the socialists.[35] The latter, like the liberals, had in Weber's view failed to appreciate the autonomy political institutions could acquire and their capacity to influence the social and political environment in which they were set. The Marxists and liberals had treated politics as a dependent variable of economics and had seen the political as "secondary and derived."[36]

The political mistakes and delusions of German socialism stemmed directly from this intellectual error, which had led them to ignore the dynamics of bureaucratic development and the consequences of a ramifying division of labor in German society. Specifically, the socialists had failed to understand the implications of the division of labor for their own program. They expected that the conquest of power by the proletariat would lead to atrophy of the state and elimination of the very sources of political power itself (mainly, inequality in access to economic

34. Anthony Giddens, *Politics and Sociology in the Thought of Max Weber* (London: Macmillan, 1972), 33–34.

35. Giddens notes: "A key theme in Weber's writings is his emphasis upon the independent influence of the 'political' as opposed to the economic" (*Politics and Sociology*, 32). According to Freund, Weber held that "the political aspects of a phenomenon are never exclusively conditioned by the economy." He rejected the tendency in Marxism to "reduce the explanation of all cultural phenomena to an economic substratum" (Julien Freund, *The Sociology of Max Weber* [New York: Pantheon Books, 1968], 153, 157).

36. Giddens, *Politics and Sociology*, 32–33.

resources). In reality, Weber argued, the socialization of the economy proposed by the radicals would probably lead to an enlargement of the bureaucracy. In the same way, the mass parties organized by the radicals and socialists were themselves bound to become bureaucratized, and the closer they came to nominally controlling the apparatus of the state, the more the latter would impose its own interests and operating principles upon them.[37]

Thus the folly of the socialists was to assume that economic power could be mustered to reshape the state in accordance with the program of a particular class and its leaders. Bureaucracy could be directed and in fact needed leadership (which the German middle class had failed to provide).[38] But it was necessary to recognize the fundamental drive toward greater division of labor in all capitalist societies, the way in which such division established the state as an independent interest, and the degree of initiative which the component bureaucracies of the state consequently enjoyed. Indeed, according to Anthony Giddens, Weber saw the division of labor as expanding from the political sphere into the economic.[39] Moreover, he insisted that specific types of social relationship were best seen as constituting "spheres of political domination," rather than as reflections of particular dispositions of economic power.[40] He went on to make his well-known distinctions between types of domination ("traditional," "legal-rational," and "charismatic"), arguing that charismatic domination—the rule of the politician—was necessary to provide guidance to the proliferating bureaucracies.

In all of this, however, it was vital to recognize that the rationalization and specialization of social life were irreversible processes and that all programs of reform and revolution had to be conceived in acceptance of this reality. The state would not "wither away," and bureaucracy had profound roots in broader processes of social change that had been under way since the late Middle Ages. The state itself was not merely an appendage of a

37. Ibid., 33, 36.
38. Ibid., 24, 35.
39. Ibid., 35.
40. Ibid., 30.

social class. It could not be identified as serving some "ethical" purpose, but only in terms of the scope and character of its power. The former was territorial, the latter coercive: the state was a comprehensive organization enjoying a legitimate monopoly of force within specific territorial boundaries.[41]

STATE CORPORATISM IN THE THIRD WORLD

After Weber's death, the idea of the supremacy of the state became associated with theories of the corporate state as established notably in Spain, Portugal, Italy, and Germany itself. In the process, *corporatism* became a theoretical synonym for *fascism*. This association was unfortunate so far as later application of the term to European politics was concerned. *Corporatism* inevitably bore connotations of totalitarian dictatorship obviously irrelevant to the type of interest representation that emerged in the advanced industrial countries.

Such connotations could also distort discussions of corporatism in the Third World. But at least in developmental terms, there was, as has already been suggested, some similarity between the experiences of the late-developing and peripheral European capitalist countries and those of some Third World societies actually in the throes of industrialization. Certainly, in Latin America many such societies had inherited legal and philosophical beliefs that gave preeminence to the state; and such preeminence had been reinforced by the aloofness and authoritarianism of colonial government.

In Latin America, the circumstances of development in the nineteenth and early twentieth centuries typically brought about real, sharp changes in the holders of power: landowning oligarchies were displaced by populist regimes, usually directed by previously excluded members of the intelligentsia. Populism was, in turn, supplanted in the 1950s and 1960s by military and "bureaucratic authoritarian" governments.[42] The state appara-

41. Ibid., 34.

42. See, for example, James M. Malloy, "Authoritarianism and Corporatism in Latin America: The Modal Pattern," in *Authoritarianism and Corporatism in Latin*

tus expanded throughout this process, being continually enlarged to cope with tasks of economic development and (as importantly) to provide mechanisms for managing relations with the complex of organized interests that development generated.

As in the late-developing societies of Europe, the preeminence of the state (and the authoritarianism accompanying it) was partly a historical legacy and partly a result of a weakness of the "national bourgeoisie," which made a liberal, private-enterprise style of development unworkable. As O'Donnell argues, the middle class "is a viable national bourgeoisie only if it finds a state which shelters it to a degree unknown in previous cases of capitalist development."[43] In Latin American and other Third World cases, the creation of a middle class was impeded by the domestic power of a landed oligarchy and by the external control wielded by foreign firms. Before it obtained political power, the middle class was mainly confined to employment in the liberal professions and the bureaucracy.[44] Once it obtained power, it adopted a nationalist rhetoric against both the displaced oligarchy and the outside interests held responsible for "dependence" (a concept discussed in more detail in the next chapter).

The populism embraced by this middle class did not imply any loosening of control or loss of initiative on the part of the state. Indeed, the state took on new functions as it became involved in managing external economic relations and in providing money,

America, ed. J. Malloy, 6–9; and O'Donnell, "Corporatism," 66–67. O'Donnell's "bureaucratic authoritarian" thesis is set out most fully in his *Modernization and Bureaucratic Authoritarianism: Studies in South American Politics* (Berkeley: Institute of International Studies, University of California, 1973). See also his article, "Reflections on the Patterns of Change in the Bureaucratic Authoritarian State," *Latin American Research Review* 12, no. 1 (Winter 1978): 3–28. A useful symposium on O'Donnell's argument and its implications is *The New Authoritarianism in Latin America*, ed. David Collier (Princeton, N.J.: Princeton University Press, 1979).

43. O'Donnell, "Corporatism," 63. Stepan writes similarly that in Latin America "the national bourgeoisie has not been able to attain a hegemonic situation comparable to that achieved by the bourgeoisie in England, the United States, and some other countries in Europe, nor has a hegemonic industrial proletariat emerged" (*The State and Society*, 23).

44. Malloy, "Authoritarianism and Corporatism," 7.

roads, and other types of public support for domestic industrialization. In external relations, the posture of most populist regimes was, as Malloy points out, "neomercantilist": in domestic politics, their attitudes and policies were paternalistic.[45] Like European corporatists of the 1920s, the populists rejected the formulas of both capitalism and socialism. They emphasized national over class interests and saw their duty as one of leading the workers and peasants out of underdevelopment. Their strategy was "to seize the state and create a base so as to render it [the state] capable of acting as an autonomous factor shaping both its internal and external environment."[46]

Malloy remarks that the philosophy and policies of populism were "based on an implicit *corporatist* image of socio-political organization."[47] It assumed that the state could represent a national interest higher than any sectional interest, and that in pursuit of the national interest it was necessary to shape and stabilize relations between the state and the various organized interests that appeared and proliferated as industrialization and the "emancipation of the masses" proceeded. The question was whether "state corporatism" thus conceived would have a more or less democratic character. Would the various interests concerned (such as business and labor) keep some independence? And would control from above extend to all forms of public expression (apart from the main economic interests)?

State corporatism has typically left some autonomy to the main organized interests and is therefore not totalitarian.[48]

45. Ibid., 11.

46. Ibid., 13.

47. Ibid., 12 (emphasis in original). Elsewhere, Malloy refers to populism as a "general and amorphous concept": it was, he suggests, "the ideological product of the highly bureaucratized and largely dependent Latin American middle class which found its previously secure position threatened by the multiple effects of the exhaustion of the export-oriented growth model" (ibid., 9).

48. However, as a review of the Collier symposium points out, "the new authoritarianism" differs from its predecessors in not offering the prospect of a return to civilian democratic government. For this reason, and because they are more "rational" and efficient, they tend to be more systematically oppressive: such regimes "actively pursue the demobilization of the lower classes, to induce political quietude through repression and terror . . . [they] are a chilling combi-

Usually, it has affected some sectors more than others. In O'Donnell's view, it generally works to curb or even suppress popular demands, while providing formalized procedures for favored interests to influence or even control policymaking in specific areas.[49] Whatever the variations between particular regimes, the common trait is an assertion of the right of the state to determine who may participate in politics and on what terms. Corporatism is thus "a mode of organizing state and society through strong, autonomous government structures that enforce a limited pluralism of authoritatively recognized groups."[50]

It has been most apparent and thoroughgoing in societies which have ceased to be mere exporters of agricultural or mineral commodities and have achieved extensive and advanced industrialization.[51] In such societies, industrialization has produced a complicated and sophisticated pattern of organized interests and a demand for continuous improvements in opportunities and standards of living. Corporatism represents (Malloy suggests) a compromise that channels and controls the demands made of the state while accepting their legitimacy. It is conceived

---

nation of brutality and rationality" (Douglas C. Bennett and Kenneth F. Sharpe, "Capitalism, Bureaucratic Authoritarianism, and Prospects for Democracy in the United States," *International Organization* 36, no. 3 [Summer 1981]: 637). Argentina, Chile, and Uruguay are the most obvious examples of such "rational" repression.

49. O'Donnell, "Corporatism," 48, 68.

50. Monson, "Corporatist Approaches," 22, paraphrasing Malloy, "Authoritarianism and Corporatism," 4. Schmitter defines corporatism as "a system of interest representation in which the constituent units are organized into a limited number of singular, compulsory, noncompetitive, hierarchically ordered and functionally differentiated categories, recognized or licensed (if not created) by the state and granted a deliberate representational monopoly within their respective categories in exchange for observing certain controls on their selection of leaders and articulation of demands and supports" ("Century of Corporatism?" 93). For other definitions, see Cawson, "Pluralism," 179, where the organic imagery sustaining corporatism is emphasized); O'Donnell, "Corporatism," 47, 49; Douglas Chalmers, "The Politicized State in Latin America," in *Authoritarianism and Corporatism in Latin America,* ed. Malloy, 34; and Schwartzman, "Back to Weber," 93.

51. O'Donnell, "Corporatism," 48, 54, 60.

as a way of ensuring the political stability leaders consider essential for further development (and therefore for satisfying popular demands).[52]

Some radicals criticize such an interpretation of corporatism for failing to identify what they consider the main factor shaping the domestic regime, namely, the wishes and interests of foreign businesses.[53] They argue that "political stability" is not desirable for its own sake, may actually be undesirable in some instances, and does not of itself contribute to economic progress. It becomes a priority only when governments adopt policies that increase dependence on multinational corporations and other sources of investment, technology, and manpower.

CORPORATISM AND STATISM: THE PHILIPPINES AND TAIWAN

An example of such a perspective on state corporatism (and one that, for a change, refers to a region outside of Latin America) is Robert Stauffer's account of the "New Society" inaugurated by President Marcos in the Philippines in the mid-seventies.[54] Following the imposition of martial law in 1972, Marcos formulated a design for his country that closely resembled, in its ideology and institutions, the corporatist model elsewhere. A set of central economic planning and development agencies were to be set up (answerable to the president) and the state itself was to move into sectors of economic activity that it did not wish to see controlled by multinational corporations but that Filipino entrepreneurs were unable to enter successfully for lack of resources or experience.[55] The state would also take on the marketing of

52. Malloy, "Authoritarianism and Corporatism," 5. On the connection between phases and sequences of economic development and the occurrence of populist and "bureaucratic authoritarianism," see the essays in *The New Authoritarianism in Latin America,* ed. D. Collier, many of which are critical of O'Donnell's association of a particular sequence and crisis with "bureaucratic authoritarian" regimes.

53. It should be said that both Malloy and O'Donnell emphasize the influence of external forces in generating corporatism.

54. Robert B. Stauffer, "Philippine Corporatism: A Note on the 'New Society,'" *Asian Survey* 17, no. 4 (April 1977): 393–407.

55. Ibid., 397.

some crops, while it would limit competition and "waste" in other sectors.

Overall, Philippine society would be "rationalized." A hierarchy of organizations was created, each enjoying a formal monopoly by virtue of government recognition. There were to be peak associations for labor and business, as well as an overarching "National Tripartite Congress of Labor, Management and Government." The professions were to be similarly organized (from above, if need be). Thus, Stauffer reported in 1977, "each of the two major sectors of the media is organized into an integrated association of all those working in the industry ('Kapisanan ng mga Broadkaster sa Philipina' for radio and TV, for example)."[56] In return for submitting to such regulation, professional bodies were guaranteed participation in government policymaking on revelant matters. Rationalization was also to extend to political life itself, initially through the removal of opposition leaders and the destruction of their organizations and subsequently through the creation of a complex of representative assemblies, including both "Citizens' Assemblies" (territorially based) and sectoral groupings (providing notably for representation of youth, the professions, "capital," and labor). Stauffer concludes: "The result is an imposing framework having symmetrical balance, order, and hierarchy, and providing for effective government penetration through its participation as a coordinating partner . . . or through its regulatory role. The total pattern is strongly corporatist in design and execution."[57] It is accompanied by an ideology (spelt out in a series of speeches by Marcos) that emphasizes hierarchy, discipline, and national welfare as objectives dictated by the "organic harmony of interests," which the New Society is to generate.

Stauffer claims that such corporatism is in reality paradoxical, since the nationalism it so monotonously preaches actually serves very well the interests of international business and finance:

> Rather than contributing to the enhancement of "national economic and political autarky," corporatist tendencies in the Philippine econ-

56. Ibid., 398.
57. Ibid., 400.

> omy have been associated with a more complete integration of the Philippine economy into the world market system, greater penetration into the economy by transnational corporations and a variety of multilateral banking consortia, "advisory" groups, national and multinational funding agencies, etc., than at any time in Philippine history.[58]

Stauffer implies that such association is more than coincidental by remarking that "transnational and multinational networks of influence . . . require (functionally) the very types of guarantees that can only be assured by authoritarianism." But he does not specify the logic behind such requirements, show how premartial law politics failed to satisfy them, or indeed show that anxiety to meet them was an important factor promoting establishment of the New Society.

Taiwan provides a very different example both of state domination and of international influence. In this case, it would be misleading to apply the label *corporatist* insofar as this term implies a junction between the state and well-established labor and business interests. Yet, contrary to some views of the island as a fortress of free enterprise, Taiwan is clearly a society in which state control of the economy is extensive and entrenched. Alice Amsden argues, indeed, that "the forceful manipulation of Taiwan's political economy by the state" is an inheritance both of the Japanese occupation in the interwar years and of the Chinese imperial conception of "bureaucratic capitalism."[59]

Statism in Taiwan has involved two waves of land reform (under the Japanese and the Guomindang) and intimate control of agriculture by government. The old landowning class was dispossessed, and an extreme fragmentation of land ownership ensued. The mass of smallholders has been "beholden to the state"

58. Ibid., 397–98.

59. Alice H. Amsden, "The State and Taiwan's Economic Development," unpublished paper, 48. See also Amsden's article, "Taiwan's Economic History: A Case of Etatisme and a Challenge to Dependency Theory," *Modern China* 5, no. 3 (July 1979): 341–80, and the important studies by John C. H. Fei, Gustav Ranis, and Shirley W. Y. Kuo, *Growth with Equity: The Taiwan Case* (New York: Oxford University Press for the World Bank, 1979), and R. E. Barrett and M. K. Whyte, "Dependency Theory and Taiwan: Analysis of a Deviant Case," *American Journal of Sociology* 87, no. 5 (March 1982): 1064-89.

for credit and for the supply of fertilizer: in return, while their productivity has risen sharply, the farmers are taxed heavily, if indirectly, through the operation of state marketing monopolies in rice and other products. A "superexploitative state" has not only extracted a large surplus from the rural sector (which it has mainly reinvested in industry), but, by ensuring the equal distribution of resources to peasants, it has prevented the development of a class of wealthy farmers who might challenge the regime and create resentment on the part of smallholders.[60]

The government's control of industry is also extensive. During the so-called liberalization of the late fifties and early sixties, Taiwan switched from a policy of import-substitution to one of "export-led growth," based on labor-intensive industries. However, as Amsden remarks, such liberalization "should in no way be interpreted as a restoration in Taiwan of a 'market economy.'"[61] Government-owned firms dominate the major industrial sectors such as steel production, shipbuilding, engineering, chemical and petroleum processing, and development of semiconductors. Virtually all banks are state-owned, and the government controls the operation of the private sector by regulation of trade and finance, encouraging the creation of cartels and even requiring prior official approval of foreign loans and technical agreements.

What does such involvement say about the political character of the regime and the identity and interests of those dominating it? The interesting aspect of the Taiwanese case is its apparent transformation from a garrison-state, dominated by Chiang Kai-Shek and his military associates (who were fairly indifferent to economic growth). into a bastion of outward-oriented, if *étatiste,* development. Up to a point, there is no contradiction: a productive agriculture and the establishment of a heavy industrial sector were quite compatible with the priorities of the military. They could be seen (along with suitably protectionist measures) as a form of mercantilism.[62] Yet outward-orientation and a de-

60. Amsden, "The State and Taiwan's Economic Development," 16–27.

61. Ibid., 32. In 1980 the state's share of Gross Domestic Product was roughly 50 *percent* (down from 62 *percent* in 1958).

62. Amsden points out that Taiwan was especially guarded about giving multinational corporations entry to domestic production (ibid., 37).

pendence on foreign trade inevitably make a society more vulnerable to political as well as economic pressures from outside.

How, then, was the military establishment in Taiwan persuaded to accept "liberalization?" The answer is partly that such liberalization was selective: in particular, the state's self-sufficiency in armaments and related equipment was not reduced.[63] But the economic success of the Guomindang state seems to have changed the perspective of the elite, giving it more confidence in its capacity to hold the island—as well as a direct interest in its development, through the wealth its members have derived from liberalization. A corresponding redefinition of geopolitical interests has followed, the obsession with reconquering the mainland yielding to a preoccupation with establishing the legitimacy and viability of the state as widely as possible in Asia and beyond.[64]

In more theoretical terms, this change, as Amsden notes, tends to confirm Engels's view, quoted earlier, that "economic development" invariably breaks down "political force." The reality, however, is more complex and seems to indicate a more interactive interpretation. Taiwan "is a case which demonstrates the reciprocal interaction between the structures of the state apparatus and the process of economic growth."[65] The character of the state was certainly changed by the form of economic development that occurred. But the state, despite its unpromising militaristic beginnings, itself was largely responsible for transforming the island's economy, and its history demonstrates the possibilities for "political" control of economic development, even under a regime that many outsiders seem to regard as a devotee of liberal economic principles.

The theories and cases reviewed in this chapter have in common the belief that power and political institutions can and do influence economic life; in some cases, the belief that they should define the national or public interest and enforce it

63. Ibid., 52–53.
64. Ibid., 54–55.
65. Ibid., 55.

against the self-interested claims of individuals, cartels, and classes; and, in certain cases, the belief that the state is a higher entity endowed with this duty. They also assume that the nation-state provides the appropriate framework for analysis and prescription. This is true whether we are talking about very general explanatory theories, about normative theories (such as mercantilism) that urge the primacy of politics, or about more limited analytic categories (such as corporatism) that depict regimes in which the state is accorded preeminence over sectional interests and has created institutions to express and reinforce such dominance.

Before considering theories that employ a global or international framework, it is worth asking what distinguishes "politicist" theory and what are its strengths and weaknesses. The unifying *assumption* of politicist writing is clear enough: it is that politics and political institutions can be independently influential, that they are not simply dependent on economic processes, and that power may be a decisively important dimension of the economic system itself. But who are the politicist *theorists*? If we classify the material in this chapter, we find that we have empirical classifications (those describing, for instance, particular types of regime); we have normative theory (sucy as "organic" theory) which urges the desirability of putting political interests first); and we have power-oriented views of economics.

What is striking, however, is the lack of a general politicist theory (equivalent to liberalism or Marxism) claiming that political considerations are (or should be) the key to behavior and institutions, not only now but throughout human history. It is hard to think of a latter-day successor of Dühring. Certainly, in international relations there are plenty of "realists" and "neorealists" eager to assert the necessary supremacy of states' interests over international economic exchange. But domestic politicist theory is in short supply. One reason is undoubtedly the dominance of liberalism in Western societies, and another is that its main rival in many countries—Western and non-Western—is socialism in its various "democratic" rather than "national" forms. To a great extent, socialism has occupied the ideological and intellectual terrain available for theory that sets the pursuit of a collective interest over that of individual interest. Its main competitor, the organic, conservative belief in the primacy of the political order and its institutions *irrespective* of their democratic or distributive character, has been pushed into the position of an ideological minority, surviving in more reactionary forms of nationalism.

In any case, from an analytic point of view, politicist theory is no better than economistic theory as a solution to the problem of relating politics and economics. Logically, it makes as much or as little sense to say that politics or power is a fundamental factor shaping social organization as to say that economics is. One formula is the mirror image of the other. Just as economism (in its liberal and paleo-Marxist forms) ignores the influence of political structure upon the maximization of individual or class interest, so politicism begs the question of how power itself is generated and why a particular political structure and distribution of power has come about in the first place. I shall return to this question in the last chapter, for it raises the fundamental problem of political economy—how to break out of the logical circle in which politics and economics revolve, each attached to the other's tail.

In ending, we may note that just as politicist theory is an exact logical counterpart of economistic theory, so it is open to some of the criticisms aimed at economics. "Moral" critics of economics claimed that it enshrined the pursuit of individual affluence, ignoring moral questions relating to the distribution and uses of wealth. A moral critique can also be aimed at politicist thought. Why should political rationality be allowed a self-sufficiency denied to economic rationality? The preservation or amassing of power for its own sake is surely not intrinsically more acceptable, from the moralists' point of view, than the accumulation of wealth. Both must presumably be evaluated according to how they are pursued and how they are used.

In the next two chapters, we move from analysis conducted within a national framework to examine analysis using a global or international framework—interdependence and dependency theory, world-systems theory, and Marxism.

FIVE
INTERNATIONAL POLITICAL ECONOMY

If political economy is generally fashionable, no branch of it is more fashionable than international political economy. The reasons for this preoccupation are fairly clear, can be quickly summarized, and are not in themselves a matter of significant disagreement. The real question is how satisfactorily theorists of international political economy have dealt with the relationship between economic and political processes. Are models of "international political economy" essentially internationalized versions of models conceived to deal with domestic relationships? If so, does their application to international relations remove or merely emphasize the weaknesses they manifest in the domestic context? In this chapter I shall raise these questions in relation to liberal, mercantilist, "realist," interdependence, dependency, and "world-systems" approaches, reserving for chapter 6 the concepts and issues raised by Marxism.

WHY "INTERNATIONAL POLITICAL ECONOMY" IS NECESSARY

Non-Marxist writing on international economic relations abounds in calls for a "political economy perspective" and complaints about the mutual indifference of the academic economics and international relations disciplines.[1] (Marxists have always

1. One writer declared: "The decade of the 1970s may well be remembered as the renaissance of political economy in the literature of international politics"

considered themselves preeminently "internationalist," though, as we shall see, this commitment does not enable them to avoid the analytic and strategic questions of relations between "external" and "internal" factors which face non-Marxists.)

The usual criticism of academic treatments of international economic relations is that the world has changed and theory has failed to keep up with it. Specifically, developments in international relations have not only undermined some key concepts and assumptions of particular approaches; they have also subverted the premises on which disciplinary separation itself rests.

Thus, in 1970, even before the disturbances to the international economic system associated with American withdrawal from the gold standard and the Arab oil boycott, the British scholar Susan Strange called for greater cooperation between economists and students of international relations, pointing to "the pressures which a fast-growing international economy is exerting on a more rigid international political system."[2] The old assumption, embodied in the Bretton Woods agreement and other post–World War II arrangements, that the "high" politics of diplomacy and strategic affairs could and should be separated from the "low" politics of international economic relations, was no longer valid.[3] The volume of commercial transactions be-

---

(Maurice A. East, "The Organizational Impact of Interdependence on Foreign Policy-Making: The Case of Norway," *The Political Economy of Foreign Policy Behavior,* ed. Charles W. Kegley, Jr., and Pat McGowan, Sage International Yearbook of Foreign Policy Studies, vol. 6 [Beverly Hills, Calif: Sage Publications, 1981], 137). A widely used textbook on international economic relations contains a typical complaint: "in the twentieth century the study of international political economy has been neglected. Politics and economics have been divorced from each other and isolated in the analysis and theory, if not the reality, of international relations" (Joan E. Spero, *The Politics of International Economic Relations* [London: St. Martin's Press, 1977], 1.

2. Susan Strange, "International Economic Relations: A Case of Mutual Neglect," *International Affairs* 46, no. 2 (April 1970): 310.

3. See, for example, Christopher Brown, "International Political Economy: Some Problems of an Inter-Disciplinary Enterprise," *International Affairs* 49, no. 1 (January 1973): 53; and Edward L. Morse, "Interdependence in World Affairs," in *World Politics: An Introduction*, ed. James W. Rosenau, Kenneth W. Thompson, and Gavin Boyd. (New York: The Free Press, 1976), 668; and Spero, *Politics of International Economic Relations*, 3.

tween countries had grown enormously, but, more significantly, the range of people and organizations involved in international affairs had broadened, the rise of multinational corporations being only the best-known instance.[4]

During the seventies, the demand for reappraisal of the analytic frameworks used in studying international relations became more insistent. A report on a conference sponsored by the Royal Institute of International Affairs in London noted agreement among participants that "the international political economy is in a state of crisis which can only be understood by bringing political and economic analysis into some form of relationship with each other."[5] The "stresses and strains of interdependence" that had contributed to the crisis had also exposed the irrelevance of academic theory. They had highlighted the folly of economists in assuming that "political factors and attitudes simply did not exist, and could be brushed aside as some kind of curious quirk or aberration of dim-witted politicians."[6] They had also revealed the narrowness and redundancy of the standard "realist" model of international relations, which rested on a belief in the sovereignty of nation-states, the primacy of traditional diplomatic and security issues, and the efficacy of force as an instrument of foreign policy.

CRITICISMS OF INTERNATIONAL ECONOMICS

The demand for international political economy has thus involved both criticism of existing disciplines and proposals for in-

4. Thus in 1980 K. J. Holsti wrote that "*interdependence* is the most pervasive and fundamental result of rapidly growing *transaction* rates between societies. The development of closer and multidimensional contacts between societies . . . constitutes one of the fundamental forms of system change in the twentieth century" ("Change in the International System: Interdependence, Integration, and Fragmentation," in *Change in the International System,* ed. Ole R. Holsti, Randolph Siverson, and Alexander L. George (Boulder, Colo.: Westview Press, 1980), 23 (emphases in original). Holsti, it should be said, did not accept that greater peace would necessarily result from interdependnece or that the nation-state was *dépassé.*

5. Brown, "International Political Economy," 54.

6. Strange, "International Economics," 309.

novation. The orthodoxy in international relations and its critics are examined later in the chapter (in connection with the realist and interdependence schools). The weaknesses of international economics were the objects of attack from several quarters and provide a useful starting point for discussion, since they pick up from some of the criticisms of orthodox economics mentioned in chapter 2.

Some critics of international economic theory argued merely that the intertwining of politics and economics was a novel or exaggerated aspect of current international affairs. But the more radical suggested that they had always been intertwined and that it was only in quite exceptional circumstances that the "heroic and unrealistic assumptions" of liberal economics—notably its abstraction from politics—even temporarily approached credibility for anybody except professional economists.[7]

Critics especially attacked the apolitical character of international trade theory, with its view that mutually and equally beneficial relations arose from every country's pursuit of the "comparative advantage" nature gave it for the production of particular commodities. Such theory was used to explain current trading patterns and to support doctrines of free trade. But, argued the critics, the explanations were partial and the doctrine was somewhat disingenuous. Trade could be free without being equally advantageous, and where its benefits were unequally divided the reason was often political. Quite frequently (even in the case of Anglo-Portuguese relations used by Ricardo), the conditions and even the actual occurrence of trade were "the result of the extensive use of military coercion and the manipulation by the stronger state of the weaker state's political posi-

7. Charles P. Kindleberger, *Power and Money: The Politics of International Economics and the Economics of International Politics* (New York: Basic Books, 1970), 19 (cited in R. Barry Jones, "International Political Economy: Perspectives and Prospects—Part II," *Review of International Studies* 8, no. 1 [January 1982]: 46). On the dangers of "abstraction from politics" by economists, see Douglas Rimmer, "The Abstraction from Politics: A Critique of Economic Theory and Design with Reference to West Africa," *Journal of Development Studies* 5, no. 3 (April 1969): 190–204.

tion."[8] Trade could be free yet be costlier for some than for others.

This observation does not seem to invalidate "comparative advantage" as an ideal basis for international trade, as a standard or an objective to be achieved. But it obviously diminishes its use in explaining current patterns of trade and makes liberal acceptance of them seem complacent. To the extent that liberal trade theory appeared to imply that societies had freely determined how (and whether) they would take part in international commerce, it almost seemed to embody an international economic version of the social contract. Clearly, such an assumption was wrong as a historical explanation for the entry of colonial territories into the world economy and, so far as political pressures have been applied, of the roles played by others as well. In a world of perfect competition, comparative advantage would provide perfect explanations and an achievable ideal. Otherwise, however, it is actually of little use to account for current patterns of trade or to explain change in them. As Barry Jones remarks, "employing simplifying initial assumptions, [liberal trade theory] offers a logically consistent argument that actually amounts to little more than the assertion that successful international competition in any goods or services follows from the possession of endowments that permit such competitive production and trade."[9] In other words, comparative advantage is a necessary but not a sufficient condition of success: the other conditions presumably include noneconomic factors. The tendency to exclude such factors does not mean that such theory has no political content or implications. But it is *considered* apolitical because it prefers the market to determine the distribution of power, wealth, and privilege rather than governments.

Both the original model and the criticisms made of it recall the

8. Nazli Choucri, "International Political Economy: A Theoretical Perspective," in *Change in the International System,* ed. Holsti, Siverson, and George, 111. On the Anglo-Portuguese case, see T. Baumgartner and T. R. Burns, "The Structuring of International Economic Relations," *International Studies Quarterly* 19, no. 2 (June 1975): 126–59.

9. Jones, "International Political Economy," 46.

political critique of liberalism by institutionalists, Keynesians, and "radicals." The modifications and alternatives proposed were also similar. They involved a recognition "that economic life is as much, if not more, characterized by various forms of power and their use as by perfect competition" and an acceptance of the reality of state intervention in international (as well as domestic) affairs.[10] The obvious question is whether theories of international political economy deal any better with the relationships entailed than did their domestic counterparts.

MODELS OF INTERNATIONAL POLITICAL ECONOMY

The various models of international political economy closely resemble the main alternatives offered to replace or reform apolitical, liberal economics, They tend, however, to be more complicated because they have to cope with a dimension that is missing from some domestic versions. The missing dimension is the relationship between international (or "external") forces and domestic (or "internal") processes. Theories of international political economy typically deal with several kinds of relationship between the political and the economic. They can perhaps best be indicated in the form of questions:

1. How does the international economy influence the "high politics" of international relations and vice versa?
2. How does the international economy influence internal political processes and vice versa?
3. How does the international state system influence internal political processes?
4. How does the international economy influence domestic economies?

Clearly the last two questions are not strictly political economy questions at all: they are exclusively political or economic in conception. But, as we have already noted, theories of political economy often *are* undisciplinary wolves in interdisciplinary clothing, and have to be considered, not least when they are popular and flawed. Also, even when not trading under the name of politi-

10. Ibid., 47.

cal economy, they represent important alternative perspectives and standpoints from which theories of political economy are criticized.

In the following sections I review the ways in which the main schools of international political economy differ in answering the questions posed above.[11]

The Liberal School

The main premises and concepts of this school have already been discussed, and their implications for a political economy approach to international relations are fairly clear. As in domestic developmental matters, the liberal approach to international relations tends to be economistic. Specifically, while liberal values (notably freedom of the individual) are prominent in discussions of objectives, discussions of means tend to stress the beneficial impact of the free market upon the nominally "political" problems of international conflict.

Similarly, when explaining changes in international relations (or, more exactly, changes in national policies), liberals are apt to adopt what John Odell calls a "market explanation":

> This approach identifies international market conditions as the chief, or a major, source of change in policy content. . . . In general, a market explanation for policy changes claims that international market conditions changed so as to make it economically irrational for a government to continue prevailing policy, and it was for this reason that the government yielded and adopted a new policy more in conformity with market signals.[12]

11. In comparing the approaches concerned, I have been greatly aided by the lucid and helpfully coincidental classifications suggested by Peter Gourevitch in his excellent article, "The Second Image Reversed: The International Sources of Domestic Politics," *International Organization* 32, no. 4 (Autumn 1978): 881–911; Robert O. Keohane and Joseph S. Nye, Jr., in their book *Power and Interdependence: World Politics in Transition* (Bostom: Little, Brown, 1977); and John S. Odell in his study *U.S. International Monetary Policy: Markets, Power, and Ideas as Sources of Change* (Princeton, N.J.: Princeton University Press, 1982)—a model of clear exposition.

12. Odell, *Monetary Policy,* 18. Gourevitch remarks that liberalism generally offers a "very apolitical analysis" and tends to "attribute considerable importance to the international economy" ("Second Image," 891).

Given their faith in the benevolence, rationality, and irresistible strength of market forces, liberals tend to be impatient of "irrational" political considerations and to believe, in the late Harry Johnson's words, that "in the longer run economic forces are likely to predominate over political" and even that "ultimately, a world federal government will appear as the only rational method for coping with the world's economic problems."[13] In short, the international economy is seen as dominant in shaping both overall patterns of international relations and the policies of particular states and in imposing changes on both, "regardless of domestic politics, or the ideology or skill of the rulers, or domination by foreign governments."[14]

Liberals are not as unsympathetic to (for example) nationalism as the preceding statements imply. They do, however, distinguish between the specifically *political* goal of "self-determination" (which is good) and the *economic* goal of "national development." The latter, in their view, is best realized through an opening to outside aid, investment, and technology. "Enlightened nationalism" (autonomy within the constraints of interdependence) is thus preferable to "narrow nationalism" (autarky). The first entails a sophisticated acknowledgment of the sovereignty of international economic forces: the second an artificial, "politically motivated" attempt to frustrate them, a triumph of irrational "ideology" over rational "development."

The Realist and Mercantilist School

The mercantilist position was outlined in the previous chapter. It has a close affinity with the realist view of international relations in stressing the subordination of economic forces to political interests and specifically in emphasizing the reality and primacy of "national interest." The general premise of this school is that of international anarchy tempered by war and diplomacy. It envisages "a world not of markets but of states," a

13. Harry G. Johnson, *International Economic Questions Facing Britain, the United States and Canada in the Seventies* (London: British-North American Research Association, June 1970), 24 (cited in Odell, *Monetary Policy*, 24).

14. Odell, *Monetary Policy*, 19.

world in which economic policy is a weapon in the continual struggle for dominance and security between nation-states.[15]

Thus in mercantilism and realism, it is clearly politics that constrains economics. It is not the "international state system" that constrains international economics, because the word *system* suggests an order and even an international interest which mercantilism and realism deny.

The overriding commitment to national security that characterizes this school also has implications for domestic economic activity. For example, "realists," though in some eyes political conservatives and therefore friends of established business interests, actually argue for the right of the state to regulate economic activity.[16] They may, for example, oppose unrestricted expansion by multinational corporations, either into the domestic market or abroad. In the first case, they fear that foreign interests may acquire the ability to manipulate the domestic economy or to deny supplies of strategically important materials, or may in some other way reduce the nation-state's effectiveness and room for maneuver in international affairs. In the second case, they fear that heavy investment in areas of little strategic or diplomatic importance may at some time lead to pressures for intervention that would entail distraction of attention from vital interests, as well as a dissipation of resources. Just as importantly, they might argue that national security demands a concentration of investment at home rather than its dispersal abroad, regardless of whether the rates of return abroad are higher or not.

The "power perspective" is thus opposed at all important points to the assumptions and values of liberal trade theory and practice. It is skeptical about the benefits of free trade (E. H. Carr, a critic of utopian internationalism, once described laissez-

15. Ibid., 30.

16. Gourevitch, "Second Image," 895. For a neomercantilist approach to American interests, see Stephen D. Krasner, "The Great Oil Sheikdown," *Foreign Policy* 13 (Winter 1973–74): 123–38, and the same writer's *Defending the National Interest: Raw Materials, Investment and U.S. Foreign Policy* (Princeton, N.J.: Princeton University Press, 1978).

faire as "the paradise of the economically strong").[17] It is skeptical of claims that "economic interdependence" has made the nation-state obsolete and impotent: "In general, whenever states assert their views they are able to prevail over international organizations [including multinational corporations]. Interdependence derives from state policy, not the other way round: that is, it exists because states allow it to exist. Should states refuse to do so, the constraining quality of that interdependence would be broken."[18] The nationalism of this school is unequivocal. It places politics—the interest of the state—over economics at both the international and the domestic levels, and it does so in both explanatory and prescriptive spheres. That is, it suggests that economistic explanations are likely to be wrong and that policies based exclusively on economic arguments or pieties about "international economic cooperation" are likely to be disastrous.

Nevertheless, the downright tone of the "realist" approach sometimes conceals a subtler, more ambiguous analysis of power. Thus Robert Gilpin, in his study *U.S. Power and the Multinational Corporation,* adopts a definition of *political economy* that is interactive, despite his earlier emphasis on the significance of power in international relations.[19] He argues that "the economic motive and economic activities are fundamental to the struggle for power among nation-states" and suggests that this view corresponds to the classical mercantilist view. Therefore, any opposition of "political interests" and "economic interests" is misconceived: indeed, the expansion of the world economy had

17. E. H. Carr, *The Twenty Years Crisis, 1919–1939* (New York: Harper & Row, 1964), 60.

18. Gourevitch, "Second Image," 894, paraphrasing Robert Gilpin in his *U.S. Power and the Multinational Corporation: The Political Economy of Foreign Direct Investment* (New York: Basic Books, 1975). K. J. Holsti is equally skeptical about the probability of interdependence removing conflict and domination from international affairs: "The argument that increased interdependence is likely to reduce international conflict is . . . open to serious question. . . . Increased transaction flows can lead to dependency, exploitation, conflict and violence as well as to more collaboration and mutual knowledge" ("Change in the International System," 28).

19. Gilpin, *U.S. Power,* 34–35.

depended on the existence of centers of economic power (such as Great Britain in the nineteenth century). Liberals are wrong to assume that such an economy simply arose through the apolitical pursuit of individual economic interest and the recognition of comparative advantage: "Rather, every economic system rests on a particular political order; its nature cannot be understood aside from politics."[20]

But how do we understand *politics*? On what, if not on itself, does the political order rest? Gilpin's answer is to posit a reciprocal relationship between power and wealth. He writes:

> political economy in this study means the reciprocal and dynamic interaction in international relations of the pursuit of wealth and the pursuit of power. In the short run, the distribution of power and the nature of the political system are major determinants of the framework within which wealth is produced and distributed. In the long run, however, shifts in economic efficiency and in the location of economic activity tend to undermine and transform the existing political system. This political transformation in turn gives rise to changes in economic relations that reflect the interests of the politically ascendant state in the system.[21]

This formulation seems a neat squaring of the circle (indeed, Gilpin claims to have successfully combined the "strengths" of liberalism, Marxism, and mercantilism). One problem it presents is the need to understand the logic of the "short run" and the "long run." Why should power be dominant only in the short run and economics only in the long run? And how is the transition made? If political dominance (meaning, presumably, the ability of a state to change the behavior of another by the threat or deployment of force) is so effective in the short run, why does the short run ever end? Why is it that shifts in the location of economic power are *allowed* to occur? Obviously, such shifts do happen: Britain, for example, did not or could not prevent technological development in Germany before World War I nor the loss of her control of world markets to the United States. Yet she

20. Ibid., 40. See, for a further development of this view, Gilpin's more recent work, *War and Change in International Politics* (Cambridge: Cambridge University Press, 1981).

21. Ibid., 43.

was able earlier to force the practice of free trade on Latin American countries.

What Gilpin seems to have done is to solve the problem of identifying the mechanisms by which economic power and political power are connected and converted by arbitrarily allocating each to a distinct *chronological* sphere of influence. Gilpin does not justify such an allocation, and it does not help us understand why a state can get its way at one time but not at another. Take away the short-run/long-run distinction, and what is left is the general proposition that the political framework affects economic activity and economic activity shapes the distribution of power. In empirical terms, we are no further along in explaining particular historical outcomes. We have answered, abstractly, the question of whether but not the question of how.

The "Interdependence" School

In terms of an intellectual dialectic, interdependence theory represents a reaction against realism with its emphasis on the nation-state. In the work of Robert Keohane, Joseph Nye, and others, it challenges certain central assumptions of realism. First, it challenges the assumption that states are coherent units and thus represent a satisfactory lowest common denominator for analytic purposes. It suggests that there may be considerable disagreement between officials and departments in defining "the national interest" and therefore conflict over objectives and specific policies. For purposes of understanding why a certain policy was adopted or why it was changed or abandoned, it may be important to explore such conflicts, and a perspective that assumes the nation-state is an actor in its own right, with a clear, objective interest and an undivided will, discourages such inquiry.[22]

Further, interdependence theory questions the assumption that nation-states are necessarily the most important actors in international relations and that the military force they wield is always a relevant, usable instrument for imposing their will. Since 1945 (it is argued) the growth in the volume and breadth of in-

22. Keohane and Nye, *Power and Interdependence*, 23.

ternational exchange has created very complicated patterns of interdependence that make the definition of national interest more difficult, increase the points at which conflict may occur, and simultaneously make a simple resolution by force less feasible and attractive.[23] Countries are linked in many ways and a corresponding multiplicity of interests has developed, many of them outside the apparatus of the state. The best known example is the multinational corporation, the assets and incomes of which frequently exceed those of the less affluent members of the United Nations.[24] Such private-sector organizations may be accountable to no national government and may, indeed, be able to influence the policies of individual states, whether by alliances formed with domestic interests or by playing one state off against another. According to interdependence theorists, the growth of multinational or supranational organizations has justified their downgrading of the nation-state as the central actor in international affairs.

Recent events have also justified their view that the realists'

23. Ibid., 3–5, 27.

24. On relations between multinational corporations and Third World governments, see, for example, Raymond Vernon, "The Power of Multinational Enterprises in Developing Countries," in *The Case for the Multinational Corporation*, ed. Carl Madden (New York: Praeger, 1975), pp. 151–83; Theodore Moran, "Multinational Corporations and Dependency: A Dialogue for Dependentistas and Non-Dependentistas," *International Organization* 32, no. 1 (Winter 1978): 170–200; Stephen Krasner, "Transforming International Regimes: What the Third World Wants and Why," *International Studies Quarterly* 25, no. 1 (March 1981): 119–48; Franklin B. Weinstein, "Multinational Corporations and the Third World: The Case of Japan and Southeast Asia," *International Organization* 30, no. 3 (Summer 1976): 373–404; Thomas J. Biersteker, *Distortion or Development? Contending Perspectives on the Multinational Corporation* (Cambridge, Mass.: MIT Press, 1978); Peter F. Drucker, "Multinationals and Developing Countries: Myths and Realities," *Foreign Affairs* 53, no. 1 (October 1974): 121–34; and a useful recent case-study, Joseph M. Grieco, "Between Dependency and Autonomy: India's Experience with the International Computer Industry," *International Organization* 36, no. 3 (Summer 1982): 609–32. Two important country case-studies are: Peter Evans, *Dependent Development: The Alliance of Multinational, State, and Local Development in Brazil* (Princeton, N.J.: Princeton University Press, 1979); and Richard L. Sklar, *Corporate Power in an African State: The Political Impact of Multinational Mining Companies in Zambia* (Berkeley: University of California Press, 1975).

emphasis on the traditional subordination of economic to diplomatic and strategic matters is redundant (if it was ever, indeed, appropriate). The appearance of commodity cartels such as OPEC and the impact of arcane processes of international finance have shown how constrained diplomacy and strategic affairs are by movements in economic markets. Such markets cannot necessarily, or at least immediately, be brought to heel by threats of force, and they may provide a weapon by which states that are weak in traditional military and political terms can obtain a compensating—even commanding—leverage over those more powerful in conventional terms.

The implication of these observations and developments for study of international relations is that analysis must be more discriminating and contextual. Instead of the brusque confrontations of force and the encircling anarchy depicted by realists, the international world has to be seen as one of complex interdependence, in which the nature and effectiveness of power vary according to what the issue is, how other issues and priorities are related to it by the participants, how skillfully the participants bargain, and how well they can bring into play resources and inducements unrelated to those engaged initially. Interdependence theory thus discounts the brutal simplicities of realism without discounting (as liberals have) the equally brutal reality of power. Instead, it sees the substance of international economic relations as consisting of "regimes"—conventions governing economic exchange that are shaped partly by market forces and partly by the distribution of geopolitical power between states.[25]

As this formulation suggests, the result is a model of change in which neither "politicism" nor "economism" prevails. On the one hand, interdependence (mainly, but not exclusively, economic interdependence) "severely constrains the freedom of action of governments" and may affect domestic politics both

25. Keohane and Nye define "regimes" as "networks or rules, norms, and procedures that regularize behavior and control its effects" (ibid., 19). For useful critiques of this concept, see the review by Susan Strange in *International Affairs* 53, no. 2 (April 1977): 270–73, and the same author's article, "*Cave! hic dragones:* A Critique of Regime Analysis," *International Organization* 36, no. 2 (Spring 1982): 479–96.

within and outside the apparatus of government.[26] On the other hand, governments are not mere puppets: their negotiating skills are crucial in determining whether or not a state realizes the value of the assets it has for promoting itself in the international pecking order.

In one of the best-known analyses of interdependence, Keohane and Nye present a model of "regime change" that depicts this process. They recognize that interdependence does not connote an equal distribution of the benefits of trade between countries and that the inequalities that exist are at least partly due to the exercise of political pressure by stronger states upon weaker. They argue, indeed, for a distinction between two degrees of interdependence ("sensitivity" and "vulnerability") which is essentially a distinction between states of susceptibility to power. Whether a country is "vulnerable" or merely "sensitive" depends on what range of alternatives it enjoys and how severe the costs of adopting them would be.[27] Faced with, say, a partner's threat to withhold some raw material or to close a market for its commodities, can it at acceptable cost switch to another supplier or another market? Can it at acceptable cost switch to another raw material or to another commodity? Obviously, the examination of alternatives and costs will yield a continuum of individual situations, stretching from extreme latitude of choice (with minimal costs attached) to extreme vulnerability (with minimal choices, all with high costs). But a continuum of situations is not necessarily a spectrum of countries: a country may be highly vulnerable to another in one respect yet be quite strongly placed in another. Whether it can use such strength to reduce or compensate for its vulnerability in particular areas is a matter not just of economic feasibility but of political skill and determination.[28]

As we saw, neither liberal trade theory nor realism (at least in Gilpin's version) has an adequate model of how change occurs in international economic relations. Keohane and Nye deal with this problem by identifying four models of change, namely:

1. *Economic processes* (meaning that change is caused by techno-

26. Gourevitch, "Second Image," 892.

27. Keohane and Nye, *Power and Interdependence,* 12–15.

28. Ibid., 180.

logical development and growing economic interdependence);

2. *Overall world power structure* (meaning that change is caused by alterations in the distribution of military power, by the erosion of one state's hegemony and the rise of challengers);
3. *The power structure within issue areas* (meaning the particular disposition of resources and the particular relationships characteristic of a certain sector of exchange, such as precious minerals or textiles);
4. *Power capabilities as affected by international organizations* (meaning change attributable to the independent influence of the "world political structure" and to the deference paid by states to the institutions that comprise it—the United Nations being the most conspicuous example).[29]

Keohane and Nye then suggest that, in order to explain "regime change" in particular cases, these models should be invoked consecutively and cumulatively. If the change is not explained sufficiently by economic processes (and the authors do not expect it will be), then the next step is "to add politics in the simplest possible way by seeing whether the overall structure model, alone or in conjunction with the economic process model, can explain change."[30] Again, the authors consider that this analytic ploy will be unsuccessful, because it rests on the false assumption that the states most powerful in conventional terms can get their way on all issues to an equivalent degree. But battleships do not necessarily intimidate bankers, and it is usually imperative to move on to the third model (or level). If exploration of the "issue structure" itself does not provide, in combination with the others, a satisfactory explanation, then it may be necessary to refer to the "international organization model."

The Keohane and Nye framework is, in fact, a sophisticated attempt to bring together the market explanation and realism, supplementing them to take account of the differentiation of is-

29. Ibid., 38.

30. Ibid., 58. Elsewhere they remark (accepting the political critique of liberalism) that "a departure from perfect competition *always* introduces political factors into the analysis. . . . To explain regime change, we will have to use models with explicit political assumptions" (ibid., 39; emphasis in original).

sue areas and the development of international organizations, which the authors see as distinctive features of complex interdependence. Moreover, the authors are clear-sighted about the probable limitations of each model, and they bring out the merits and defects of each by a series of case studies. The synthesis they present makes an interesting comparison with Gilpin's neomercantilist version. Whereas Gilpin solves the problem of political economy by vesting politics and economics with different temporal sovereignties (the short run and the long run), Keohane and Nye in effect stack one on top of the other, and then add two more models to complete the edifice. Though they argue that the economic process should be considered first, and they conclude that reference to it is "necessary for understanding most of the changes in international regimes" considered in their book, Keohane and Nye also find that "it never provided a sufficient explanation." The world power structure model helps to account for some changes but by itself is a poor predictor of change. Issue structure provided clear prediction of change in specific areas, but only so long as the influence of the world power structure was excluded.[31] International organization comes out as the weakest explanatory framework and is assigned an essentially residual role.

Where does this synthesis stand as a form of international political economy? Its authors note the criticisms made of both economism and politicism and accept the premises of much aspirant political economy. But they explicitly reject any claim to have proposed a comprehensive theory (the term *political economy* is scarcely, if at all, used in the book).[32] They also stress the limits to any theory centering on complex interdependence. While holding that interdependence creates greater opportunities for bargaining than traditional theory assumes, they acknowledge that such bargaining depends on conditions obtaining mainly in the advanced industrial, non-Communist world. (Such an acknowledgment is not made by advocates of "the new political economy," which shares some of the assumptions of in-

31. Ibid., 222.

32. "We do not claim . . . to have developed a general theory of world politics under conditions of complex interdependence" (ibid., 224).

terdependence theory.) Extreme inequality between states will normally minimize the prospects for bargaining, as will the advent of regimes—Communist or rigorously mercantilist—that restrict international contracts or subordinate them to their own strategic objectives.[33]

Interdependence theory, at least as formulated by Keohane and Nye, is not and does not claim to be a comprehensive theory of international political economy. (Keohane and Nye are, in fact, more concerned with developing a framework that will guide policy analysts than with formulating grand theory.) However, it is a significant and influential response to the problem of how internal and external factors are related in contemporary international relations. It clearly stands with those who are critical of the statist tradition, who see the state as a complex entity—highly susceptible to international economic pressures over which it has little control, divided by feuding bureaucratic interests, and vulnerable to alliances of domestic and foreign business interests. But interdependence theory is not as naively economistic as classical liberal theory or as uncompromisingly economistic as some of the dependency and Marxist theories considered later and in the last chapter.

A wider interest in interdependence has generated a large literature on regimes.[34] This literature suffers in some ways from the same vices of fashionability that afflict "political economy." The one main problem is a tendency to treat the concept of a "regime" as all-explanatory and to use it to assert the occurrence of changes in international relations that may be less significant and durable than its advocates believe. The concept itself is broad to the point of woolliness (as, for example, in the definition of a regime as "a set of principles, norms, rules, and procedures around which actors' expectations converge").[35] More-

33. Ibid., 226.

34. See, notably, the symposium on international regimes in *International Organization* 36, no. 2 (Spring 1982); Ernst B. Haas, "Why Collaborate? Issue-Linkage and International Regimes," *World Politics* 32, no. 3 (April 1980): 357–405; and Oran R. Young, "International Regimes: Problems of Concept Formation," *World Politics* 32, no. 3 (April 1980): 331–56.

35. This definition was used by contributors to the *International Organization* symposium.

over, critics have complained that strong emphasis on regimes risks discounting the very large areas of international relations in which conflict persists and is too severe to be susceptible to management. They also suggest that such emphasis complacently ignores the vulnerability of regimes to changes in markets and in perceptions of national interest: either can, overnight, destroy the conditions on which apparently stable arrangements for international negotiation have rested.[36]

Nevertheless, students of regimes argue, somewhat convincingly, that they have identified a form of international management which is qualitatively different from the transient treaties and bilateral arrangements of earlier times. In effect, they argue that what is new is the existence of standing arrangements to negotiate, sustained by an enduring sense on the part of actors that self-interest dictates mutuality rather than isolation and confrontation.[37] They do not claim that specific resulting arrangements will be equitable or that mutuality is possible in all areas. But they do claim that regimes represent a form of international political economy insofar as they show the impact of an increasingly complex set of international economic relationships upon governments and relations between states. In this sense, writing on regimes represents an attempt to conceptualize, in political economy terms, the implications of complex interdependence.

The Dependency School

Just as the interdependence school generally concentrates on relations between industrialized countries, so the dependency school focuses overwhelmingly on conditions in the Third World and on north-south relations. (Indeed, as we shall see,

36. Susan Strange, "*Cave? hic dragones,*" 490. This article is an admirably clear and trenchant appraisal of the regime literature.

37. An interesting case of weaker countries persisting in negotiation and actually profiting by an avoidance of confrontation is that of newly industrializing countries (such as Taiwan, Korea, Singapore, and Hong Kong) in their responses to American protectionism. In this connection, see the excellent work of David Yoffie, notably his article, "The Newly Industrializing Countries and the Political Economy of Protectionism," *International Studies Quarterly* 25, no. 4 (December 1981): 569–99, and his book, *Power and Protectionism: Strategies of the Newly Industrializing Countries* (New York: Columbia University Press, 1983).

one criticism of the school is that it has made too sharp a distinction between the developed and the underdeveloped worlds).

Dependency theorists do not adhere to a single theory, but they share certain general assumptions, analytic priorities, and values, and are subjected to similar criticisms.[38] The great majority of theorists in the school have been Latin American or have been concerned with the special problems of Latin American development. Indeed, the dependency framework is best seen as one response to the crisis that also led to corporatism in theory and in practice.[39] The central issues in the related debate between liberals and radicals have been, first, how Latin America can achieve improved living standards given the openness of Latin American economies to outside political and economic influence; and, second, what political strategies are required to ensure development.

Although there are significant differences within the dependency school, its members share a perspective that emphasizes

38. Philip O'Brien argues that the theory of dependency is really "a higher level or general hypothesis whose objective is to define the problem or area of interest and to try and show how lower level, more specific *ad hoc* hypotheses fit within this framework" ("A Critique of Latin American Theories of Dependency," *Occasional Papers*, no. 12, Institute of Latin American Studies, University of Glasgow, n.d., 2; also published in Ivar Oxaal, Tony Barnett, and David Booth, eds., *Beyond the Sociology of Development: Economy and Society in Latin America and Africa* [London: Routledge and Kegan Paul, 1975], 7–27). Ian Roxborough also comments that "the notion of dependency defines a paradigm rather than a specific theory. . . . Within the paradigm there are a number of competing theories and explanations of the nature of dependency." *Theories of Underdevelopment* (London: The Macmillan Press, 1979), 43–44.

39. On the genesis of dependency theory, see, for example, Gabriel Palma, "Dependency: A Formal Theory of Underdevelopment or a Methodology for the Analysis of Concrete Situations of Underdevelopment?" *World Development* 6 (July/August 1978): 896–909; J. Samuel Valenzuela and Arturo Valenzuela, "Modernization and Dependency: Alternative Perspectives in the Study of Latin American Politics," *Comparative Politics* 10, no. 4 (July 1978): 535–57; C. Richard Bath and Dilmus D. James, "Dependency Analysis of Latin America: Some Criticisms, Some Suggestions," *Latin American Research Review* 11, no. 3 (1976): 6–11; Colin Leys, "Underdevelopment and Dependency: Critical Notes," *Journal of Contemporary Asia* 7, no. 1 (1977): 97; and James H. Street, "The Latin American 'Structuralists' and the Institutionalists: Convergence in Development Theory," *Journal of Economic Issues* 1, nos. 1–2 (June 1967): 44–62.

the subjection of Latin American economies to an international system dominated by the advanced capitalist countries of Western Europe and North America. They thus reject the optimism of liberal trade theory and argue that domestic development requires a political initiative to reduce and remove the disabilities to which their countries are subject as the result of a long historical process marked by direct control or manipulation from outside. "Moderate" *dependencistas* (such as Prebisch, Furtado, and Sunkel) looked to existing elites for the required initiative and claimed that specific economic strategies, notably import substitution and related tariff policies, could assure greater autonomy for Latin American states. When their strategies—collectively known as "the ECLA approach"—began to falter in the sixties, a more radical dependency analysis appeared that envisaged Latin America as the victim of a deeply rooted malignancy, with ramifications in the political, social, and cultural spheres: the societies in the region therefore needed more radical surgery than the moderates had proposed.[40] The analysts concerned dismissed the strategies of the moderates as the tinkering of bourgeois technocrats and proclaimed that a domestic social revolution and the establishment of socialism were absolute prerequisites for an escape from dependency.

This conclusion also challenged the views of the established Left in Latin America. Adopting orthodox Marxist analysis, the Left had concentrated on developing ties with the industrial working class and forming alliances with "progressive" middle-class elements, on the assumption that socialism could only follow the unfolding of the "bourgeois mode of production," the corresponding formation of an industrial proletariat, and the emergence of a revolutionary movement within that proletariat.[41] The duty of the Left was to encourage the bourgeois to hasten its own demise: capitalism had to build the nest from which the proletarian cuckoo would eventually eject it.

The radicals held that such analysis was as misconceived and

40. "ECLA" stands for the United Nations Economic Commission for Latin America. Useful accounts of this period are given in Roxborough, *Theories of Underdevelopment*, 27–41, and Palma, "Dependency," 906–09.

41. See, for example, Palma, "Dependency," 897–98.

ethnocentric as that of the liberals and moderate *dependencistas*. The very character of dependency meant that although Latin America was completely in thrall to capitalism, capitalism had its center elsewhere. Latin America was on the periphery of a system that had its core in Europe and North America. The Latin American satellites could not develop an indigenous capitalism because it was in the interest of the core (or the metropolis) to keep its satellites as raw-material-exporting economies and as markets for its own manufactures. It had, moreover, long since established alliances with domestic commercial and landowning classes within the Latin American countries that also profited from existing relationships: sociologically, these interests could be categorized as feudal or *comprador* (intermediary). In neither case had they the interest, incentives, or pressures to perform the role of a historic bourgeoisie. Moreover, the very basis of domestic capitalism—surplus value—was continually being drawn off to the core, which appropriated profit from the satellites. And, applying the logic of orthodox Marxism itself, if there was no basis for a domestic capitalist class and little hope for sustained and autonomous industrial growth, there could accordingly be little prospect of a significant industrial proletariat and thus little prospect of an effective proletarian revolutionary movement.[42]

Latin America, then, was doomed to stagnation. Penetrated to the innermost Andean village by foreign capitalism, there was no chance even of "dependent capitalist development." Penetrated as they were not only geographically but culturally, it was unrealistic to expect revolutionary initiative from the consumerist urban classes, which would otherwise have provided the growth, the exploitation, and the organized anger necessary for a socialist revolution. The revolutionary process would therefore have to start elsewhere—among the peasants (ignored by liberals and the Left alike) or at the core itself, by confronting capitalism in its lair.

42. Good summaries of the radical dependency approach are given in Ernesto Laclau's critique of André Gunder Frank, "Feudalism and Capitalism in Latin America," *New Left Review* 67 (May/June 1971): 20–22, and in Robert Brenner's broader survey, "The Origins of Capitalist Development: A Critique of Neo-Smithian Marxism," *New Left Review* 104 (July 1977): 27–29.

ECONOMISM AND DETERMINISM IN DEPENDENCY THEORY

The above summary is a broad simplification of dependency theory, excluding both details of argumentation and the historical cases on which analysis rested. It is impossible (and unnecessary) to review here all the debates and criticisms to which dependency has given rise. I shall therefore concentrate on aspects of dependency theory that affect its status as a form of political economy and distinguish its treatment of relations between domestic politics and the international system.

On the latter question its posture is unequivocal. As Peter Gourevitch remarks, compared with other brands of international political economy, dependency theory attributes "less weight to purely national, internal factors such as specific historical conditions, institutions, economic forms, and politics." It sees the underdeveloped country as caught in "a system of pressures which sharply constrain, indeed, wholly determine the options available."[43] Compared with interdependence theory, dependency theory sees the asymmetry of international relations as extreme and, under current conditions, irreversible. Dependency, in the words of Theotonio Dos Santos, is "an historical condition which shapes a certain structure of the world economy such that it favors some countries to the detriment of others, and limits the development possibilities of the subordinate economies."[44] In the work of André Gunder Frank and others, "shaping" is replaced by "determining." In either case, the direction of influence is clear.

On the questions of the relationship between economics and politics, dependency theory also tends to be emphatic. Just as domestic politics is shaped by the international system, so the political system is shaped by its economic base—an echo of the Marxist strain, which blends, rather uneasily, with nationalism in dependency theory. Such economism can be traced (as Gabriel Palma points out) through an entire lineage of radical writers, notable among them Paul Baran, Paul Sweezy, André Gunder

43. Gourevitch, "Second Image," 888.

44. Theotonio Dos Santos, "The Structure of Dependence," in *The Political Economy of Development and Underdevelopment,* ed. C. K. Wilber (New York: Random House, 1973), 109.

Frank, and (latterly) Immanuel Wallerstein (whose work is considered separately below).[45] Thus Baran and Sweezy, in their book *Monopoly Capital,* declared that "the modes of utilisation of surplus constitute the indispensable mechanism linking *the economic foundation of society with its political, ideological, and cultural superstructure.*"[46] (Baran and Sweezy do not try to support this assertion, nor indeed do they subsequently specify how this "indispensable mechanism" works.)

André Gunder Frank, whose *Capitalism and Underdevelopment in Latin America* made him (perhaps undeservedly) the best-known dependency writer in the English-speaking world, wrote, for example, that "the domestic economic, political and social structure of Chile always was and still remains determined first and foremost by the fact and specific nature of its participation in the world capitalist system."[47] Indeed, economism has not been limited to the radical *dependencistas.* The writing of Prebisch, as two critics of dependency theory have pointed out, "is almost exclusively technical and impersonal. Reference to social or class differences are often couched in terms of income groups. . . . He uses history in his analysis, but in a cursory way, usually referring to the macro-level and rarely with penetrating depth."[48] Many critics have commented on the implications—and costs—of this double determinism in dependency writing, at least in the way in which it is presented.[49] For, quite

45. Palma, "Dependency," 900.

46. Paul Baran and Paul Sweezy, *Monopoly Capital: An Essay on the American Economic and Social Order* (New York: Monthly Review Press, 1966), 21 (cited in John Taylor, "Neo-Marxism and Underdevelopment—A Sociological Phantasy," *Journal of Contemporary Asia* 4, no. 1 (1973); 9.

47. André Gunder Frank, *Capitalism and Underdevelopment in Latin America: Historical Studies of Chile and Brazil* (New York: Monthly Review Press, 1967), 29.

48. Bath and James, "Dependency Analysis," 7.

49. Leys, for example, comments that underdevelopment theory "tends to be economistic in the sense that social classes, the state, politics, ideology figure in it very noticeably as derivatives of economic forces, and often get very little attention at all" ("Underdevelopment and Dependency," 95). For similar criticisms, see Taylor, "Neo-Marxism," 12; Palma, "Dependency," 900; and Tony Smith, "The Underdevelopment of Development Literature: The Case of Dependency Theory," *World Politics* 31, no. 2 (January 1979): 262, 264.

apart from the specific merits of the propositions of dependency theory, there is a fundamental problem in evaluating it because of the apparent indifference of some *dependencistas* to mundane questions of definition and evidence.

THE MEANING OF "DEPENDENCE"

What, after all, does *dependence* mean? If it just means a need to import and export, then most economies in the world are to some degree dependent, and dependence is indistinguishable from interdependence.[50] If it refers (as it generally seems to do) to "asymmetrical reliance" ("vulnerability" in Keohane and Nye's language) that results in one country acquiring power over another, then it needs to be shown why such asymmetry is uniquely characteristic of relations between northern and southern countries. "'Being limited' is a common affliction"; and inequality is, and has always been, a general feature of international relations.[51] France and Monaco do not meet on equal terms, nor do Nigeria and Benin, nor (for that matter) do the United States and Canada.

Nor, indeed, do the Soviet Union and Poland, which raises a question about the connections assumed by this school between dependency and capitalism.[52] Moreover, if it is capitalism that

50. For criticisms of dependency theory's failure to "confront the abiding realities of the contemporary international economic system," see Robert L. Ayres, "Economic Stagnation and the Emergence of the Political Ideology of Chilean Underdevelopment," *World Politics* 25, no. 1 (January 1972): 59; David Ray, "The Dependency Model of Latin American Underdevelopment: Three Basic Fallacies," *Journal of Interamerican Studies* 15, no. 1 (February 1973): 7, 13–18; W. Arthur Lewis, *The Evolution of the International Economic order* (Princeton, N.J.: Princeton University Press, 1978), 69; Richard Leaver, "The Debate on Underdevelopment: On Situating Gunder Frank," *Journal of Contemporary Asia* 7, no. 1 (1977): 113; Bath and James, "Dependency Analysis," 35.

51. Leaver, "Underdevelopment," 113.

52. David Ray argues that "there is a striking similarity between the economic dependence which has been imposed upon Latin America by the United States and the economic dependency which has been imposed upon Eastern Europe by the Soviet Union" ("The Dependency Model of Latin American Underdevelopment," 8). For an attempt to compare the scale and consequences of dependence in the two cases, see James Lee Ray, "Dependence, Political Compliance, and

generates the generic form of dependency apparently suffered by Third World countries, then several problems arise. One, as Sanjaya Lall has shown to devastating effect, is that many of the features of dependency on the periphery can also be found in the core. Dominance by foreign capital is more a feature of the Canadian and Belgian economies than it is of the Indian and Pakistani economies.[53] High profit rates are gleaned by multinational corporations in Europe as well as in the Middle East. Capital-intensive techniques, so widely deplored for their failure to cure unemployment, are a universal feature of certain industries: they may be a response to high labor costs (which are certainly not a general feature of the Third World) or a reflection of the educational and technical requirements of the industry concerned. (One aspect of the mindlessness of much argument on this subject is the lack of attempts to show how, for instance, control and management of the major processes in a petroleum refinery or a pharmaceutical plant could, without loss of efficiency or periodic explosions, be reorganized so as to provide employment for people with only a primary-school education). Dependence on foreign technology is not restricted to Third World countries. As Lall points out, "the proportion of patents taken out by foreign corporations as compared to local ones is almost as high, or higher, in Canada or Belgium as, say, in India or Brazil, and the extent of technological 'dependence' in

---

Economic Performance: Latin America and East Europe," in *The Political Economy of Foreign Policy Behavior*, ed. Kegley and McGowan, 111–36. For a Marxist view, see Christopher Chase-Dunn, "Socialist States in the Capitalist World-Economy," *Social Problems* 27, no. 5 (June 1980): 505–25. Further analysis of Soviet relations with Eastern Europe is found in P. Marer, "The Political Economy of Soviet Relations with Eastern Europe," in *Testing Theories of Economic Imperialism*, ed. Steven Rosen and James Kurth (Lexington, Mass.: Lexington Books, 1974); Uwe Stehr, "Unequal Development and Dependency Structures in Comecon," *Journal of Peace Research* 14, no. 2 (1977): 115–28: and William Zimmerman, "Dependency Theory and the Soviet–East European Hierarchical Regional System," in *The Foreign Policies of Eastern Europe: New Approaches*, ed. Ronald Linden (New York: Praeger, 1982), 159–85.

53. Sanjaya Lall, "Is 'Dependence' a Useful Concept in Analysing Underdevelopment?" *World Development* 3, nos. 11–12 (November/December 1975): 803.

Denmark is probably just as great as, say, in Colombia or Taiwan."[54] Monopolies and cartels do not uniquely affect the Third World, nor (as OPEC has shown) are they limited to the developed world.

Ian Roxborough has suggested that it is useful to distinguish between dependency as a relationship between systems, and dependency "as a conditioning factor which alters the internal functioning and articulation of the elements of the dependent social formation."[55] But it is up to the dependency theorists to show how such a social formation is different from any found, now or earlier, in the developed world, how the conditioning occurs, and how it prevents an escape from underdevelopment. Apart from the phenomena noted above, it is easy to find in advanced industrial countries groups or regions that have features, and face problems, like those of dependent social formations south of the equator. Unproductive agriculture, overpopulation, the diploma disease, consumerism, rentierism, corruption, inefficient bureaucracies, authoritarianism, and military intervention are neither unknown nor extinct in Western and Southern Europe.

Another problem arising from the association of dependency and underdevelopment with capitalism is that some countries on the periphery of capitalism have in fact achieved a high level of industrialization. What, then, has enabled Canada, Australia, South Africa, and Japan (not to mention such recent additions as Taiwan, Brazil, South Korea, and Mexico) to achieve industrialization and a significant degree of indigenous capitalism?[56]

54. Ibid., 804.

55. Roxborough, *Theories of Underdevelopment,* 44.

56. For criticism of dependency theory's failure to account for these and other escapes, see Lall, "Is 'Dependence' a Useful Concept?" 807; Palma, "Dependency," 904; Bill Warren, "Imperialism and Capitalist Industrialization," *New Left Review* 81 (September/October 1973): 3–44; Michael Barratt Brown, *The Economics of Imperialism* (Harmondsworth: Penguin, 1974), 264–84; Holsti, "Change in the International System," 39–41. For an alternative explanation of the causes of development and underdevelopment, see Lewis, *Evolution of the International Economic Order,* passim. On the interesting recent cases of industrialization in East Asia (the so-called Gang of Four—Taiwan, South Korea, Hong

The stock answer of some nationalists—namely, absence of the malign hand of colonialism—clearly fails to solve this problem, for many of the countries mentioned above were themselves colonies. Moreover, as Sir Arthur Lewis remarks, Ethiopia, Liberia, and Thailand (none of which suffered under prolonged colonial rule) have not, according to conventional indicators, done any better at vanquishing underdevelopment than such victims of imperialism as Kenya, the Ivory Coast, and Singapore.[57] They may well be freer of "colonial mentality," but they are not in any obvious way better off materially.

If dependent underdevelopment were a matter of imposition by the core, we would expect to find it limited to the periphery; but it is not. If dependent underdevelopment were imposed by the core, we would not expect to find any development or industrialization in countries influenced by the core; but we do. If dependent underdevelopment were a result of colonial rule, we would expect to find its manifestations limited to ex-colonies; but we do not.

Such disappointments do not rule out the possibility of discovering general patterns or developing theories to explain them. They do reveal some serious intellectual flaws in dependency theory. It is worth identifying them, not because such identification is new (critiques of dependency theory abound), but because the same flaws exist in the work of the critics.

INTELLECTUAL WEAKNESSES OF DEPENDENCY THEORY

The main flaw in much dependency theory is the lack of empirical grounding—even empirical reference. The theory is offered as a high-level hypothesis without sufficient definition or supporting material to make testing (or even argument) possible. Indeed, some *dependencistas* have objected to the attempts of American social scientists to evaluate dependency theory by se-

Kong, and Singapore), see the valuable analysis by Stephan Haggard and Tun-jen Cheng, "State Strategies: Local and Foreign Capital in the Gang of Four," paper presented at the annual meeting of the American Political Science Association, Chicago, September 1–4, 1983.

57. Lewis, *Evolution of the International Economic Order,* 10.

lecting measurable variables on the ground that they destroy "the very basic characteristic of dependency studies—the emphasis on global analysis." Measurement (argue Cardoso and Faletto) is irrelevant to dialectical analysis, for "history becomes understandable when interpretations propose categories strong enough to render clear the fundamental relations that sustain and those that oppose a given structural situation in its globality."[58] In other words, the only relevant criticism is to produce another equally general and abstract theory. This convenient doctrine— which resembles forms of self-defense found in the work of Samir Amin and some Marxists—means that the theory is immune to apparently contradictory evidence, partly because it does not offer close definitions or detailed interpretations susceptible to disproof, and partly because its authors consider a "structural" or "global" interpretation to be immune to mere empirical evaluation.[59]

58. Fernando H. Cardoso and Enzo Faletto, *Dependency and Development in Latin America* (Berkeley: University of California Press, 1979), xii.

59. The *dependencistas'* objection to attempts to measure dependence is defended by the Valenzuelas ("Modernization and Dependency," 544–55). Such attempts include Patrick J. McGowan, "Economic Dependence and Economic Performance in Black Africa," *Journal of Modern African Studies* 14, no. 1 (March 1976): 25–40; Christopher Chase-Dunn, "The Effects of International Economic Dependence on Development and Inequality: A Cross-National Study," *American Sociological Review* 40, no. 6 (December 1975): 720–38; R. R. Kaufman, D. S. Geller, and H. I. Chernotsky, "A Preliminary Test of the Theory of Dependency," *Comparative Politics* 7, no. 3 (April 1975): 303–30; Sheila M. Smith, "Economic Dependence and Economic Empiricism in Black Africa," *Journal of Modern African Studies* 15, no. 1 (March 1977): 116–18; Richard Vengroff, "Dependency, Development, and Inequality in Black Africa," *African Studies Review* 20, no. 2 (September 1977): 17–26; Richard Vengroff, "Dependency and Underdevelopment in Black Africa: An Empirical Test," *Journal of Modern African Studies* 15, no. 4 (December 1977): 613–30; Richard Rubinson, "The World Economy and the Distribution of Income within States: A Cross-national Study," *American Sociological Review* 41, no. 4 (August 1976): 638–59; Tom Travis, "A Comparison of the Global Economic Imperialism of Five Metropoles," in *The Political Economy of Foreign Policy Behavior,* ed. Kegley and McGowan, 165–89; Volker Bornschier, Christopher Chase-Dunn, and Richard Rubinson, "Cross-national Evidence of the Effects of Foreign Investment and Aid on Economic Growth and Inequality: A Survey of Findings and a Re-analysis," *American Journal of Sociology* 84, no. 3 (November 1978): 651–83; and Steven Jackson, Bruce

This attitude expresses a disturbing degree of intellectual arrogance. It is also self-impoverishing as far as the refinement of the theory itself is concerned—a criticism made by Marxists as well as by conservatives and liberals. As Philip O'Brien has noted, the tendency to assert rather than to argue, prove, or persuade has stranded dependency theory on a plateau of banality. It rarely tries to show how the "actual mechanisms of dependency" work and tends therefore "to lose the parts in the totality":

> Everything is connected with everything else, but how and why often remains obscure. . . . One looks in vain through the theories of dependency for the essential characteristics of dependency. Instead, one is given a circular argument: dependent countries are those which lack the capacity for autonomous growth and they lack this because their structures are dependent ones.[60]

According to other Marxists, the shallowness of dependency theory goes deeper, so to speak. It is not actually a substantively new theory but merely a reversal, a mirror image of the orthodoxy it replaces. Whereas liberal theory saw the global expansion of the market as bringing modernization and development, dependency theory regards it as "enforcing the rise of economic backwardness."[61] Dependency theory ignores the dynamics of

Russett, Duncan Snidal, and David Sylvan, "An Assessment of Empirical Research on *Dependencia*," *Latin American Research Review* 14, no. 3 (1979): 7–29; On Samir Amin's methodology, see Sheila Smith, "The Ideas of Samir Amin: Theory or Tautology?" *Journal of Development Studies* 17, no. 1 (October 1980): especially 11–12, and idem, "Class Analysis versus World Systems: Critique of Samir Amin's Typology of Under-development," *Journal of Contemporary Asia* 12, no. 1 (1982): 10–11. Smith's witty description of Amin's main tactic as "assertion plus threat" applies to others of the school.

60. O'Brien, "Theories of Dependency," 14. For similar criticisms of the methodological faults of dependency theory, see Lall, "Is 'Dependence' a Useful Concept?" pp. 799–800; Bath and James, "Dependency Analysis," 26; Laclau, "Feudalism and Capitalism," 34; Leys, "Underdevelopment and Dependency," 95 ff.; and Jones, "International Political Economy," 45–46.

61. Brenner, "Capitalist Development," 27, 91. The same point is made in Frank T. Fitzgerald, "Sociologies of Development," *Journal of Contemporary Asia* 11, no. 1 (1981): 10.

class struggle as well as misrepresenting the relationship between commerce and capitalism.[62]

For Marxists and non-Marxists, the globalism or holism of dependency theory has disturbing intellectual implications. It greatly limits the capacity of the theory to explain or take account of deviant cases, and it results in the use of categories so broad as to strain credibility. As Colin Leys observes, the center-periphery metaphor "is seldom if ever replaced by a concrete typology of centres and peripheries."[63] There are said to be different kinds of dependence, but actual relationships are rarely developed beyond the most simplistic dichotomies. In sum, "the empirical meaning of 'underdevelopment' has to be pretty slight if it must embrace India and Brazil as well as Haiti and Tanzania."[64]

LEFT AND LIBERAL CRITIQUES OF DEPENDENCY THEORY

For non-Marxists, the idea of dominance of the whole over the parts has ominous political implications in addition to exhibiting intellectual superficiality. Anthony Smith, in particular, has complained that dependency theory exaggerates the power of the international system and demeans the historical individuality and political capacities of Third World countries: "Too many writers of this school make the mistake of assuming that since the whole (in this case the international system) is greater than the sum of its parts (the constituent states), the parts lead no significant existence separate from the whole, but operate simply in functionally specific manners as a result of their place in the

62. See, for example, Leys, "Underdevelopment and Dependency," 98; Brenner, "Capitalist Development," passim; John Browett, "Out of the Dependency Perspectives," *Journal of Contemporary Asia* 12, no. 2 (1982): 146–48; and Theda Skocpol, "Wallerstein's World Capitalist System: A Theoretical and Historical Critique," *American Journal of Sociology* 82, no. 5 (March 1977): especially 1078–81; and the essays in *Dependency and Marxism: Toward a Resolution of the Debate,* ed. Ronald H. Chilcote, Latin American Perspectives Series no. 1 (Boulder, Colo.: Westview Press, 1982).

63. Leys, "Underdevelopment and Dependency," 95.

64. Ibid., 95.

greater system."[65] Not only does such an assumption leave underdevelopment theory powerless to explain "escapes" and "experiments" (the Japans, Taiwans, and Cubas), but it implicitly degrades the identities of all the countries concerned. For its effect is "to deprive local histories of their integrity and specificity, thereby making local actors little more than pawns of outside forces . . . [this approach] seeks to specify universal laws or processes in blatant disregard of the singular or the idiosyncratic. [It] refuses to grant the part *any* autonomy, *any* specificity, *any* particularity independent of its membership of the whole. Such writing is tyrannical."[66] Ironically, for the Marxists it is precisely a lurking *excess* of nationalist sympathies that makes dependency suspect. As O'Brien remarks sternly, "the eclecticism of a theory which can straddle petty bourgeois nationalism and socialist revolution should be a concern for reflection."[67] "Straddling" may even be overcomplimentary, as the other aspect of dependency theory's abstraction concerns the vital question of how countries can escape from dependent underdevelopment.

THE TRAPS OF DEPENDENCY THEORY

While *dependencistas* have been loud in condemnation of the core, scornful of "bourgeois reformism," and patronizing toward unreconstructed Marxists, their own strategies and prescriptions are far from clear. Their outrage implies the possibility of an alternative, and the alternative mentioned is invariably socialism, with revolution as the means toward it. But on the actual meaning of socialism, how it will enable countries to escape dependency, and how the revolution is to be launched dependency theory has been curiously modest. As one writer generally sympathetic to the school has written in exasperation: "After more than a decade its only positive contribution is to write, in specialist books and journals in a language that few can, or care to, understand (or have access to) on the necessity for a socialist revolution."[68]

65. Smith, "Underdevelopment of Development Literature," 252.
66. Ibid., 257, 258 (emphasis in original).
67. O'Brien, "Theories of Dependency," 11.
68. Browett, "Dependency Perspectives," 148. For other criticisms of the in-

This failure might be attributable to characteristics of the Latin American intelligentsia were it not for the fact that the North American *dependencistas* tend to be just as simplistic. Dependency theory is a crucial failure both politically and intellectually: politically, because it raises expectations of progress without showing how such progress is to be made; and intellectually, because it draws attention to the trap that a rhetorical, overmechanical, and economistic style of analysis creates for its alter ego, the tribune of revolution. This trap is set by overselling dependency, emphasizing the universal, iron grip in which it holds Third World countries, and portraying its tentacles as stretching into the culture and the moral fibre of societies. The trouble is that the more impressive and persuasive such a portrayal is, the more utopian and fanciful talk of progress, certainly of revolution and socialism, is bound to seem. How could such a dragon ever be slain? Who, indeed, is to slay it? After all, the bourgeoisie is feeble and in collusion with the metropolis. The urban working class is threatened by unemployment, seduced by multinational corporations, and by definition incapable of developing into a mature industrial proletariat. The peasants may be revolutionary material, though the experiences of movements on the mainland of Latin America seem to suggest that peasant uprisings occur under very specific conditions and involve very specific demands, and the Left has traditionally had a rather suspicious attitude toward peasant movements.

In light of these deficiencies, it is important to set out exactly what questions have to be answered if dependency theory (and indeed any theory of underdevelopment) is to be taken seriously. I suggest that the following are among the fundamental questions to be answered:

1. What, precisely, does *dependency* mean? What exactly are the mechanisms that produce this phenomenon?
2. What is the relationship between political and economic elements in dependency?

---

conclusiveness of dependency theory, see Jones, "International Political Economy," 46; O'Brien, "Theories of Dependency," 15; Bath and James, "Dependency Analysis," 9; Leys, "Underdevelopment and Dependency," 92, 98; Ray, "Latin American Underdevelopment," 14–15; Fitzgerald, "Sociologies of Development," 10.

3. How, precisely, do external forces shape domestic institutions?
4. Is dependency exclusively and unavoidably linked to capitalism, or can it arise from any relationship of economic and political inequality?
5. What would constitute an escape from dependency? Is autarky the only solution? What would its costs be? Is interdependence the desired alternative, and how might it be achieved?
6. What, given the answers to questions 2, 3 and 4, would be a feasible program and political strategy for overcoming dependency on both the domestic and international levels?
7. What, exactly, is meant by *socialism* in the context of underdevelopment? Is it achievable without a global change in the international system? How compatible are socialism, political independence, and economic growth?

These are very large questions, but questions that theory claiming global and revolutionary credentials should at least try to answer. I want to conclude this chapter by considering how some of them are dealt with in two bodies of work deriving from dependency theory and widely regarded as important developments of it. The first is the writing of Fernando Henrique Cardoso (or, more exactly, his book *Dependency and Development in Latin America,* written in association with Enzo Faletto).[69] The second is the writing of Immanuel Wallerstein on world-systems.

CARDOSO AND "DEPENDENT DEVELOPMENT"

Within the dependency school, the work of Cardoso is regarded as distinctive on several counts. First, he denies the stagnationist view of Frank and others (the view that development is

69. Related writing by Cardoso available in English includes "Dependency and Development in Latin America," *New Left Review* 74 (July/August 1972): 83–95; "Associated-Dependent Development: Theoretical and Practical Implications," in *Authoritarian Brazil,* ed. Alfred Stepan (New Haven: Yale University Press, 1973), 142–76; "The Consumption of Dependency Theory in the United States," *Latin American Research Review* 12, no. 3 (1977): 7–24; and "The Originality of the Copy: The Economic Commission for Latin America and the Idea of Development," in *Toward a New Strategy for Development.* A Rothko Chapel Colloquium (New York: Pergamon Press, 1979), 53–72.

incompatible with dependence). Cardoso argues that "forms of dependency can change." Indeed, he believes that a new dependency has emerged in Latin America that involves industrialization and a growth of productive forces, though he also concludes that dependent development has not reduced the constraints of dependency and has in some ways sharpened the choices facing Latin American countries.

Second, Cardoso denies the possibility of a dependency theory as such, suggesting that there are *situations* of dependency. Instead of trying to create a general theory (which is impossible), scholars should work at "concrete analyses of specific characteristics of dependent societies."[70] *Dependency and Development* is an essay headed in this direction. It compares the histories of a number of Central and South American countries and suggests a broad distinction between societies in which export production was concentrated in enclaves controlled by foreign investors (especially mining interests) and those in which exports (typically cash-crops) were developed and controlled by domestic groups.

The comparison is meant to illustrate Cardoso's belief that earlier dependency theory was simplistic and overmechanical.[71] He and Faletto call for a return to the ideal of a comprehensive social science, with politics and economics treated as aspects of a single process. Similarly, they criticize the propensity of dependency theory to treat domestic politics as merely a product of external forces. Oppressed groups can, in their view, challenge dominant structures: "organization, will, and ideology"—in short, politics—can make a difference.[72] Cardoso and Faletto therefore set out to discover "how internal and external processes of political domination relate to one another" and "external factors are interwoven with internal ones," as well as "to determine the links between social groups that in their behavior actually tie together the economic and political spheres."[73]

Clearly, these aims promise some kind of political economy, as

70. Cardoso and Faletto, *Dependency and Development,* xxiii, xiv.

71. The authors specifically criticize the ECLA school for failing to develop "an analysis of social process" and particularly for not taking account of "the asymmetric relations among classes" (ibid., viii, xiv).

72. Ibid., ix, xi, xiv, xv, 173.

73. Ibid., xviii, 15, 21.

well as a serious effort to remedy the defects of dependency theory. But the results are often confusing and even contradictory, not only because of the authors' ornately Hegelian style, but also because of intellectual weaknesses in their analysis.[74] These weaknesses broadly replicate those previously identified in examining dependency theory. They concern, first, the relationship between theory and evidence; second, the relationship between economics and politics; and third, strategies for escape from dependence.

Theory and Evidence

The organization of *Dependency and Development* detracts from its authors' claims to be engaged in serious historical comparison. Two opening sections, a conclusion, and a "Post-Scriptum" enclose, without illuminating, a series of descriptive chapters that comprise long passages of bald narrative interspersed with interpretations.[75] Large theoretical assertions, statements of intention, and broad conclusions are presented, but there is little serious attempt to put them to the test of the cases offered, much less to examine the conflicting evidence offered by conflicting interpretations. This is not to say that the interpretations intrinsically lack credibility, but merely that the authors seem to disdain the work of demonstrating it. There are few references to sources and little effort to give empirical substance to the concepts used. For instance, Cardoso and Faletto declare that "a system is dependent when the accumulation and expansion of capital cannot find its essential dynamic component inside the system."[76] But they do not describe this dynamic component or

74. Translation may have magnified the stylistic problem, represented by such mind-straining sentences as "the style of the development of the possibility of alternatives depends upon the resolution of this question of the state" (ibid., p. 212).

75. See, for instance, the remarkable piece of apparently inconsequential political history on page 49, where the campaigns of rival Argentine warlords are described. One reviewer overpolitely described much of the analytic content of the book as "highly stylized economic history" (Carlos F. Diaz-Alejandro, review, *Journal of Economic History* 39, no. 3 [September 1979]: 804).

76. *Dependency and Development,* xx.

say what the specific signs of frustration of capital are. Furthermore, they argue that dependency represents "the conditions under which alone the economic and political systems can exist and function in [their] connections with the world productive structure."[77] But they do not specify these conditions, tell us how to recognize them, or say how they would have to change in order for the systems to enjoy alternative ways of connecting with the world productive structure.

These and other cases of disjuncture between theory and empirical evidence seem to stem from the authors' commitment to structural analysis. Attempts to test theory would offend the "globality of dialectical analysis." As a result, their theories are immune to empirical contradiction. But this position has considerable (if politically immaterial) intellectual costs. It leaves little ground for legitimate argument and gives no incentive for revisionism, radical or otherwise. As Lall has remarked, such theory "ceases to offer an independent and verifiable explanation of the processes at work."[78] It does, however, offer scope for ideologically resounding conclusions (such as the authors' assertions about the basic objectives of American foreign policy).[79]

Economics and Politics

As we have seen, Cardoso and Faletto emphasize the potentiality of "organization, will, and ideology" for directing and obstructing economic forces. They do, in fact, give politicist interpretations of several historical episodes, arguing, for example, that in the period after independence in Latin America the es-

77. Ibid., 18.

78. "Is 'Dependence' a Useful Concept?" 800.

79. Ibid., 199. Cardoso and Faletto assert that Latin American countries "remain dependent and assure an internal social order favorable to capitalist interests and consequently fail to challenge one of the basic objectives of American foreign policy. Multinational enterprises continue to receive support from the foreign policies of their countries of origin, as well as from local states." The reader is left to conclude that advancing the interests of capitalism (specifically, those of multinational corporations) is a "basic objective" of American policy, but no evidence, argument, or clarification is provided. Indeed, despite the authors' claim to be concerned with international relations, they give little space (and less rigor) to examining such relationships in the book as a whole.

tablishment of an agricultural exporting sector depended on a political alliance between the exporting interest and the nonexporting landowners (who kept order in the hinterland and whose control of farmland ensured a steady supply of landless or impoverished wage laborers for the plantations). Similarly, they attribute differences in patterns of exporting between countries to differences in dominant political coalitions.[80]

Even more striking are the authors' "political" explanations of the timing and incidence of industrialization in Latin America. They argue that in Brazil, for example, industrialization was a deliberate political act, or rather, an economic solution to a political problem. The elite was faced with the problem of large numbers of people who "were mobilized without effective employment." The agricultural sector was in decline and the private sector could not create new jobs quickly: creation of jobs by the state was therefore the surest way to avoid political trouble. If the elite had been influenced only by economic considerations, it would (the authors suggest) have preferred a slower form of growth arising from an expansion of the domestic market, without (presumably) any involvement of the public sector.[81]

Enclave economies (such as that of Chile) were marked by a different kind of political domination. Here the controllers of economic power (the foreign companies) were in alliance with the holders of political power (the domestic elites): "economic exploitation was effected politically." The political oligarchy depended on foreign enterprises for the royalties and taxes that financed its government. The government in turn guaranteed "an internal order that would ensure the supply of labor and natural resources."[82]

Cardoso and Faletto thus use a distinction between the political and the economic which is very helpful in explaining different paths of development and especially in accounting for changes that seem irrational from a narrowly economistic point of view. The problem is that the book is also laden with state-

80. Ibid., 67–68, 80.
81. Ibid., 139–40.
82. Ibid., 102, 103.

ments, even asides, which assume, imply, or directly state a completely contrary view, a fairly crudely economistic view of a Marxian kind. Thus, on the surface the authors continually assert the possibility of independent political influence and even refer to the state as having "a political line"[83]; yet there is a powerful groundswell beneath the surface that plainly moves the analysis toward quite different conclusions—a view of politics as instrumental to class interest.

Often such economism appears in close proximity to assertions of the primacy of politics. In their introduction, for instance, the authors' claim to "stress the socio-political nature of the economic relations of production" (itself a revealing formulation) is followed by the comment that differences between countries are partly due to the ways in which "sectors of local classes" have historically "organized different forms of state."[84] While asserting that economic processes should be seen as social processes, Cardoso and Faletto also hold that "an economic class or group tries to establish through the social process a system of social relations that permits it to impose on the entire society a social form of production akin to its own interests. . . . The modes of economic relations, in turn, set the limits of political action."[85] And again: "Political institutions at a given moment can only be fully understood in terms of the structures of domination because these express the class interests behind political organization."[86]

Similar economism appears in interpretations of specific historical cases. For instance, having told readers that expansion of the export economy in the nineteenth century "was more a political than an economic problem," the authors assert that "national political institutions *had to serve* not only the interests of the 'modernizing' groups created by the export system itself but also the interests of the regional oligarchies."[87] In countries such as Brazil after World War I, it was the "dominant agro-

83. Ibid., 142.
84. Ibid., ix, xvii.
85. Ibid., 15.
86. Ibid., 14.
87. Ibid., 68.

exporting group" that "tried to exercise monopoly through a system of single-commodity production which assured it almost absolute political control." (Indeed, Cardoso and Faletto later refer to "the agro-export political system.")[88]

Using such Marxian formulas, Cardoso and Faletto inevitably run up against the question of the relative autonomy of the state that has troubled Marxist analysis of politics (and is considered in the next chapter). In examining the import-substitution phase (when the state became actively interventionist), they veer between seeming to attribute an independent interest to the state and conceiving it as "a tool for the fortification of the economic order."[89] It apparently became such a tool after the exhaustion of populism. Yet previously, at least in the case of Peronism in Argentina, the state had been an "arbitrator for the class struggle and was used as a mechanism for income distribution both within the entrepreneurial class and downward."[90] Cardoso and Faletto do not, however, seriously pursue the possibility of the state standing above the classes. Instead, their treatment of relations between economics and politics simply alternates between unsubstantiated allusion to the primacy of politics and equally allusive comments of a quite crudely economistic kind.

Escaping from Dependence

Cardoso and Faletto differ from other dependency theorists in believing that development (including industrialization) is possible. But they think that such development will merely redefine the links of dependency, and that it will mainly benefit the wealthier consumers and indeed will aggravate income inequality. Beyond a certain point, there are "necessary structural limitations" on such a style of development, and further industrialization will require "profound political-structural change":

> When a political crisis in the system prevents an economic policy of public and private investments for development, the only alternatives are opening the market to foreign capital or making a radical political

88. Ibid., 76, 81, 99.
89. Ibid., 200.
90. Ibid., 134.

> move toward socialism. . . . It is not realistic to imagine that capitalist development will solve basic problems for the majority of the population. . . . The important question . . . is how to construct paths toward socialism.[91]

But the authors neither consider what socialism would mean nor ask how a radical political move toward socialism might come about. They do suggest that there is a tension between nationalism, played upon by the bourgeois state, and socialism, and they refer to "the difficulty in conceiving a political passage to socialism by a strictly proletarian route, given the structural conditions of industrial capitalism in the periphery."[92] Since the advent of dependent development, the choice between entrenched dependence on foreign interests and "the popular interest" has actually become clearer, and populism would not now bridge the gap.

Yet, given the supposed starkness of the choice facing Latin America, Cardoso and Faletto's vision of the desirable alternative is rather foggy. They claim that some countries (such as China and the Soviet Union) have broken out of dependency and have kept "a reasonable degree of autonomy." While acknowledging that there are "forms of dependent relationships between socialist countries," they dismiss the issue with the remark that "the structural context that permits an understanding of these is quite different from that within capitalist countries and requires specific analyses."[93] Their conclusion is similarly inconclusive, proclaiming the struggle as one "between technocratic elitism and a vision of the formative process of a mass industrial society which can offer what is popular as specifically national and which succeeds in transforming the demand for a more developed economy and for a democratic society into a state that expresses the vitality of truly popular forces, capable of seeking socialist forms for the social organization of the future."[94] In the light of this passage, to say that Cardoso and Faletto have not "actually provided a base for policy recommen-

91. Ibid., xxiii, 155.
92. Ibid., 213.
93. Ibid., xxiii.
94. Ibid., 216.

dation for Latin America" is extreme understatement, irrespective of whether the policies envisaged are reformist or revolutionary.[95] Like so much else in dependency theory, their work is a curious mixture of theoretical grandiosity and rhetorical stridency with empirical and prescriptive shallowness—a fanfare without notation, instrumentation, or coda.

WORLD-SYSTEMS THEORY

Immanuel Wallerstein's writings on world-systems theory adopt the basic premises of dependency theory concerning the relationship between core and periphery. But they go beyond contemporary and regional issues of development to present an extended historical interpretation of the expansion of European capitalism and its consequences for peripheral societies.[96]

Wallerstein distinguishes between "world systems" and "world empires." A world system (which does not necessarily encompass the entire globe but has global dimensions) is "a unit with a single division of labor and multiple cultural systems." A world empire is such a unit converted into a single political structure: in world empires the central political authority imposes itself upon the economic system, extracting and redistributing resources according to the imperatives of imperial survival and growth.[97]

In Wallerstein's view, the peculiar features of the period since the Renaissance have been the dynamism of capitalist expansion and the failure of any single state to seize control and create a new world empire. The Hapsburgs (more exactly, the emperor Charles V) had such an ambition but failed. Thereafter, domin-

95. See Charles J. Stokes, review, *Journal of Economic Literature* 18, no. 2 (June 1980): 600.

96. The most important work is Wallerstein's *The Modern World-System: Capitalist Agriculture and the Origins of the European World-Economy in the Sixteenth Century* (New York: Academic Press, 1974). Many of his major essays have been reissued in a collection, *The Capitalist World-Economy* (Cambridge and Paris: Cambridge University Press and Editions de la Maison des Sciences de l'Homme, 1979).

97. "The Rise and Future Demise of the World Capitalist System: Concepts for Comparative Analysis," in his *Capitalist World-Economy*, 5–6. See also "Three Paths of National Development in Sixteenth-Century Europe," in ibid., 37–38.

ance within the world system was contested, and even the hegemony of the British in the nineteenth century was transient. Such stability as now exists depends upon the assertion of power by the core and the complicity of countries making up the "semiperiphery"—upwardly mobile members of the periphery that have experienced some development and have been coopted economically and ideologically by the core. The semiperiphery gives legitimacy to a system that the core (the cluster of industrialized capitalist countries) maintains by the exercise of power (though it is itself dependent on the economic exploitation of the periphery). Core, semiperiphery, and periphery all have their respective economic roles.[98]

In the following sections, Wallerstein's historical analysis is examined under broadly the same headings used to evaluate Cardoso and Faletto. What is his general theoretical approach? How does he relate politics and economics? And how does he conceive an escape from dependency?

Theory: The Dominance of the Whole

Wallerstein is much more concerned than Cardoso and Faletto with exploring particular situations, and he provides extensive documentation for some very detailed case-studies. Yet he shares the deductive, holistic approach of the dependency school. Indeed, he carries it to an extreme, arguing that for analytic and evaluative purposes only the world system is real, as a social as well as an economic entity. Other seeming entities are derivative from the world system and can only be understood by reference to its development and needs. This view embodies both the organic tradition in which, as a sociologist, Wallerstein is heir to Durkheim, and the Marxist tendency to adopt a method of totality emphasizing the domination of the whole over the parts.

More important than its intellectual lineage are the remarkable denials to which this attitude leads. Once self-sufficient "minisystems" have disappeared, the only kind of social system is

98. Ibid.; "Rise and Future Demise," in Wallerstein, *Capitalist World-Economy,* 22–23, 26–31; *Modern World-System,* 178–79, 355.

a world system. Classes, "ethno-nations," and ethnic groups are "phenomena of world economies": states and cultures are "nonsystems." Thus, the role and interests of a class, such as industrial workers, are "determined by their collective relationship to the world economy." States are merely "one kind of organizational structure among others within this single social system."[99] As it is improper to speak of nations in isolation, "there is no such thing as 'national development.'" And since "in the nineteenth and twentieth centuries there has been only world system in existence, the capitalist world economy," there cannot logically be socialist systems either: "There are today no socialist systems in the world economy any more than there are feudal systems because there is one world system. It is a world economy and it is by definition capitalist in form."[100]

Economics and Politics: Strong and Weak States

Wallerstein's theoretical position is highly deterministic, not to say dogmatic, and it has a constricting impact on the author's historical analysis and his ideas of political strategy. Everything that has happened, has not happened, and will happen is explained by reference to the needs of the world system; exceptions tend to be explained away as accidents. Obviously, the result is some circular and self-confirming argument. In particular, political development is attributed to a country's role in the world system. Peter Gourevitch describes the approach thus:

> States [in Wallerstein's view] are the concrete precipitates from the system, not the component units of it. . . . The international division

99. "Rise and Future Demise," in *Capitalist World-Economy,* 7, 24; *Modern World-System,* 7. Wallerstein declares in the latter work that he "abandoned the idea altogether of taking either the sovereign state or that vaguer concept, the national society, as a unit of analysis. I decided [*sic*] that neither one was a social system and that one could only speak of social change in social systems. The only social system in this scheme was the world system." As Ian Roxborough remarks, Wallerstein thus solves the problem of relating "internal" to "external" factors by abolishing the distinction and the problem (*Theories of Underdevelopment,* 51). Wallerstein seems completely indifferent to what the members of societies may feel and to the implication that systems he sees as unreal might be real for them.

100. "Rise and Future Demise," in *Capitalist World-Economy,* 35.

> of labor determines how much variance in political forms is allowed the component units. Position in the division of labor determines the type of form: states at the core must be strong; states at the periphery must be weak.[101]

But why should the strength or weakness of states matter, since they are dependent variables of the system? Because (paradoxically enough) differences in the power of nation-states are crucial to explaining the persistence of a system rooted in unequal economic exchange. If there was no coercion to enforce it, the victims might well revolt. In Wallerstein's own words, "Once we get a difference in the strength of the state-machineries, we get the operation of 'unequal exchange' which is enforced by strong states on weak ones, by core states on peripheral areas. Thus capitalism involves not only appropriation of surplus-value by an owner from a laborer, but an appropriation of surplus of the world economy by core areas."[102] State power thus appears as a deus ex machina to account for the survival of exploitative relationships—an ironic outcome for an approach which dismisses the nation-state as a real entity.

Yet even in this role, the strength or weakness of states is interpreted economistically. Strength is a function of surplus appropriated and taxable capacity, weakness a function of lack of either. As to the state's domestic role, Wallerstein is at some pains to deny that he is a crude instrumentalist, arguing that in the seventeenth century states were not manipulable puppets of the bourgeoisie: "The formula of the state as 'executive committee of the ruling class' is [he writes] only valid . . . if one bears in mind that executive committees are never mere reflections of the wills of their constituents."[103]

Yet Wallerstein claims that "the state machineries of the core states were strengthened to meet the needs of capitalist landowners and their merchant allies." Moreover, his distancing from simple *domestic* instrumentalism actually sustains his usual view that it was the *external* force—the world system—which was

101. "Second Image," 890.

102. "Rise and Future Demise," in *Capitalist World-Economy,* 18–19.

103. Ibid., 20.

determinant. Indeed, as Marxist critics have remarked, the system and its political derivative, the state, are more prominent as motors of history in Wallerstein's analysis than classes or class conflict.

The problem is, as the same Marxists and others have pointed out, that the neat identification of strong states with the capitalist core and of weak states with the periphery does not work, even for the period in which Wallerstein is mainly interested.[104] England and Holland were clearly among the leading capitalist economies in both the sixteenth and seventeenth centuries. Yet neither had a strong state, if this term implies a highly centralized, autocratic, and effective political apparatus and a standing army. Sweden, Prussia, Austria, Spain, and Portugal did have strong states. But the first three were on the periphery (at that time), while the latter two had extensive overseas possessions but failed to develop as capitalist economies. France, Wallerstein argues, was both core and periphery, and a strong state had to develop there in order to hold together capitalist groups whose interests differed.[105] But, as Zolberg has pointed out, it can just as plausibly be argued that the strength of the French state (and the strength and weakness of other states) was a reaction to the pressures of the European state system. Strong states developed in response to external threat.[106]

Moreover, while Wallerstein generally (if inconsistently) produces particular explanations for apparently deviant cases, the reader is left wondering why the United States—the core of the core—has such a feeble state apparatus, with a constitutionally entrenched division of power and substantial vested authority in states and local governments. What kind of strong state is it that allows private citizens to possess firearms, lets them calculate

104. Skocpol, "Wallerstein's World Capitalist System," 1083–87; Peter Gourevitch, "The International System and Regime Formation: A Critical Review of Anderson and Wallerstein," *Comparative Politics* 10, no. 3 (April 1978): 422–25; Brenner, "Capitalist Development," 61–66; Smith, "Underdevelopment of Development Literature," 262–64.

105. *Modern World-System,* 263–69, 283 ff.

106. Aristide Zolberg, "Origins of the Modern World System: A Missing Link," *World Politics* 33, no. 2 (January 1981): 263 ff.

their own taxes, and allows them access to the files of the bureaucracy? Every such exception and accident is bound to undermine the general force of Wallerstein's argument, and the argument is crucial to explaining the growth and survival of the world system.

In terms of his treatment of the relations between politics and economics, then, Wallerstein is both exceptionally holistic and unusually economistic. He tends to treat domestic political processes as determined externally or as reflections of domestic economic interests, and he does so in a sweeping and mechanical fashion. Yet he reintroduces politics (and the nation-state) as a decisive factor in accounting for the maintenance of a system of unequal exchange of which they are supposedly also the product.

Escaping from Dependence

Wallerstein's holism also dominates his view of how the capitalist world economy can be overturned. Its implications are obviously rather gloomy: if the whole is dominant over the parts, there can be no significant change until the entire system is changed. If the Chinese and Russian revolutions have not established socialist systems, what hope is there for the Tanzanias and Nicaraguas?

Wallerstein and his disciples are, indeed, quite blunt and consistent on this point. Autarky and nationalization are not enough. They cannot lead to socialism so long as the capitalist world system survives: "A state which collectively owns all the means of production is merely a collective capitalist firm as long as it remains—as all such states are, in fact, presently compelled to remain—a participant in the market of the capitalist world economy."[107] This is, in fact, the familiar state capitalism critique applied originally to the Soviet Union by Maoists, but it must logically apply to any "national" road to socialism. For, according to the world-systems view, "the capitalist mode of production . . . is a feature of the world system as a whole. If this is

107. "Dependence in an Interdependent World: The Limited Possibilities of Transformation within the Capitalist World-Economy," in *Capitalist World-Economy*, 68–69.

true, then strategies that try to move toward socialism at the national level may only reproduce capitalism . . . China, the Soviet Union, Cuba, etc., are important experiments in the attempt to build socialism, but they are not separate islands of the socialist mode of production."[108] For socialism as a mode of production can only come about "within the single division of labor that is the world-economy and . . . that will require a single government."[109] Thus Wallerstein ends up, like the liberal Harry Johnson, envisaging world government, except that his would be a "single" government, whereas Johnson looked forward to a federal system.

Less logical, and again ironic, is Wallerstein's suprisingly reformist answer to the question, What should be done? Revolutions not only create but depend on hope, and the world-system view offers, at best, infinite deferment. Not so, says Wallerstein: "What sensible men can do is to use the subtleties of careful intelligence . . . to push those changes that are immediately beneficial and to coordinate with others elsewhere the long-run strategies that will permit a more fundamental transformation."[110] As strategic advice, this injunction seems reasonable enough, and certainly less metaphysical than the peroration of Cardoso and Faletto's work. But in terms of Wallerstein's own theoretical framework it is hard to see why any sensible man would waste his time working for a global revolution when states as powerful and populous as the Soviet Union and China have apparently had so small an impact.

Wallerstein is involved in a double paradox. To explain the survival of an exploitative world system, he falls back on the nation-state, the significance of which he otherwise dismisses. To kindle hope for its overthrow, he falls back on the coordination and careful intelligence of sensible men—an extraordinary

108. Christopher Chase-Dunn, "A World-System Perspective on *Dependency and Development in Latin America*," *Latin American Research Review* 17, no. 1 (1982): 169.

109. "Dependence in an Interdependent World," in *Capitalist World-Economy*, 91.

110. Ibid., 92.

retreat into individualism for someone so unequivocally global and collectivist in attitude!

The variety and complexity of the material examined in this chapter lead to three general conclusions about the quest for international political economy. The first is that casting the problem of relations between politics and economics onto an international plane makes for greater complication, not for easier answers. The second is that, just as there is no single domestic model of political economy, so there are competing forms of international political economy, most of which derive their assumptions and concepts from well-established schools of thought. The third is that the intellectual energy which this enterprise has consumed in recent years indicates a pressing need for relevant and reliable analysis of a set of global relationships that have changed radically while continually growing more complex.

The situation of international political economy resembles the plight of a man trying to swallow the sea to save himself from drowning. It not only has to find an adequate conceptualization of relations between political and economic processes, but it also has to depict the relationship between external and internal processes. It has to deal with the problems facing economists, political scientists, and students of international relations, and to satisfy critics of these specialists that it has more to offer than any single group of them.

The criticisms made here of international political economy should therefore be set against the extreme difficulty of the task confronting scholars in this field. It is hardly surprising that most of them opt for models which are fundamentally economistic or politicist: the need for a basic organizing principle to establish order among the intricacies of international relations is powerful. Nor is the attraction of all-explanatory global theories hard to fathom: it derives from the very character and direction of the processes described, and from the same need to simplify in order to explain.

By virtue of being ambitious, global theories are more vulnerable than theories of more modest application. But this does not invalidate their ambition or their force, least of all when we are dealing with relations between developed and underdeveloped areas. Of the approaches examined here, that employed by Keohane and Nye is in some ways the most intellectually appealing. It offers a procedure for successively applying entirely different approaches and provides for discrimination among different aspects of relations among countries. Yet, by the authors' own admission, this procedure is not universally applicable, any more than the interdependence it is intended to highlight is characteristic of relations among all states or, necessarily, of all relations between any two.

There may, in other words, be relationships in which the elements of domination and inequality stressed by realism and dependency theory are more evident. To say that dependency theory distorts by its insistence on their powerlessness is not to deny that dependence exists or that inequality reinforces it. In short, an approach that is intellectually flawed may nevertheless illuminate certain relationships better than one that on many counts is conceptually more elegant and logically sounder. This paradox emphasizes the value of looking not just at the internal content of theories but at the political contexts in which their creation and popularization occur.

In the next chapter, I am concerned with a body of theory in which domination, conflict, and inequality are major themes—Marxism. In particular, I shall examine applications of the Marxist tradition to the political economy of the Third World. What is distinctive about the Marxist treatment of politics and the state? What problems does it create? And how do Marxists deal with such problems when analyzing the politics of underdeveloped countries?

SIX
MARXISM AS POLITICAL ECONOMY

In looking for an authentically political political economy, it is natural to seek it within the capacious framework of Marxism; for Marxists have always claimed that comprehensiveness—the connection of all kinds of apparently distinct social institutions—is a special merit of their approach (in contrast to the deductive procedure of classical political economy, which derives explanation from a small set of axioms). They have insisted that "the world must be understood as basically a single, integrated unit . . . following Lukacs' dictum that the essence of Marxism is not any idea of economic base, but the method of totality."[1] Yet even the method of totality has to start somewhere: it has to make some assumptions on which to build a structure of explanation and prescriptions. Moreover, the pursuit of totality entails difficulties and temptations of its own. It inspires a tendency, for example, to treat the behavior of individuals and small groups as determined and explicable by total, even global, processes, and a consequent indifference to ideas and policies that are partial or "merely reformist."

In this chapter I first summarize the assumptions Marxists have brought to analysis of relations between political and other structures, as well as the problems to which their approach has given rise and attempts to solve them. Then I examine the re-

1. Aidan Foster-Carter, "Neo-Marxist Approaches to Development and Underdevelopment," in *Sociology and Development*, ed. Emanuel de Kadt and Gavin Williams (London: Tavistock 1974), 82.

cent development of Marxist treatment of the political-economic complex in the setting of Third World countries, using for illustration debates about the nature of class and politics in African countries.

POLITICS AND THE STATE IN MARXISM

The more sophisticated Marxists reject vehemently the notion that Marxism's central tenet is a mechanical determination of the political (and social, ideological, and cultural) "superstructure" by an economic "base." They insist that such economism violates the dynamic, interactive quality of Marxist thought (words such as *insist*, *must*, and *correct* litter Marxist analysis, reflecting its didactic and often dogmatic character). Yet such insistence tends to detract from the robust simplicity that has made Marxism so appealing and dramatic as political rhetoric. It also creates a tension with the equally insistent imperative of Marxology to refer back to what Marx said and to seek truth in exegesis. For what Marx said on the subject of the state and politics was limited, rather dismissive, and quite economistic. Like liberals of the period, he tended to see the state and political processes in general as secondary and probably transient.[2] Transient, because just as for liberals the state was a reminder of the propensity of human imperfection to generate and abuse power, so for Marxists it reflected the asymmetries of class relations in a bourgeois society, to be ended with the advent of socialism. Neither school was apt, therefore, to treat the state seriously, and both tended to assume that a proper resolution of economic conflict would put an end to political conflicts and, ideally, to the institutions that profited from it.

Limited though they are, Marx's comments on the significance of politics are, with one notable exception, plainly economistic. The short form is the well-known statement in the *Communist Manifesto* that "the Executive of the modern state is but a

2. See, for example, Anthony Giddens, *The Class Structure of the Advanced Societies* (London: Hutchinson, 1973), 124–25; and Frank Parkin, *Marxism and Class Theory: A Bourgeois Critique* (London: Tavistock, 1979), 119, 121–22.

committee for managing the common affairs of the whole bourgeoisie." A larger form occurs in *Capital*, where he declares:

> The specific economic form in which unpaid surplus labor is pumped out of direct producers, determines the relationship of rulers to ruled. . . . It is always the direct relationship of the owners of the conditions of production to the direct producers—a relationship always naturally corresponding to a definite stage in the development of the methods of labor and thereby its social productivity—which reveals the innermost secret, the hidden basis of the entire social structure, and with it the political form of the relation of sovereignty and dependence, in short the corresponding specific form of the state.[3]

The stages referred to were conceived as a succession of "modes of production" (notably, the feudal, capitalist, and socialist), each of which comprised the material "forces of production" and a corresponding set of "social relations of production." A particular society ("social formation") in a given historical period would normally be shaped by one dominant mode of production; but in the dynamic historical dialectic envisaged by Marxist change it was the result of one mode of production supplanting another, so that there might well be the remnants of, for instance, the feudal mode in a society dominated by the capitalist mode. Conversely, and of even greater theoretical importance, each new mode of production grew out of the contradictions of its predecessor, though outside forces might be crucial to its development. Thus a central issue in Marxist theory was that of transition—from feudalism to capitalism, and from capitalism to socialism: how, for example, did capitalist forms establish themselves and finally prevail in the materially and ideologically hostile environment of the Middle Ages?

The role of the state in this perspective was that of providing "the political and coercive conditions essential for the maintenance of any mode of production" short of socialism.[4] It served

3. Karl Marx, *Capital*, ed. Frederich Engels (New York: International Publishers, 1967), 3: 791.

4. John Lonsdale, "The State and Social Processes in Africa," paper presented to the Twenty-Fourth Annual Meeting of the African Studies Association, Bloomington, Ind., 21 October 1981, 3.

the ruling class both directly—by keeping the exploited direct producers in their place—and indirectly—by providing a mystifying rationale for existing relationships, an "ideology" which falsely represented reality as natural, divinely ordained, or in some other way legitimate. In short, the state's role was to exercise power and authority, but the source of its influence lay outside of the personnel and institutions that comprised the state, that is, in the ruling class constituted by the material forces and social relations of production. Hence the distinction between base and superstructure:

> legal relations as well as forms of state are to be grasped neither from themselves nor from the so-called general development of the human mind, but rather have their roots in the material conditions of life. . . . The sum total of these relations of production constitutes the economic structure of society, the real foundation, on which rises a legal and political superstructure and to which correspond definite forms of social consciousness. The mode of production of material life conditions the social, political, and intellectual life process in general.[5]

Politics was the medium through which the ruling class exercised and legitimized its control, but it was also the channel through which contradictions were expressed and resolved. Change involved tension between developing forces of production and existing social relations, the latter becoming redundant as the former expanded and altered. "Objectively," any political action that effected a reconstitution of social relations to accommodate the development of forces of production might be considered progressive. But such an accommodation was not assured: "reactionary" social forces (for example, a feudal or landowning aristocracy) might try to hold back or reverse the objective logic of the historical dialectic. Political initiative, backed by a correct theoretical analysis, was therefore always necessary and might require compromise and alliance with forces (for instance, the bourgeoisie) that, while themselves

5. Karl Marx, *Contribution to the Critique of Political Economy*, in Karl Marx and Frederich Engels, *Selected Works* (New York: International Publishers, 1968), 182.

exploitative of the direct producers and the proletariat, represented an objective progression from existing conditions. History was a dialectic between oppressor and oppressed. At each stage, the objective requirements of progress had to be distinguished from the superficial, contingent appearances of subjectivity. Objective judgment might indicate support of groups whose attitudes and interests were ostensibly at odds with those of the proletariat and detachment from groups that regarded themselves as progressive. History, like God, moved in mysterious ways; but, unlike God's, those of history were quite intelligible to those capable of conducting a correct theoretical analysis and able to discern the shifting historical boundary between impersonal constraints and the terrain open to political action. Men make their own history, but not as they choose: excessive determinism and excessive "voluntarism" equally deform analysis and derail action (praxis).

In all this, an appreciation of the "class character" of the state is important. While it is normally, according to Engels, a machine for keeping down the oppressed, exploited class, there may be moments in which it appears to stand above the class struggle.[6] In particular, Marx suggested that periods of transition, when rising and falling classes were temporarily in balance and eclipsed each other, provided opportunities for the rise of leaders who both benefited and suffered from the lack of a clear class hegemony and for the related aggrandizement of the state apparatus. He identified such a situation in mid-nineteenth century France, where Louis Napoleon had emancipated himself from the bourgeoisie and had succeeded in playing it off against the peasantry and the working class.[7] Such autonomy was, however, precarious and temporary: it was precarious, because Louis Napoleon needed class support and had to take actions to get it that would strengthen the power of one of the classes, thereby threatening both his power and the equilibrium among the classes upon which it rested. It was temporary by definition,

6. Frederich Engels, *The Origin of the Family, Private Property, and the State*, in Marx and Engels, *Selected Works*, 591.

7. Marx, *The Eighteenth Brumaire of Louis Bonaparte*, in Marx and Engels, *Selected Works*, 97–180.

for eventually the equilibrium would pass and a new class hegemony (bourgeois or proletarian) would be established to which the leader would have to submit. Engels later generalized this phenomenon, arguing that, although the state was normally an instrument of the ruling class,

> By way of exception, periods occur in which the warring classes balance each other so nearly that the state power, as ostensible mediator, acquires, for the moment, a certain degree of independence of both . . . such was the Bonapartism of the First, and still more of the Second French Empire, which played off the proletariat against the bourgeoisie and the bourgeoisie against the proletariat. The latest performance of this kind . . . is the new German Empire of the Bismarck nation: here the capitalists and workers are balanced against each other and equally cheated for the benefit of the impoverished Prussian cabbage junkers.[8]

With respect to politics, the intellectual inheritance of Marxism thus consists of a major instrumentalist tradition, which conceives political insitutions as instruments of class power, and a minor autonomist tradition, which suggests that in some circumstances the state may acquire a significant degree of independence from the class struggle. We now examine criticism and recent developments of these traditions.

Instrumentalism is in effect a form of economism, treating political institutions and ideas and change in both as a dependent variable of modes of production.[9] Rhetorically, it has obvious merits, clearly indicating who are the oppressed, who the oppressors, how oppression is carried out, and how it can be ended. Analytically, it points to examination of the social and political ties linking the personnel who man the state apparatus

8. Engels, *The Origin of the Family*, in Marx and Engels, *Selected Works*, 588.

9. Miliband, for example, writes: "In the Marxist scheme, the 'ruling class' of capitalist society is that class which owns and controls the means of production and which is able by virtue of the economic power thus conferred upon it, to use the state as its instrument for the domination of society" (Ralph Miliband, *The State in Capitalist Society* [New York: Basic Books, 1969], 22). Sweezy writes, in a similar vein, that the state is "an instrument in the hands of the ruling class for enforcing and guaranteeing the stability of the class structure itself." Paul M. Sweezy, *The Theory of Capitalist Development* (New York: Monthly Review Press, 1968), 243.

with the ruling class—those who own the means of production, exchange, and distribution.

Such analysis, and the assumptions underlying it, however, have been heavily criticized by Marxists and non-Marxists. Critics claim that it is narrow, question-begging, and redundant. It assumes (unconsciously aping liberal assumptions) that the state is no more than the sum of individual politicians and civil servants and the expression of their collective socialization (the ideas and values they picked up from their [bourgeois] families, schools, and other extrapolitical associations).[10] It ignores the structures within which political personnel operate and relations between nominally political and nominally nonpolitical structures (such as the media) that lie outside personal relationships (for example, financial ties and legal relationships).

More fundamentally, instrumentalism provides a static analysis and seems incapable of explaining change. If politics merely reflects the asymmetries of class power, and the state enforces those asymmetries, how can class struggle ever occur? At most, an instrumentalist view is merely a kind of social register of the class struggle: it records without explaining; it indicates an outcome but not the dynamics which produced—and may change—that outcome. In fact, it is circular: the bourgeoisie (for example) commands power, therefore those who exercise power are members or dependents of the bourgeoisie.

Further, such analysis can be faulted on its own ground. Not only have bourgeois states (like bourgeois corporations) been controlled by people who cannot plausibly be regarded as members or progeny of the class owning the means of production, but they have also taken actions which have been loudly and actively opposed by spokesmen of that class. The entire history of welfare legislation and state capitalism since the early nineteenth century has been marked by a struggle between the bourgeois state and organized bourgeois interests opposing change in the name of the central bourgeois values of freedom and individual

10. See, for example, David A. Gold, Clarence Y. H. Lo, and Erik Olin Wright, "Recent Developments in Marxist Theories of the Capitalist State," *Monthly Review* 27, no. 5 (October 1975): 33–35; and Nicos Poulantzas, "The Problem of the Capitalist State," *New Left Review* 58 (November–December 1969), 69–70.

initiative.[11] The tendency of the state to intervene in the economy in both advanced industrial and underdeveloped countries seems as persistent under liberal as under socialist regimes.

The usual explanation of such phenomena is that the bourgeois state takes such actions to preempt opposition or to provide conditions for its further expansion. Public housing and free health care are intended to buy off the proletariat, to deceive them into accepting capitalism, and even into regarding it as benevolent; state capitalism relieves the bourgeoisie of the costs of creating its own infrastructure, often relieves it of the pain of facing its own failures, and sometimes directly subsidizes it. Whatever the truth of such arguments, they do not solve the problems that such cases of state initiative raise for instrumentalist analysis. For they raise the possibilities of conflict between the bourgeois state and representatives of the bourgeoisie and of such conflict being resolved in favor of the state.

STRUCTURALISM AND THE RELATIVE AUTONOMY OF THE STATE

The problem of the relationship between the bourgeoisie and the state has attracted Marxists who are critical of the instrumentalist approach. They object to an approach that seems to reduce "the exercise of power and the formation of state policy . . . to a kind of voluntarism on the part of powerful people."[12] They call for one that incorporates the assumption of class struggle and allows for the possibility of the state acting independently of the supposed ruling class, "on behalf" of that class, perhaps, but not "at its behest."[13] As conceived by Nicos Poulantzas and other "structuralists," such an approach emphasizes the func-

11. Gold, Lo, and Wright, "Marxist Theories," 35; Parkin, *Marxism*, 123–25. On the general question of the ability of states to raise themselves above the class system, see Theda Skocpol, *States and Revolutions* (Cambridge: Cambridge University Press, 1979).

12. Gold, Lo, and Wright, "Marxist Theories," 35.

13. Ralph Miliband, "Political Forms and Historical Materialism, in *The Socialist Register 1975*, ed. Ralph Miliband and John Saville (London: Merlin Press, 1975), 316.

tions or roles of the state relative to capitalism and claims that such functions impose themselves on the personnel of the state: "If the *function* of the state in a determinate social formation and the *interests* of the dominant class in this formation *coincide*, it is by reason of the system itself."[14] And if the personnel of the state happen to be members of the ruling class, such coincidence is an effect or symptom of the structural relationship, not the cement that creates and holds it together.

But whereas the functions of the state are determined by the structures of the society (shaped by the process of surplus-value production), the state itself enjoys "relative autonomy." Such autonomy is necessary because the ruling class is often divided internally (a possibility that instrumentalism would find it hard to deal with) and is often unable to recognize or ensure the conditions necessary for the continuing expansion of capitalism. The state thus acts as "'the intelligence' of the bourgeoisie": "by virtue of its social distance from the class it serves, the state is all the more able to orchestrate and plan the strategies for bourgeois survival."[15] Specifically, the state performs three tasks. One is to push through those social reforms which are in the long-term interest of the bourgeoisie, even if some of its politicians resist them. The second—much helped by the first—is to break up the political unity of the working class. The third is to project the rationale of capitalism as being in the interests of the entire community—an ideological task which involves invoking the symbolism of "the nation" or "the public interest" and is more effectively performed when the state is seen to be, however intermittently, independent of the ruling class. The state, in the jargon of this school, "symbolizes the unity of the social formation"; but the unity is, of course, unreal.[16]

The structuralist approach is a serious attempt to deal with the inadequacies of instrumentalism and thereby to protect the overall intellectual credibility of Marxism. Nevertheless, it pro-

14. Poulantzas, "Capitalist State," 73.

15. Parkin, *Marxism*, 124.

16. John S. Saul, "The State in Post-Colonial Societies: Tanzania," in *The Socialist Register 1974*, ed. Ralph Miliband and John Saville (London: Merlin Press, 1974), 351.

vokes serious doubts on both conceptual and empirical grounds. For example, it has a troubling and ironic affinity with functionalism, which has been attacked ad nauseam as a conservative methodology when applied by social scientists.[17] The notion that structures "cause" and functions "require" people to act quite properly strikes readers as at best metaphysical and at worst downright mischievous and threatening. As several critics have pointed out (and structuralists have indeed declared), consciousness, intention, and action themselves have no explanatory significance in structuralist theory. The prime mover is the mode of production anthropomorphized, and consciousness is a product of a complex set of structural relationships.[18] Analysis is thus able to transcend the contingency of individual actions and misapprehensions and to achieve a clearer, more farsighted vision of the working of social forces. As Parkin puts it, with obvious incredulity:

> Notions such as the mode of production make their claims to explanatory power precisely on the grounds of their indifference to the nature of the human material whose activities are structurally determined . . . [To] introduce questions such as the ethnic composition of the workforce is to clutter up the analysis by laying stress upon the qualities of social actors, a conception directly opposed to the notion of human agents as *träger* or embodiments of systematic forces.[19]

Indeed, structuralism represents a significant advance for the concept of false consciousness, since its view of the state rests on the high probability that the bourgeoisie, as well as the proletariat, will fail to recognize its true interest. Thus, as Parkin notes, the state intervenes to save the bourgeoisie from itself, just as the

17. Lonsdale ("State and Social Processes," 1) remarks that "structural-functional political science of unimpeachable conservatism bears an uncanny resemblance to the more structural brands of Marxism."

18. For criticism on these grounds, see Frank T. Fitzgerald, "Sociologies of Development," *Journal of Contemporary Asia* 11, no. 1 (1981): 15; Gold, Lo and Wright, "Marxist Theories," 38–39; and Amy Beth Bridges, "Nicos Poulantzas and the Marxist Theory of the State," *Politics and Society* 4 (Winter 1974): 182, 186, 189.

19. Parkin, *Marxism*, 37.

vanguard party guides the masses toward socialism.[20] The only snag in the theory is how to explain the miraculous escape of theorists and intellectuals generally from the snares and pitfalls of false consciousness: only they seem to be, so to speak, tenured in objectivity.[21]

On empirical grounds, demonstrating the relative autonomy of the state has raised further problems. Such demonstration requires establishing, first, that "the incumbents of state offices form a corporate political elite with distinct aims and interests of its own," and, second, that the aims and interests of this elite are clearly contrary to those of the ruling class (those dominant within a particular mode of production).[22] Such a demonstration is possible for absolutist and fascist states, which had a distinct political apparatus and quite firmly squashed the presumptions and trimmed the power of the ruling class (the aristocracy in the former case, the bourgeoisie in the latter). Krasner has argued that such an elite is identifiable in American government.[23] But in the examples most commonly cited by structuralists—the introduction of welfare legislation, the regulation of business, and the inception of state capitalism—it could be argued that a progressive element within the bourgeoisie prevailed over its more reactionary wing. Historically, each reform had its advocates *within* the bourgeoisie, and the outcome was decided by the usual processes of bourgeois democracy.[24] If such an interpretation is persuasive, it makes resort to the idea

20. Ibid., 125.

21. As Bridges remarks, Poulantzas's theory of ideology, "by asserting that as a result of ideological practice, the social whole is obscured to people, claims a mental passivity for them which is uncomfortably reminiscent of behavioralist theories of socialization. This is particularly striking when it is recalled that while this is the experience of 'agents,' we intellectuals (at least Poulantzas) are presumably not so deluded" ("Poulantzas and the Marxist Theory of the State," 182).

22. Parkin, *Marxism*, 129. For a useful discussion of the concept of a strong state, see Eric A. Nordlinger, *On The Autonomy of the Democratic State* (Cambridge, Mass.: Harvard University Press, 1981), especially 21ff.

23. Stephen D. Krasner, *Defending the National Interest: Raw Materials, Investment and U.S. Foreign Policy* (Princeton, N.J.: Princeton University Press, 1978), 55–57.

24. Parkin, *Marxism*, 133–35.

of an autonomous state imposing its will on squabbling factions unnecessary. It also restores "human agents" and their collective efforts to a more central place, thereby reinvigorating the older Marxist notion of history as class struggle.

Indeed, though structuralism claims to be thoroughly Marxist, the implications of positing a relative autonomy for the state should be alarming to Marxists. Logically, what is to ensure that relative autonomy does not become absolute autonomy?[25] In positing the possibility of a state elite cutting loose from its immediate class commitments, the structuralists are giving ground dangerously to the politicist idea of politics imposing upon economics. If the state elite is able to redefine the interests of capitalism, why should it not go further and redefine all interests as subordinate to its own? If the structuralists retort that such absolute autonomy is inconceivable given the functional constraints on the state to act in the interests of capitalism, it seems fair to ask them to indicate, for once, the mechanisms that would prevent such a development, especially in the light of the record of fascist and state corporatist regimes in this century.

HEGELIAN-MARXISM: THE ROLE OF CONSCIOUSNESS

Both instrumentalism and structuralism take a rather slighting view of the role of ideas and culture generally, typically regarding them as vehicles of class power, as products with very little independent and no decisive influence on the struggle between exploiter and exploited. A third school, largely indebted to the work of Antonio Gramsci and sometimes labeled Hegelian-Marxist, stresses the importance of cultural hegemony in maintaining class power. It takes up the fundamental matter of legitimacy, which is usually avoided or ignored by the other schools, and asserts that the questions of consciousness and ideology are crucial to understanding both the consolidation and the decay of the capitalist state.[26] The latter certainly serves the interests of the ruling class, but it does so partly by persuading the proletariat that class conflict is insignificant or is soluble

25. Ibid., 126–28.

26. Gold, Lo, and Wright, "Marxist Theories," 40.

within the framework of a common, typically "national" interest represented by the values and traditions of a common culture. The process of mystification is traceable partly in the rhetoric of politicians but also (and perhaps more importantly) in the institutions of cultural domination—the media, educational institutions, the family, and the arts.

While such theory promises a much broader, less economistic working-out of Marxist assumptions and methods than the other two schools, it often seems to remain at a generalized, abstract level, referring generically to capitalist society, rather than exploring actual processes in particular capitalist societies. Moreover, this approach, though in fact very relevant to the problems of Third World societies, has mostly been applied to advanced capitalist societies.

This section (following the typology of Gold, Lo, and Wright) has dealt with three strands of interpretation in Marxist analysis of relations between politics and economics. First, there is an instrumentalist tradition, which is heavily economistic but in Marxological terms undeniably authentic. Second, there is a structuralist tradition (a tradition insofar as it has discernible roots in Marx's discussion of Bonapartism), distinguished by its assertion that the state can and sometimes must act independently of the class whose economic power it is structurally bound to preserve. Third, there is a school that emphasizes the central role of cultural processes in legitimizing class power and the central role of the state in generating the symbols of hegemony which give authority and credibility to class power.

The next questions are: How has Marxism adapted to the history and present conditions of the Third World? And how specifically have these views of the politico-economic complex fared in the attempt to adapt Marxism to the circumstances of the underdeveloped world?

MARXISM AND UNDERDEVELOPMENT

Many elements of the Marxist view of relations between the capitalist core and the underdeveloped periphery were presented in the discussion of dependency theory in the previous chapter. The crucial question, increasingly debatable as the twentieth century progresses, has been that of the probability of capitalism reproducing itself in the colonial or satellite economies of the Third World. As Palma has so clearly shown, the orthodox position on this issue has retreated continually from Marx's own confidence, shown in his work on India, that Europe held up to the tropical territories an image of their own future.[27] Lenin's theory of imperialism suggested that industrialization in the colonies would be opposed by the monopolies, which would want to keep the colonies as sources of raw materials and as markets for their products. Further, experiences elsewhere indicated that precapitalist modes of production might survive and create obstacles to penetration by capitalism. Specifically, the problem might be an alliance between traditional elites and the forces of imperialism obstructing the establishment of a "national bourgeoisie."[28] The obvious way to break such alliance would be to support movements for colonial independence, and to this end Stalin called for a "popular front" strategy in support of both liberation movements and "progressive" elements in the national bourgeoisie.[29]

After 1945, however, the official view of colonial elites fluctuated. Stalin's "two-camp" doctrine affirmed that the national bourgeoisies in colonial territories were unworthy of support, a position he maintained despite the spectacular advances of nationalist movements in Asia and Africa. Under Khrushchev, a more forward policy was adopted, involving an acceptance of the "objectively progressive" role of the national bourgeoisie. Such acceptance was, nevertheless, grudging. A conference in Moscow in 1955 concluded that "as far as the national bourgeoisie is concerned, the achievement of independence is its ultimate

27. Gabriel Palma, "Dependency: A Formal Theory of Underdevelopment or a Methodology for the Analysis of Concrete Situations of Underdevelopment?" *World Development* 6, nos. 7–8 (July/August 1978): 885–97.

28. Ibid., 897.

29. Fritz Schatten, *Communism in Africa* (London: George Allen and Unwin, 1966), 72.

aim, and it consists in the establishment of their undivided rule in a sovereign State."[30]

While faith in the reproduction of capitalism and its contradictions persisted in orthodox Western Marxist writings (such as those of Jack Woddis), one effect of anticolonial nationalism was a growing tendency to question or even reject the "ethnocentric" concepts and prescriptions of received Marxism. Intellectually, this trend appeared in theories (among them dependency theory) that assert the impossibility of an implantation of the capitalist mode of production, its attendant industrialism, and its corresponding social and political forms in the Third World. At the least, such theories denied that this process could follow the same route as in Western Europe. Partly in reaction against dependency theory (with its emphasis on global commerce as a motor of underdevelopment), Marxists have leaned toward a rather economistic analysis turning on modes of production. A common view is that the persistence of precapitalist modes of production in colonial and ex-colonial countries has produced a peculiar "articulation" of the capitalist mode with the earlier forms. (Related to this view is the notion of a special colonial mode of production.)[31] The implication is that capitalism is likely to be

30. Report of meeting on "the particular characteristics of the national-revolutionary movement in the colonial and dependent countries of the East," *Mezhdunarodnaya Zhisn* (Moscow), vol. 3 (1959) (cited in Schatten, *Communism in Africa*, 77). For other accounts of Soviet attitudes toward nationalism in the Third World, see, for example, Ishwer C. Ojha, "The Kremlin and Third World Leadership: Closing the Circle," in *Soviet Policy in Developing Countries*, ed. W. Raymond Duncan (Waltham, Mass.: Ginn-Blaisdell, 1970), 9–28; Helen Desfosses Cohn, *Soviet Policy toward Black Africa: The Focus on National Integration* (New York: Praeger, 1972); and William Zimmerman, *Soviet Persepctives on International Relations, 1956–1967* (Princeton, N.J.: Princeton University Press, 1969).

31. On the identity of "modes of production" in colonial and postcolonial societies, see Hamza Alavi, "India and the Colonial Mode of Production," in *The Socialist Register 1975*, ed. Ralph Miliband and John Saville (London: Merlin Press, 1975), 160–91; and Bernard Magubane, "The Evolution of the Class Structure in Africa," in *The Political Economy of Contemporary Africa*, ed. Peter C. W. Gutkind and Immanuel Wallerstein (Beverly Hills, Calif.: Sage Publications, 1976), 169–97.

weak or to be concentrated in certain sectors (notably commerce), and that a strong, indigenous, entrepreneurial bourgeoisie is unlikely to develop. There may well be a wealthy dominant class, but its interests and attitudes will be quite different from those of the classical bourgeoisies of the industrialized world. It will not challenge, except rhetorically, the continuing power of foreign capital. It may, indeed, collaborate with international capitalism, which can then shape development policy according to its own preferences.

MARXISM AND THIRD WORLD POLITICS

Given the perspective just outlined, what is the nature of the class struggle in underdeveloped countries, and what is the class character of the state?

The first injunction of Marxist analysts in treating these questions is that the only meaningful framework is an international one. They reject the premise of most "bourgeois" writing on "modernization" and "nation-building" that domestic processes can be understood using a national framework. Thus the first editorial statement of the radical *Review of African Political Economy* called for an approach that "sees the dynamic of African societies as a complex result of internal and external forces which distort and limit the development of the forces of production under capitalism."[32] In practice two ambiguities mark this position. One is an ambiguity about the desirability of capitalism. As Colin Leys has remarked, much dependency theory is infused with an implicit hankering for "true" capitalist development.[33] But the same ambivalence is present in much Marxist writing, and quite naturally so, given the uncertainty in Marx's successors about the possibility of achieving socialism without capitalism to expand production and create a proletariat.

32. "Editorial," *Review of African Political Economy* 1 (1974): 3.

33. Colin Leys, *Underdevelopment in Kenya: The Political Economy of Neo-Colonialism* (London: Heinemann, 1975), 13; and idem, "African Economic Development in Theory and Practice," *Daedalus* 3, no. 2 (Spring 1982): 104. For a critique of the ambiguities of radical theory in Africa, see Björn Beckman, "Imperialism and the 'National Bourgeoisie,'" *Review of African Political Economy* 22 (October–December 1981): 12–13.

The other ambiguity concerns the national and international credentials of theory itself. Specifically, it concerns the acceptance of Marxism by intellectual nationalists in the Third World. "Bourgeois" theory is denounced as "cultural imperialism," because it presumes a global process is under way that will generalize the experiences and structures of the Western industrialized countries to the underdeveloped world. It equates modernity and development with acquisition of the institutions and values of the liberal capitalist world. Critics argue that such theory offends the integrity and independence of ex-colonial countries by excluding the possibility of development on lines different from those of liberal capitalism. The obvious question is why Marxism, which also originated in the West (albeit as a dialectical adversary of capitalism), which also assumes the preeminence of international processes and the dominance of international forces, and which is even more peremptory in its treatment of nationalism, should be so warmly embraced by so many intellectual nationalists in the Third World, not to mention radicals in the first world.

To explain this interesting paradox would involve some burrowing into the cultural dilemmas of Third World intellectuals. The point of noting it is simply to identify a tension apparent in actual discussions of Third World politics. The tension is one between the external and internal dimensions, which, as remarked in the last chapter, is characteristic of much international political economy, but which takes on a particular idiom in Marxist analysis. Here the tension expresses itself (to use Lonsdale's useful distinction) as one between capital logic and class logic. "Capital logic" means that "the main determinant of action by the capitalist state are the systematic requirements of capitalism in general." "Class logic" means that "the state's, and capitalists', freedom to choose more productive techniques and so on is crimped by the existing class relations of power and production."[34] One way of understanding Marxist debates about

34. Lonsdale, "State and Social Processes," 16. Lonsdale argues that this distinction is artificial: it does, however, correspond to a real distinction in analytic emphasis.

Third World politics is to conceive them as pulled, broadly, between these competing logics. To oversimplify, one camp sees the logic of international capitalism as the main dynamic in the development of Third World countries. It thus adopts a clearly externalist view and sees domestic politics as instrumental to the needs and purposes of international capitalism. This view satisfies both the internationalism of Marxism and the intellectuals' yearning for a universal theory of cause and effect. The other camp is uneasy about the mechanical character of such argument and its implied depreciation of the significance of domestic politics. It therefore wants a framework that recognizes the realities of external influence but accords more prominence to internal class struggle. It seeks, if not in so many words, to inject a note of voluntarism, to assert that while Third World peoples may not make their history as they choose, they do nevertheless make it. Such an assertion satisfies the nationalism of Third World intellectuals and also restores a sense of political efficacy to arguments about Third World politics.

In order to make this abstract distinction intelligible, I shall now examine the specific arguments between Marxists about the nature of politics and the state in Africa, an area with which I am relatively familiar and one in which an active, if occasionally theological, debate has occurred in the two decades since independence.

MARXISM AND THE AFRICAN STATE

Two quite divergent themes compete in Marxist analysis of African politics. One, arising from the capital logic view, represents the class structure of African societies as shaped by international capitalism. In this perspective, the dominant class in African countries is not a true bourgeoisie, nor is it a true ruling class (the latter is, in fact, the bourgeoisie of the European and North American core). The dominant class in the African state is a *comprador* group, an auxiliary bourgeoisie, in terms of Marx's original formulation, "a kind of sub-committee of the metropolitan committee for managing the affair of the bourgeoisie."[35]

35. Leys, *Underdevelopment in Kenya*, 10.

The subordination of the African state to capitalism follows ineluctably and is often described in the language of structural Marxism. Thus Michaela Von Freyhold writes of Tanzania:

> The colonial and post-colonial state are both the agents of parts of the bourgeoisie, but the ways in which they *fulfill their function and the tasks they have to perform* are rather different and require a substantial transformation of the state in the process of decolonization . . . [the postcolonial state] is faced with the task of disorganizing the direct producers who have begun to assert their class interests . . . the actual dynamics of economic and social development . . . are determined by the metropolitan bourgeoisie irrespective of the form in which it intervenes.[36]

Writers taking the externalist, capital logic view tend to be uninterested in detailed examination of domestic political life in African societies. Just as earlier, liberal writers of the nation-building school concentrated on elites, so many Marxists concentrate on the character of dominant classes, since they are seen as crucial agents for the penetration and stabilization of capitalism. Because, in this view, domestic politics is essentially a product of larger forces, it holds little interest for the theorist.

The other theme, often associated with the class logic view (and more agreeable to radicals with nationalist sympathies), stresses the systemic autonomy of African states. Writers drawn to this perspective often argue that the major characteristic of the postcolonial elite is its possession of political power. They accept that this elite is not a true bourgeoisie and they may also agree that it is neocolonial in character.[37] However, they assert that the lack of a true bourgeoisie does not imply the existence of such a bourgeoisie elsewhere but a very different basis for class formation in Africa. *Power, not control of the means of production is the basis of class formation and class conflict*: the dominant class is therefore to be seen as a "political class," a "bureaucratic" or "managerial" or "organizational" bourgeoisie. Class logic is

36. Michaela von Freyhold, "The Post-Colonial State and Its Tanzanian Version," *Review of African Political Economy* 8 (January–April 1977): 79, 80, 81 (emphasis added).

37. See, for example, Shivji's argument that the "bureaucratic bourgeoisie" in Tanzania is subordinate to "international capitalism." Issa G. Shivji, *Class Struggles in Tanzania* (New York: Monthly Review Press, 1976).

thus preserved, but by inverting the classical Marxist conception of the relationship between economics and politics. Power determines access to wealth, rather than wealth determining access to power.[38]

Such observations are often accompanied by the notion that class formation occurs downward. The state provides the organizational foundation any class needs to move from being a "class-in-itself" (a group with identifiable common interests, problems, and values) to a "class-for-itself" (a group that has recognized such community and has started to create collective organizations). Therefore, class formation has proceeded more rapidly within the elite than among the peasants and workers, who are dispersed and lack such an organization ready to hand. The state, then, can be regarded as "a preformed class organization in waiting": "There was thus [at independence] no need for those at the upper levels of society to constitute an organization to represent their class interests—they had the State."[39] The externalist (capital logic) perspective and the internalist (class logic) perspective are not altogether mutually exclusive. They do, nonetheless, constitute distinct ways of dealing with two sets of questions to which a Marxist approach to international political economy gives rise. One set concerns the relationship between international capitalism and the Third World state: is the latter merely a tool of the former, or does it enjoy relative auton-

38. Robin Cohen argues that five major variables—all of them political in character—have influenced class differentiation in Africa, and comments: "Unlike in Western industrial societies wealth or status do not customarily precede power; rather power and status are isochronous, while wealth more often than not increases with power. . . . The behavior and activities of the ruling groups in office show their overt indebtedness to the political process as a means of developing class crystallization and solidarity. For this reason we term them . . . the political class." ("Class in Africa: Analytical Problems and Perspectives," in *The Socialist Register 1972*, ed. Ralph Miliband and John Saville [London: Merlin Press, 1972], 247–48). For a similar exposition of the idea of power as a basis for class differentiation, see Richard L. Sklar, "The Nature of Class Domination in Africa," *Journal of Modern African Studies* 17, no. 4 (December 1979): 531–52.

39. Michael G. Schatzberg, "The Emerging Trialectic: State, Class, and Ethnicity in Africa," paper presented to the African State Colloquium, Institute of International Studies, University of California, Berkeley, 25 May 1982.

omy? The other set concerns the relationship between the state and domestic interests: is this relationship shaped by the exigencies of international capitalism, or is it subject to dynamics that are local in origin, perhaps involving forces other than those generated by capitalism? Are the external imperatives of economic power congruent with the internal imperatives of getting and holding onto power, or may these two sometimes conflict?

It is impossible to answer such questions in a categorical way, though theorists yearn for generalizations. What we can do is show how the perspectives outlined above tend to produce different interpretations of particular situations and problems. I shall illustrate such difference by considering two debates. One—the debate about development in the Ivory Coast—essentially refers to the broader question of the state and international capitalism. The other—the debate about ethnicity—refers to the character of domestic interests. In reality, the issues overlap, since the contending approaches have clear implications for both external and internal relationships.

METROPOLITAN BOURGEOISIE OR POLITICAL CLASS: THE PROBLEM OF THE IVORY COAST

First, let us recapitulate the capital logic view as it applies to the typical underdeveloped country. This view proposes that, since international capitalism shapes the political and social structures of Third World societies, the rulers of such societies are not the true ruling class but only the dominant class. The true ruling class (the owners of the means of production and distribution) lives in Europe and North America. Capitalist underdevelopment "requires the presence of domestic classes whose interests converge with those of foreign capital and will enforce their political dominance . . . [the local dominant class] uses state protection to entrench itself as an enthusiastic auxiliary of foreign capital."[40] This argument occurs in both simple instru-

40. "Editorial," *Review of African Political Economy* 3 (May–October 1975): 7. The editorial goes on to suggest that "a government, as in Tanzania, may initiate policies intended to diminish the foreign stake and to constrain the growth of

mentalist forms (the local elite is a direct and knowing agent of capitalism, which installed it) and in more refined structuralist forms (the identity and specific interests of ties of politicians and bureaucrats are irrelevant; what matters is that the postcolonial state is structured to fulfill the roles capitalism assigns to it). Instrumentalists are liable to argue that international capitalism actively intervenes in domestic politics, "to help the friendly factions, and to destroy those that are hostile."[41] Structuralists tend to suggest that the state's function is to mediate between different modes of production:

> the State takes on the central role of managing and representing the myriad encounters and struggles between classes and agents of the different modes. The State provides economic, social and political services for capitalist penetration, orchestrates the de- and re-structuring of elements of the pre-capitalist mode . . . and 'copes,' so to speak, at the level of cohesion of the whole formation, with the dislocative consequences of the expansion of the capitalist mode.[42]

Both versions, however, cleave to the same basic premise: that international capitalism shapes and directs domestic politics and policymaking. Class logic—and the proponents of the idea of a political class—suggests by contrast, that domestic politics is a distinct process with a distinct rationale that may push policymaking in directions contrary to the interests of international capitalism: defiance of external forces may be both possible and politically expedient.

Writing on the West African state of the Ivory Coast illustrates quite sharply the differences in interpretation that capital logic and class logic approaches yield. The Ivory Coast has, indeed, been the focus of a particularly heated debate between advocates of different development strategies. A former French colony, it was generally indistinguishable from other tropical ter-

---

those domestic forces concerned to perpetuate that relationship." How this transformation can occur, and why it should do so, remains mysterious, given the supposed subordination of the local rulers to international capitalism.

41. Claude Ake, "Explanatory Notes on the Political Economy of Africa," *Journal of Modern African Studies* 14, no. 1 (March 1976): 12.

42. Steven Langdon, "The State and Capitalism in Kenya," *Review of African Political Economy* 8 (January–April 1977): 92.

ritories until the years immediately preceding independence: its economy relied heavily on exported cash-crops (mainly coffee and cocoa), grown mainly by African farmers; it had been shaken in the years after 1945 by a battle between the colonial administration and African nationalists; it had come to self-government through an accommodation made between the colonial power and the nationalist leadership. Two features did distinguish Ivoirien politics, however. One was the rural basis of the nationalist movement; the other was the great enthusiasm of the leaders of this movement (notably its head, Félix Houphouet-Boigny) for cooperation with the former colonial power and with French business.

Since independence, such cooperation has been promoted by a policy of economic liberalism, permitting easy movement of capital and profits and easy settlement by expatriates. Very large numbers of migrant workers have entered the Ivory Coast from neighboring states, while the European population has climbed to roughly fifty thousand (with French officials and businessmen continuing to occupy senior posts in the government bureaucracy and in the private sector).

Although the Ivory Coast has enjoyed what one critic calls (without apparent irony) "notoriously rapid rates of growth," Marxist accounts of its development have been uniformly hostile and gloomy.[43] The "Ivoirien miracle" is seen by critics as a temporary phenomenon, entirely dependent on neocolonial relationships that make the state a hostage to international capitalism (as well as an affront to African nationalism). In particular, following the analysis of Samir Amin in his work *Le Développement du capitalisme en Côte-d'Ivoire*, critics have claimed that there is no true Ivoirien bourgeoisie: the heart (and the mind) of

43. Bonnie Campbell, "The Ivory Coast," in *West African States: Failure and Promise*, ed. John Dunn (Cambridge: Cambridge University Press, 1978), 92. Two French political scientists have recently remarked that the Ivory Coast is "a veritable provocation" to the Left: it "symbolizes all that is instinctively rejected in intellectual circles: outward-orientation, dependence, imperialism, cultural alienation on the one hand, bourgeoisie, money, materialism on the other." *Etat et Bourgeoisie en Côte-d'Ivoire*, ed. Y.-A. Fauré and J.-F. Médard (Paris: Editions Karthala, 1982), 11. (All translations in this section are by the author.)

Ivoirien capitalism are in France, as is therefore the true Ivoirien ruling class. The apparent rulers are merely a *comprador* group, a projection of the wealthy African planter interest that originally formed the country's sole political party (the PDCI).[44] This group supposedly guides the economy to suit its own, minority interests and those of foreign capital, but the Ivoirien state is functionally subordinate to the requirements of the metropolitan bourgeoisie and international capitalism.

The view, as restated by a Canadian scholar, Bonnie Campbell, has recently been challenged, notably by a group of French political scientists. The central issue in the argument is the class character of the Ivoirien state. Campbell argues that the latter can be deduced by establishing "the identity of the interests on whose behalf the state defines and performs its task." The identity and background of those actually in charge of the state apparatus are secondary to the roles they are required to perform for the process of surplus appropriation—a purely structuralist approach.[45] The dominant class consists of the members of "the traditionally-based planter ruling class" (who are not, of course, the *true* ruling class).[46] Despite the fact that the Ivoirien government is manned by nonplanters (mainly university graduates and technocrats), Campbell argues that the big planters control the polity; for, "as long as a few agricultural products (cocoa, wood, and coffee) represent 75 percent of the value of exports, the basis and motor of the extraverted patterns of Ivoirien growth, the socio-economic basis of state power must be sought in the interests which continue to control the organization of

44. Samir Amin, *Le Développement du capitalisme en Côte-d'Ivoire* (Paris: Editions de Minuit, 1967), 279–80: "If we can . . . speak of the development of capitalism in Ivory Coast, we are not entitled to speak of the development of Ivoirien capitalism . . . the true bourgeoisie is absent, living in Europe which provides capital and personnel." "PDCI" stands for Parti Démocratique de Côte-d'Ivoire.

45. Campbell, "Ivory Coast," 67. Campbell asserts that "the class ties or class ambitions" of politicians and bureaucrats are not necessarily the same as those of the dominant class, and the state power need not reflect their own class interests except in a secondary way" (ibid., 83).

46. Ibid., 113, 114. For her identification of the metropolitan bourgeoisie as the true rulers, see page 86.

production and commercialization of the economy's export sector."[47]

Critics, notably a group of non-Marxist French political scientists, have attacked both the logic and the content of this interpretation. They point out that it is crudely economistic: it assumes (and does not even try to prove) that those who control the major resources on which the economy depends automatically command political power. This is taken to be true by definition, leaving no room for strictly political analysis. It also leaves no room for distinguishing between regimes. If control of the state is equated with "the socio-economic basis of state power," then farmers must control all Third World countries. In this case, as Fauré and Médard remark, the Ivory Coast, Tanzania, Cuba, and Guatemala would be, for all purposes, politically identical.[48]

Moreover, such analysis—which claims to be structuralist—makes no allowance for the possibility of a relatively autonomous state, one that might impose uncomfortable policies on the bourgeoisie for its own good. It is true that the Ivoirien state has shown little inclination to frustrate the wishes of the metropolitan bourgeoisie, so that in this respect its capacity for relative autonomy is an open question. (It is, however, clear that, far from neocolonialism being forced on the Ivoirien regime, the leadership deliberately opted into such commitments and never made any secret of their preferences or concealed their probable costs.)[49]

But the state has hardly pampered the cash-crop farmers. It has (like the Taiwanese state) extracted a very large surplus from the rural sector, mainly by the use of marketing agencies that pay low prices for crops sold for substantially higher prices

47. Ibid., 83.

48. Y.-A. Fauré and J.-F. Médard, "Classe dominante ou classe dirigeante?" in *Etat et Bourgeoisie en Côte-d'Ivoire*, ed. Fauré and Médard 140.

49. Y.-A. Fauré, "Le Complexe politico-économique," in *Etat et Bourgeoisie en Côte d'Ivoire*, ed. Fauré and Médard 24: "Houphouet-Boigny does not resign himself to economic dependence . . . he chooses it, embraces it completely and tries to turn it to his profit."

on the world market. Very little is returned to farmers in the form of technical assistance. Thus in the late 1970s, agriculture, which provided some 40 percent of Gross Domestic Product and employed some 75 percent of the labor force, received only 13 percent of the Ivory Coast investment budget.[50]

How has the dominant class allowed such exploitation to occur? If Campbell is correct and the "planter bourgeoisie" controls the state (though she makes no effort to show that it does so by direct political influence), this class "must have a suicidal disposition."[51] Resources have consistently (and increasingly) been channeled into the urban and industrial sectors, away from the rural and agricultural sectors.[52]

The explanation, according to the critics, is that, whoever held power in the early days of independence, control is now exercised by an urban-based political class. The planter bourgeoisie is essentially a myth, insofar as it refers to the accumulation and use of capital by working farmers (ironically, the real planter bourgeoisie consists of civil servants, politicians, and merchants who have invested money acquired from urban pursuits in land and who are generally absentee landlords).[53] The reality (as Bates claimed) is a mass of politically disorganized smallholders, who in this case have acquiesced in heavy taxation because until now there has been enough land for them to be able to raise

50. Fauré and Médard, "Classe dominante ou class dirigeante?" 141–42; Robert M. Hecht, "The Ivory Coast Economic 'Miracle': What Benefits for Peasant Farmers?" *Journal of Modern African Studies* 21, no. 1 (March 1983): especially 42–45. In the late seventies the prices paid to producers of cocoa and coffee were 35.7 percent and 34 percent, respectively, of the "free-on-board" prices of these commodities at Abidjan. In the public investment budgets of 1977, 1978, and 1979 less than 2 percent of investment was allotted to improvements in coffee and cocoa cultivation: in the 1981 budget, 3.7 percent of investment went to this function, although 40 percent of the funds invested under that budget were drawn from marketing board surpluses, which had averaged $772 million a year between 1977 and 1979. See, in this connection, J.-M. Gastellu and S. Affou Yabi, "Un Mythe à décomposer: La 'bourgeoisie de planteurs,'" in *Etat et Bourgeoisie en Côte d'Ivoire*, ed. Fauré and Médard 175.

51. Fauré and Médard, "Classe dominante ou classe dirigeante?" 142.

52. See Michael A. Cohen's excellent work, *Urban Policy and Political Conflict in Africa: A Study of the Ivory Coast* (Chicago: University of Chicago Press, 1974).

53. Gastellu and Affou Yabi, "Un Mythe à décomposer," 150, 161.

their incomes through an expansion of areas under cultivation.[54] Nevertheless, the Ivoirien state has been able to impose itself upon the farmers and to behave in a fairly authoritarian manner toward most interests, organized or unorganized. This suggests the need for more serious examination of the state itself and of the *political* techniques by which it keeps power and maintains authority.

Instead, both in its relations with the farmers and its dealings with international capitalism, the state and politics generally are treated by both Campbell and Samir Amin in a crudely instrumental fashion. Ivoirien society is regarded as a passive object of manipulation by outside forces, and the Ivoirien state itself "is ignored, emptied of significance. It is either neglected or reduced to the role of an insignificant appendage."[55]

Such an approach is sterile in two important respects. First, it preempts all the interesting questions about the dynamics of domestic politics that the class logic approach (and, indeed, conventional political science) would raise. Who gains and who loses in Ivoirien politics, and how? How is power generated, how is it used, and how do changes in its distribution occur? Second, it preempts questions about differences between Third World regimes. If all underdeveloped countries were dominated by the logic of international capitalism, then the variety of strategies their governments would adopt would be inconceivable. If capital logicians (like some dependency theorists) reply that international capitalism only sets broad constraints, then the question of the autonomy of the Third World state becomes central: it is one with which a dogmatically instrumentalist or structuralist approach, treating regimes as "puppets" and societies as "destructured" and supine, simply cannot deal.[56]

54. Hecht, "Ivory Coast Economic 'Miracle,'" 43, 31. As both Hecht and several contributors in the Fauré and Médard symposium point out, Ivoirien farmers have now begun to "use the market against the state" reducing their commitments to coffee or cocoa or finding alternative outlets, in the ways Bates suggested.

55. Fauré and Médard, "Classe dominante ou classe dirigeante?" 141.

56. As Jean Leca comments, "The notion of 'destructuration' necessarily accompanies the stooge theory, insofar as an outside political power can only im-

ETHNICITY AND CLASS

If external forces (and specifically those of international capitalism) shape the domestic politics of Third World countries, it follows that analysis of social and political life in these societies must use categories relevant to the international struggle between capital and labor. Penetration by capitalism implies active or incipient class conflict; conflict expressed or described in terms other than those of the labor theory of value—namely, Marxism—needs to be examined with particular care for lurking elements of class conflict misconceived or misrepresented by participants or observers.

The problem of ethnicity has provided a main battleground for conceptual strife of this kind in the Third World. Orthodox Marxists have been consistently wary about (and usually hostile to) movements and philosophies grounded in concepts other than those of class struggle. As we have seen, Stalin was fairly scornful of colonial nationalist movements, and the usual line has been, as Frank Parkin succinctly describes it, to present ethnic conflict "either as a joint product of bourgeois cunning and proletarian gullibility (the *impera et divide* thesis) or as a 'displacement' of social antagonisms whose origins are to be found in the multiple contradictions of the capitalist mode of production."[57] Ethnicity is thus not "real": it represents a form of false consciousness, and usually one created or maintained by a dominant class to keep the peasants divided and obedient. This view is especially popular among those, such as Bonnie Campbell, Dennis Cohen, and Colin Leys, for whom the real mover in African societies is international capitalism. Cohen, for example, holds an instrumentalist or functionalist view of African states, claiming that the international bourgeoisie's "domination and exploitation of African producers is organized through a variety of institutional arrangements," among them "the national and international state structures of the capitalist world."[58] Just as their

---

pose itself upon a society which is internally amorphous." "Postface à J.-F. Bayart: Nuances," *Cahiers d'Etudes Africaines* 18, nos. 69–72 (1978): 38.

57. Parkin, *Marxism*, 36.

58. Dennis L. Cohen, "Class and the Analysis of African Politics: Problems and

states are subordinate to the requirements of capitalism, so the real cleavage *within* African societies is that between classes. Cohen, in fact, attacks Ali Mazrui for arguing that "tribes and races are more total identities than are economic classes." He does so with a remarkable but revealing nonsequitur that shows how heavily the imperatives of orthodoxy weigh on some minds. "Such a viewpoint," Cohen writes indignantly, "rejects the most fundamental principles of historical materialism, those relating to social determination, i.e., the relation between material reality, consciousness and behavior."[59] The "correct" line is that

> ethnicity [i.e., nationality] is a significant element in human consciousness, and that it must be analyzed and dealt with by those involved in political action. It is seen, however, not as an alternative to the class struggle, but as a force shaped by the class struggle. . . . At all times . . . the class relation must be seen as historically more important than the ethnic relation, whatever the ideological appearance of the moment.[60]

Thus, the error of Mazrui and all those Africans who feel that their main loyalty is to a clan, tribe, or nation, is to have misunderstood their true interests as revealed by historical materialism. As "human agents" in distant dependencies of capitalism, their consciousness is clearly of even less import to such Marxists than that of people in the metropolitan countries.

The parallel idea, that ethnicity is merely or mainly a product of imperialist or bourgeois manipulation, also occurs widely. For example, Colin Leys claims that "tribalism" in Kenya is a product of colonialism sustained by neocolonialism:

> "Tribalism" certainly acquires a vicious cumulative force of its own, but its genesis is recent, and can be traced to the emergence of spe-

Prospects," in *The Political Economy of Africa: Selected Readings*, ed. Dennis L. Cohen and John Daniel (London: Longman, 1981), 95.

59. Ibid., 93.

60. Ibid., 94. Cohen adds that the issue of "whether independent national development is possible in the modern epoch of global capitalism . . . constitutes a better point of departure for analysis of the 'national question' than do hair-splitting controversies over the definition of nations, peoples and ethnic groups."

> cific material conditions, namely the creation of economic insecurity and competition for security under conditions of neo-colonialism . . . tribalism is a product of colonialism, and . . . what colonialism produces, neo-colonialism reproduces . . . it is a specific form of consciousness through which the "comprador" regimes in many parts of Africa exercise a "civil hegemony" complementing the use of state power.[61]

Leys also deploys the displacement argument, suggesting that tribalism "served to displace the emerging class-consciousness of the most exploited strata of society."[62] In this case, he argues, it prevented the main challenge to Kenyatta's regime from "channelling emerging class-antagonism into a nationwide opposition movement." In the same vein, Bonnie Campbell asserts that in the Ivory Coast ethnicity is a consequence of elite manipulation, and, without any supporting evidence, she concludes: "Ethnicity, so long an instrument of control in the hands of the colonial power and those who assumed political control at independence, appears a decade later to be increasingly subordinate in importance to the emerging class struggle."[63]

Not surprisingly, scholars attracted to the class logic approach are less willing to treat domestic processes as politically and conceptually subordinate to international capitalism. They usually argue that class is a phenomenon of growing significance (both as a basis of political action and as a tool of analysis), but they are often ready to concede that other loyalties exist besides those of class, and they may (as we have noted) suggest that the basis of class differentiation itself is radically different from the economic basis posited by orthodox Marxism.

Such scholars are particularly critical of the dismissive attitude capital logicians hold toward nationalism and ethnicity. Robin Cohen, for example, has warned strongly against the temptation to attribute feelings of ethnic identity "in a blanket fashion" to the operation of false consciousness.[64] Similarly, such solid radicals as Ian Roxborough and Björn Beckman have protested at

61. Leys, *Underdevelopment in Kenya*, 252.
62. Ibid., 252.
63. Campbell, "Ivory Coast," 91.
64. Robin Cohen, "Class in Africa," 244.

the tendency of their fellow Marxists to dismiss nationalism as epiphenomenal. Roxborough suggests with exasperation that such a tendency is political and intellectual folly: "Since classes are generally formed on the national level, the concepts of class struggle and exploitation only have meaning at the level of the social formation . . . at the present time [nation-states] are in fact the arenas in which social classes are formed and fight out their conflicts."[65] Beckman likewise warns that "bourgeois nationalism is a crucial political force in the third world today. It plays a central role in the structuring of the world capitalist economy . . . it is a force in ascendancy, not in decay. It is growing in strength and independence."[66]

Recognition of the political and ideological reality of ethnicity and nationalism does not resolve the basic question of whether class analysis is compatible with analysis emphasizing ethnicity. The difficulties of such a combination are apparent in, for example, Richard Sklar's analysis of class domination in Afirca.

Sklar firmly opposes those who see Third world elites as puppets. He also rejects the orthodox Marxist assumption that class formation in Africa has an economic basis, preferring, like other believers in the political class notion, to argue that "class relations, at bottom, are determined by relations of power, not production."[67] His analysis resembles that of mainstream Marxists, however, in its implication that ethnicity is essentially a product of class formation, a contrivance of members of the emerging Nigerian political class, and, indeed, a weapon used in pursuit of their rivalries.

Sklar thus claims that alliances between regional politicians in the period before the first coup d'état in Nigeria in 1966 "served to intensify class domination. Political regionalism was a conservative strategy that facilitated the use of ethnic and sectional prejudice by dominant class elements as a political weapon against challenges from below."[68] "Conservative southerners" allied

65. Ian Roxborough, *Theories of Underdevelopment* (London: The Macmillan Press, 1979), 47, 53.

66. Beckman, "Imperialism and the 'National Bourgeoisie,'" 6.

67. Sklar, "Class Domination in Africa," 531–32, 537, 550, 551.

68. Ibid., 547–48.

with leaders of the equally conservative north and exploited ethnic sentiment to repress "radical opposition to class privilege." The aim of the conservative alliance was to preserve a form of federalism that gave the north and its associates a permanent political majority.[69]

This interpretation is persuasive insofar as the declared preferences of the northerners and conservative southerners are concerned: they wanted to keep the existing federal arrangements and said so. It is, however, questionable in some of its assumptions and implications. It suggests, for example, that the leadership was exploiting and even magnifying the fears of its followers. The clear implication is that the leadership was abusing and misrepresenting the interests of its supporters, whose true interests lay outside "ethnic and sectional prejudice" and, presumably, in solidarity with members of the underclass elsewhere. Sklar says that the soundness of his interpretation "can be demonstrated."[70] Yet he does not justify the assumptions on which it rests—namely, that the leaders were distorting, exaggerating, or indeed creating the sentiments they used, and that the supporters were victims of false consciousness. As Michael Schatzberg has pointed out, for ethnicity to be manipulated, it has to be strongly felt in the first place: "Ethnicity can be orchestrated by those who control the state, but this does not mean that it lacks analytic independence as an explanatory variable. Politicized ethnicity might well be an ideology . . . but it is an ideology fraught with meaning for most of us."[71] In other words, it is one thing for a student to describe how ethnic feelings are mobilized politically; it is another to suggest that they are artificial and wrong-headed. If the ethnicity of a minority is "prejudice," then presumably all forms of nationalism (which deny the primacy of class struggle) can be tarred with the same brush. Yet in practice Marxists have taken it on themselves to distinguish be-

69. Ibid., 548.

70. Ibid., 547.

71. Schatzberg, "The Emerging Trialectic," 18. For an exceptionally clear and readable discussion, see the same author's *Politics and Class in Zaire: Bureaucracy, Business and Beer in Lisala* (New York: Africana Publishing Co., 1980), especially chapters 2 and 8.

tween progressive and reactionary ethnic and national movements. Both this and Sklar's closely related approach involve a basic refusal to acknowledge as legitimate world views that differ from those amenable to class analysis.[72]

This incompatibility leads us back to the question of whether class analysis can coexist with analysis grounded in such categories as ethnicity and nationalism. On the whole, the two seem to be mutually exclusive. But the preceding discussion raises another, equally fundamental question, namely, whether analysis centered on the concepts of a political class and of politics as a source of class differentiation is compatible with Marxism. Again, it is hard to see how they can be reconciled. Political class analysis has obvious affinities with forms of politicism, and the fact that some of its advocates use the idioms of "radical" class analysis does not conceal the wide divergence between the approaches, both in their intellectual provenance and in their political implications.

SYNTHESIS OF EXTERNALISM AND INTERNALISM: THE CASE OF CAMEROON

Is it, then, also impossible to reconcile an externalist (capital logic) approach—one stressing the determinative power of outside forces—with an internalist approach—one stressing the relative self-sufficiency of domestic politics and the nation-state?

72. Sklar, furthermore, seems to contradict himself on the question of the politics of the political class itself. He argues (in accordance with orthodox Marxism) that this class was repressive and intent on domination in the years before 1966 and claims that subsequent military regimes "energetically served" dominant-class interests. But he then asserts that since the late seventies the Nigerian bourgeoisie has become enamored of liberal democracy, that the elections of 1979 (and presumably 1983) betokened "the existence of dominant social classes, whose members are confident of their ability to manage the affairs of society." He further generalizes from this observation to suggest that demands for liberal constitutional government in many parts of Africa "reflect the rejection of authoritarianism by bourgeois classes that are steadily consolidating their power" ("Class Domination in Africa," 538–39, 540, 542, 548, 552). Since he earlier declares that authoritarianism has been "the most common political device for dominant-class consolidation in Africa" (ibid., 540), the reader is left wondering

One very interesting attempt to forge such a synthesis has been made by the French political scientist Jean-François Bayart in his writing on Cameroon.[73] Bayart tries to escape the unidimensionality of capital logic—"stooge theory"—while keeping the Marxist framework. Even more impressively, he tries to face the questions that concern Hegelian-Marxists, those to do with the cultural dimension of politics and the creation of legitimacy.

This last effort is especially important, because all too often Marxists resort to facile and even patronizing explanations to account for the establishment and persistence of regimes they dislike. Typically, such explanations involve postulating a degree of sustained repression that few states can sustain, imputing to rulers a degree of cunning that few individuals—let alone entire classes—possess, or ascribing to the masses a degree of gullibility and ignorance that raises questions about their suitability as instruments of history. The real challenge for Marxism is thus not to identify exploitation so much as to explain its persistence.

Bayart's response is to postulate "two analytically distinct dynamic orders": "the dynamics of the world capitalist system" and "internal dynamics specific to peripheral social formations."[74] He argues that although the colonial period saw an extension of the capitalist mode of production to Africa, it did not supplement but rather blended with precapitalist modes. Precolonial "systems of inequality and domination" survived and adapted both to colonial overrule and to the constitutional arrangements of decolonization. The measure of power in precolonial societies—the number of men a leader could command—was coinci-

how the ugly repressive caterpillar of the sixties turned into the beautiful social democratic butterfly of the eighties. One possibility is that Sklar means to distinguish between the "ex-dominant" political class and the current bourgeoisie; but he does not assert any such distinction. Without it, however, the liberalization of a class whose very survival depended on monopolizing power remains inexplicable.

73. In this section I have relied mainly on Bayart's article, "Régime de parti unique et systèmes d'inégalité et de domination au Cameroun: Esquisse," *Cahiers d'Etudes Africaines* 18, nos. 69–72 (1978): 5–35. See also his book, *L'Etat au Cameroun* (Paris: Presses de la Foundation Nationale des Sciences Politiques, 1979).

74. "Régime de parti unique," 5.

dentally restored by the electoral system that provided "a technique of internalization" for capitalism and the political institutions introduced by the French.[75] Elections, and the parties engaged in them, shaped the new networks of patronage and brought about new alliances within the elite: "These mechanisms were bound to lead in the long term to the creation of a dominant national class, an auxiliary to the metropolitan bourgeoisie to which it remained organically linked, yet nevertheless independent of it insofar as it represented an organic form of the particular structure of the Cameroonian social formation."[76] Under the first president, Ahmadou Ahidjo, the potential instability of a patron–client system was reduced by the installation of a "bonapartist" presidential regime that incorporated the old regional bosses and their clans, along with other interests, and over which Ahidjo ruled as an arbitrator. Behind the facade of unity, the *parti unique* was divided internally, class, power, and economic enrichment providing the main dimensions of stratification.[77] The old distinction between "elders" and "juniors" was reproduced within the party's structure, and though there was inequality and domination, the Cameroonian state represented a complex set of relationships that "did not escape the influence of the subordinated groups and showed their influence."[78]

Thus, Bayart sees the inexorable emergence of a Cameroonian political system through the forming of ever more complex ties, with an ever larger number of individuals being assimilated into a network in which the state plays a central organic role. At an economic level, the reproduction of the capitalist mode of production has been "largely internalized by the structure of the Cameroonian social formation," which becomes continually more independent.[79]

While Bayart's analysis sometimes drifts close to the abstraction and reification of modes of production analysis, it is more

75. Ibid., 15.
76. Ibid., 16.
77. Ibid., 22–23.
78. Ibid., 26.
79. Ibid., 29.

sophisticated than much Marxist analysis in several important respects. First, Bayart claims that the dominant class in Cameroon has established "hegemonic control"—that is, it rules in its own right and has created mechanisms and myths that assure its authority among ordinary Cameroonians.[80] While it may in some respects be obliged to the metropolitan bourgeoisie, it does not owe its legitimacy or survival to any outside force. It enjoys "organic autonomy," and this fact rules out "any description of the political leaders as 'stooges' or 'puppets.'"[81] Second, politics—indeed, specific constitutional systems—have been a vital, independent factor in the shaping of postcolonial societies: "the organic contribution of political regimes to the structure of African social formations puts a great premium on their maintenance."[82] Third, the assumption on the part of "stooge theory" that neocolonial governments are fragile and transient is a delusion. Having internalized capitalism and created strong and complex relationships, such regimes have a degree of resilience. Bayart thus concludes: "Because it is a quest for hegemony, the authoritarian form in Africa may show itself durable."[83]

"THE TRANSITION TO SOCIALISM"

If Bayart is right, what are the strategic implications for socialism? Does Marxist analysis provide any clearer or more optimistic prescriptions than dependency theory?

First, it is evident that capital logic and class logic approaches point in rather different directions. The implications of a capital logic view are broadly similar to those of dependency theory,

80. Bayart argues that the new "dominant class" is trying to make the possession of a European type of education "a constituent element of its power and its prosperity." He even refers to "the intellectualization" of the regime (ibid., 29).

81. Bayart expressly remarks that "it would be wrong to ascribe to the authoritarian state in black Africa and to the social groups which control it a basis external to the societies which they claim to rule" (ibid., 6).

82. "The stabilization or overthrow of constitutional systems cannot be reduced to a secondary question. . . . The problem lies at the heart of all reflection on African societies" (ibid., 30).

83. Ibid., 31.

namely, that the likelihood of socialism short of a global revolution overturning the metropolitan bourgeoisie is fairly small.

As we have noted, however, capital logic has some serious intellectual flaws (which also resemble those of dependency theory). To start with, the very idea of a dominant class without roots in the society it supposedly rules is, as John Lonsdale has remarked, almost self-contradictory:

> What makes a class "classy" is reproduction through time. And just as the agricultural household cannot reproduce itself through time save through participation in a network of lineage relations, nor can any specific interest make the social and capital investments necessary to survival through the generations save through a network of alliance, whether face-to-face in marriage or in the club or in business, or more formally in professional bodies and rules of institutional access.[84]

The point, then, about the metropolitan bourgeoisie is less that it has kept a distant, general influence over the ex-colonies than that it failed to domesticate itself in just such ways, and was therefore easily supplanted.

Moreover, capital logic, like dependency theory, makes it very difficult to account for the variety of regimes that have emerged in the Third World except by reference to a sole variable, the degree of penetration by capitalism. How can it be possible for the same set of external pressures and constraints to facilitate the installation of alleged "puppets," such as Ahidjo, Houphouet-Boigny, Kenyatta, and Marcos of the Philippines, while allowing "radicals" such as Nyerere in Tanzania, the late President Nkrumah in Ghana, and Castro to find their way to power?

One way to deal with this discrepancy is to argue that international capitalism does not find what passes for socialism in the Third World all that threatening—indeed, it may actually welcome it in certain respects.[85] Thus critics argued that Nkrumah

84. Lonsdale, "State and Social Processes," 48.

85. A representative of a well-known computer company recently told me that he preferred dealing with Ethiopian socialists to dealing with Nigerian capitalists because the Ethiopians shared his employer's concern with efficiency, rationality, and productivity. The Nigerians were mainly concerned with such unscientific questions as how large their percentages would be.

presented a "socialist" face to Ghanaian businessmen (or rather to those who were not members of his party) but compromised substantially with multinational corporations.[86] Similar comments have been made about the privileged position of foreign mining consortia in such "socialist" states as Guinea. Likewise, some critics of the "bureaucratic bourgeoisie" in Tanzania claim that international capitalism has an interest in state capitalism: "As the governing class comes under the rule of the metropolitan bourgeoisie it is obliged to assist in the creation of some type of state monopoly capitalism in which the state develops more and more institutional ties with the metropolitan bourgeoisie and takes more and more control over the economy to facilitate the inflow of metropolitan capital.[87]

Another answer, preferred by analysts such as Saul, Murray, and Leys, is that the ruling group in African states does not have a clear class character and finds itself caught between the conflicting pressures of foreign capital, domestic capital, and the exploited (peasants and workers). This interpretation thus accepts elements of both the capital logic and class logic approaches, and some of its advocates flirt with concepts resembling that of a political class. It postulates an active class conflict in African countries and sees divisions *within* the political class as reflecting this conflict and as critical to its outcome. Thus Roger Murray argued that it was simplistic to brand Nkrumah's Convention People's Party as "state capitalist" or "petty bourgeois," because there were active, ideologically distinct wings that fought for influence over Nkrumah and control of policy.[88] Likewise, Saul suggests that the "progressive" wing of TANU (the ruling party in Tanzania) prevailed over the more conservative and bureaucratic elements on at least two occasions—in 1967, when Nyerere promulgated the Arusha Declaration (favoring self-re-

86. See Bob Fitch and Mary Oppenheimer, *Ghana: End of an Illusion* (New York: Monthly Review Press, 1966). The particular case here was the building of the Volta dam.

87. Von Freyhold, "Post-Colonial State," 80.

88. See Roger Murray, "Second Thoughts on Ghana," *New Left Review* 42 (March–April 1967): 25–39.

liance and a communitarian approach to socialism in the rural sector), and in 1971, when the party attacked the affluence of members of the political class and called for greater participation by workers in management. Such initiatives "represented real achievements in a transition towards socialism."[89] Unfortunately, Saul concludes, this transition failed because of the "petty bourgeois" deficiencies of Nyerere and his associates (notably, "a hostility to Marxism and the consequent lack of a fully scientific analysis of imperialism and class 'struggle.'")[90]

Unfortunately, also, while the postulate of class struggle provides a better explanation of the ideological variability of African states and treats them as political systems in their own right, the classes themselves (and their revolutionary capacities) remain elusive. The petty bourgeoisie (the label most commonly applied to the ruling group) is, in Marxist terms, a group in transition upward or downward ("the kinless outsiders of the capitalist mode of production," in Lonsdale's words).[91] The urban working class is sometimes dismissed as a labor aristocracy and therefore as unsuitable revolutionary material (certainly at the present stage of development, when it is numerically small).

As for the peasants, Marxists always have been and still are wary of resting heavy revolutionary responsibilities upon this group, which is not only hard to organize but is thought to be individualistic and parochial. The Tanzanian comrades are particularly insistent on the lowly revolutionary status of the peasant. Tabiso, for example, writes:

> In the African case . . . he is objectively exploited by the international bourgeoisie: this begets a limited solidarity among peasants. Therefore, the peasantry forms a *reliable ally* of the working class, albeit its mode of production does not allow it [*sic*] to seek for an *alternative* system. . . . This is what limits the revolutionary potential of the peasantry, whose most radical ideology cannot transcend the bounds of populism based on private ownership ("land to the tiller"). Hence, it cannot be a *leading* revolutionary force but only the *main* force in alli-

89. Saul, "State in Post-Colonial Societies," 362.
90. Ibid., 366.
91. Lonsdale, "State and Social Processes," 23.

> ance with the working class, the only class which can fight for revolutionary goals.[92]

It is heartening to know that there are some issues which theory can settle once and for all. Shivji, who quotes this resounding affirmation of orthodoxy, comments approvingly: "There has been no example in Africa where the peasants have played a leading revolutionary role while the workers have sided with the dominating class. . . . Those who have attempted in practice to participate in the struggle have clearly found that the workers more than the peasants have been in the forefront providing leadership."[93] Even when ostensibly radical movements have got under way, Marxists are usually disdainful of their pathetically petty bourgeois objectives. For example, Colin Leys in his work on Kenya refers disparagingly to the "petty bourgeois" socialism of Oginga Odinga and his supporters who opposed the "neocolonial" strategy of the Kenyatta government in the mid-sixties.[94] Theirs, he remarks, was "a redistributive populist position," which acquiesced in "the intense commitment of the majority of the landowning peasantry to their land."[95] Leys continues: "What the peasants wanted was private property with social justice . . . this was impossible, perhaps under any conditions, but certainly in conditions of capitalist underdevelopment."[96] The implications are unclear: did the peasants need reeducating to understand the "impossibility" of their hopes? Should they have surrendered their newly acquired family farms? Why, for that matter, should they have preferred socialism as defined in their interest by outsiders who saw their own definition of their interests as "false consciousness"?

But if the peasants—60 percent and more of the population, poor, and exploited—are unsuitable revolutionary material, the prospects for a transition to socialism must be gloomy. As

92. Nga Tabiso, "Revolution and Class Alliances," *Maji Maji* (Dar es Salaam) 12 (September 1973). Cited in Issa G. Shivji, "Peasants and Class Alliances," *Review of African Political Economy* 3 (May–October 1975): 14.

93. Shivji, "Peasants and Class Alliances," 14, 17.

94. Leys, *Underdevelopment in Kenya*, 215, 225.

95. Ibid., 221, 225.

96. Ibid., 225.

Richard Jeffries has pointed out, there is really no sign of the rural radicalism that has been so ardently sought by the Left in the manner of "Spanish explorers drifting down the Orinoco in search of El Dorado." For now "the obstacles to a concerted assertion of peasant radicalism . . . must . . . appear far greater than the followers of Fanon have suggested, notwithstanding their continued insistence that a new revolutionary movement must eventually be formed."[97]

In this chapter, we have examined the main traditions in Marxist writing about the relationship of politics to economics, noting distinctive instrumentalist, structuralist, and Hegelian-Marxist approaches. We have also explored the further developments and problems that have occurred as a result of efforts to extend Marxist methodology to analysis of societies in the Third World and of relations between developed and underdeveloped countries. In this connection, we have pursued the distinction between a capital logic and a class logic approach, the one emphasizing the subordination of Third World countries to the imperatives of international capitalism, the other stressing the salience of internal processes and the need to be conceptually flexible in the analysis of such processes.

How different in reality is Marxist political economy from other forms we have considered? If we examine carefully the various approaches described in this chapter, it seems reasonable to conclude that, apart from the specific language of Marxism and its special view of economic processes, the formulas offered concerning the relationship of politics and economics tend to fall into categories already identified. Instrumentalism—and its international variant, capital logic—are clearly forms of economism. Indeed, capital logic is really an inversion of the liberal view of the global marketplace, except that they differ in their opinions of the benefits of international capitalism.

97. Richard Jeffries, "Political Radicalism in Africa: 'The Second Independence,'" *African Affairs* 77, no. 308 (July 1978): 345. Frantz Fanon, a French-speaking West Indian, argued in his book *The Wretched of the Earth* (trans. Constance Farrington) (New York: Grove, 1965) that the peasants represented the major potential revolutionary force in underdeveloped countries.

Structuralism allows, in some versions, for the relative autonomy of the political apparatus, but its basic presumption is highly economistic, holding that the state must function to promote the interests of capitalism, even at the expense of some capitalists.

Class logic can take a crudely economistic form, but it is open to a more Hegelian-Marxist treatment, emphasizing the role of culture and ideology. Applied to underdeveloped countries, however, it runs up against the fundamental challenge of demonstrating that class interests and class solidarity are more meaningful than alternative, established collectivities such as family, clan, and ethnic group. Some scholars, in attempting to assert the validity of class analysis, have tried to reformulate its basis to take account of the primacy of politics in Third World states. The resulting emphasis on the political class obviously reflects the present character of these societies better than a rigid application of Marxist theory would. But, by the same token, it is hard to see why such analysis should be regarded as *any* form of Marxism, so different are its assumptions and implications. In fact, it is virtually indistinguishable from other forms of politicism, except for its devotion to the idiom of class conflict.

The problem which emerges with particular clarity from this discussion is that of the bearing of culture on theory. Both Marxism and liberalism aspire strongly to be philosophies of global scope: both, therefore, encounter especially acute problems in dealing with the varieties of culture expressed in ethnicity and nationalism. In the last chapter we shall examine this fundamental question of how culture and social theory are related: What makes theories relevant, useful, and popular? What, for that matter, is the moral and political significance of the search for theories of political economy?

SEVEN
CONCLUSIONS

Between 1968 and 1974, persistent drought afflicted the broad belt of savannah stretching across Africa from Senegal to Ethiopia. Whole rivers dried up, and Lake Chad sank so low that it divided into four separate ponds. By 1974, perhaps a quarter of all the cattle in this pastoralist region had died: in Mali alone about 40 percent of the cereal crop was lost, and people there and elsewhere were forced to eat leaves and seeds. Epidemics of measles and diphtheria broke out, and in some areas up to 50 percent of children were found to be suffering from malnutrition. By some accounts, as many as 100,000 people died as a result of the drought and the associated famine: most of them were children.

What use, if any, are the various theories we have examined in coping with problems of this kind or stopping them from happening again? Is their only impact to add yet more paper to an already huge and often impenetrable heap, to pile on yet more specialist works written "in a language that few can, or care to, understand?"

Such questions are completely fair and deserve proper discussion. As well as examining them, I shall try in this chapter to assess the problems and possibilities of "political economy."

THEORISTS AND ANTI-THEORISTS

The harsh problems of underdevelopment naturally make those involved in them impatient of what they see as the self-indulgence of theorists. For example, in 1970 the British development economist Dudley Seers attacked academics whose loyalty to their disciplines overrode the demands of development. Such people (in Seers's view) contented themselves with

> sitting comfortably on the sidelines, talking and teaching about development problems, but remote from any practical activity. They may indeed by a different route, come to devote their time to teaching, and carrying out research, on unidisciplinary models. Those who choose this line of escape . . . are taking on a responsibility that must appear very great indeed to anyone aware of social realities—the slum of Fatima in Cali, to take a Colombian example, where the "streets" are open sewers.[1]

Since 1970, the impatience of "practical" men with theorists may well have grown. A fashion for global theories of different types (such as "world-systems" theory) has produced ever more complex and abstract models, especially of the "political economy" genre, which not only require extensive study to master but, more importantly, must make the possibilities of effective initiative by governments, let alone lesser organizations and individuals, seem increasingly remote. It is certainly easy to share the irritation and bewilderment of an activist or policymaker who, on asking what should be done about the problems of Zaire or Mexico, is answered that their problems are products of the world capitalist system and must await the destruction or subjugation of that system. As Robert Martin has written,

> the work which has been done [by Marxist scholars] is almost entirely theoretical and, indeed, it becomes more theoretical and more abstract with each passing year. . . . Windmills come crashing to the ground and platoons of straw men are despatched. What is glaringly absent from the whole project is political practice or, in many cases, even a recognition of its significance. . . . Capitalism will not collapse under the accumulated weight of exquisite papers prepared for graduate seminars in political economy.[2]

1. Dudley Seers, "Income Distribution and Employment. A Note on Some Issues Raised by the Colombia Report," *Bulletin of the Institute of Development Studies* (Brighton, England) 2, no. 4 (July 1970): 8.

2. Robert Martin, "The Use of State Power to Overcome Underdevelopment," *Journal of Modern African Studies* 18, no. 2 (June 1980): 315–16.

Critics of "theory building" do, however, differ in important ways, a basic division being that between critics who are skeptical about *any* theory and critics who dislike particular kinds of theory, either because of excessive abstraction or because of some ideological bias. Of the "anti-theorists," some are simply anti-intellectual. A startling example is the codirector of one of the more aggressive overseas development programs in the United States, who was recently quoted as declaring: "We're only interested in results, not theory. In helping our clients solve problems. Our only academic standard is 'Does it get the job done?' We're completely open to classroom techniques like videotape and role-playing."[3] His organization, he added, shunned "ideology" and was "willing to work with any government on earth," though its strongest contacts had been with OPEC countries (among which he included Egypt).

Quite different is the case of an academic like Albert Hirschman, who thinks that the attempt to produce general statements about (in this instance) "the relationship between politics and economics" is likely to produce only "banality or frustration." For relationships at this level "are either evident and hence uninteresting, or are so complex and depend on so many other variables as to be unpredictable and inconclusive . . . it seems quite unlikely that there exists somewhere a master key which would bring into view the usually hidden political dimensions of economic relationships or characteristics in some more or less automatic or systemic manner."[4] Instead, Hirschman suggests, scholars should concentrate on finding connections in what he calls the "finer features of the economic landscape"—that is, in particular areas of policymaking or in the specific consequences of decisions.

Critics in the second category want theory that is "relevant" or "committed." We encountered them in examining critiques of orthodox economics. Seers is clearly demanding relevant analy-

3. Bruce Steele, "ITOD's Expansion Covers Campus," *University Times* (University of Pittsburgh) 15, no. 10 (27 January 1983): 9 (quoting Gaylord Obern, codirector).

4. Albert O. Hirschman, *A Bias for Hope: Essays on Development and Latin America* (New Haven: Yale University Press, 1971), 8, 12.

sis—theory that can readily be applied to the purposes of policy-making. Depending on the writer's values, such a demand may shade into a more directly political or moral demand—one that the theorist declare his own sympathies and give them an intellectual, theoretical substance. Colin Leys, for example, has advocated the adoption of a theoretical stance, "which as far as possible embraces the interests of those who are exploited and oppressed in the Third World."[5]

The same writer has also remarked, however, that "revolutionary situations are not created by intellectual analyses," which leads us straight back to the much chewed-over questions of how "values" and "analysis" and "theory" and "action" are related.[6] If we look at the theories reviewed in this book, it is quite clear that values are central to the choice of questions and to the choice of concepts with which to frame and answer the questions. But the procedures used in answering these questions can and must be strictly logical in character. This seems to be the distinction Marxists use when they refer to "ideological" and "scientific" statements. We can thus have radical or liberal political economy: the adjectives merely indicate an orientation. Whether either is any good intellectually depends on the logical rigor and the quality of evidence involved in its exposition..

From this point of view, the anti-theoretical and committed approaches are necessarily incomplete. So, as stated, is Seers's demand for relevance. This contention can be illuminated by considering the debate that revolved around the African drought of 1968–74. This episode gave rise to a range of explanations and proposals, several of which were mutually exclusive. Some saw the drought and the resulting famine as a purely meteorological phenomenon, about which nothing could be done except to provide relief for the victims and (if climatic changes proved permanent) to arrange for movement of population or changes in agriculture. Other observers saw the drought as merely a precipitant, blaming the associated human suffering on

5. Colin Leys, *Underdevelopment in Kenya: The Political Economy of Neo-Colonialism* (London: Heinemann, 1975), xi.

6. Ibid., 23.

ecological changes brought about by overpopulation, overgrazing, destructive agricultural practices, and even misconceived development schemes.[7] The corollary was that population pressure should be reduced, conservation practiced, and development schemes evaluated more carefully for probable economic and environmental consequences.

Yet another school argued that while environmental problems were the immediate cause of famine, such problems were symptomatic of more deeply rooted distortions of political and economic development in the societies concerned. In particular, critics argued (on the same lines as Robert Bates) that postcolonial governments had failed to stimulate food production (preferring in many cases to encourage production of exportable cash-crops). They showed that countries such as Tanzania and Mali, which experienced severe food shortages and rising prices, continued nevertheless to produce and export cash-crops at the same levels as in nondrought years, or indeed at higher levels. In this view, the significance of the drought was that it dramatized a wider, more deeply rooted failure of agriculture—more exactly, of agricultural policy—throughout the continent.[8]

Marxists, for their part, blamed the catastrophe on international capitalism and its derived forms of neocolonialism. Thus, two writers in the *World Marxist Review* cited with approval the declaration of the French Communist party plenum in May 1973 that "the deeper roots of this famine can be traced primarily to the policy of French colonialism, replaced in 1960 by the neo-colonialism of France and the big foreign monopolies." At-

7. See, for example, A. T. Grove, "Desertification in the African Environment," *African Affairs* 73, no. 291 (April 1974): 145–47; David Dalby, "Drought in Sudanic Africa: The Implications for the Future," *Round Table* 253 (January 1974): 58; Nicholas Wade, "The Sahelian Drought: No Victory for Western Aid," *Science* 185, no. 4147 (19 July 1974): 234; Michael H. Glantz, "The Sahelian Drought: No Victory for Anyone," *Africa Today* 22, no. 2 (April–June 1975): 57–58; R. Mansell Prothero "Some Perspectives on Drought in North-West Nigeria," *African Affairs* 73, no. 291 (April 1974): 165.

8. See, notably, Michael F. Lofchie, "Political and Economic Origins of African Hunger," *Journal of Modern African Studies* 13, no. 4 (December 1975): 554–65.

tacking the Malthusians among the ecologists who saw population control as a priority, these writers asserted that

> the cardinal task is to overcome the heritage of colonialism and free African economies from the neo-colonialist shackles of the capitalist world economy. The vociferous calls of bourgeois economists for birth control merely obscure the problem and divert attention from a searching investigation of the class, socio-economic causes of poverty and hunger in the developing countries.[9]

Given this variety of interpretations and prescriptions, how do we decide which approach is most "relevant," "committed," and likely to get "results?" All the writers concerned are undoubtedly committed to the cause of seeing that if possible such misery is not repeated. But commitment by itself does not tell us which approach is likely to be most effective. Is conservation sufficient? Or is conservation impractical without changes in farming systems? Do changes in agriculture require new forms of government incentive? Can such incentives be obtained without a change in the political coalition on which the government itself rests?

Again, it obviously makes sense, from the developmentalist's point of view, to ask for theories that are relevant. By relevant, I mean theories that contain or can easily be translated into direct relationships of cause and effect and that indicate where action is likely to be effective and where it is not. The meteorological theories of famine are "relevant" because they provide a plausible and rigorous explanation and indicate quite clearly the limits of human intervention, thus concentrating people's attention and energy on what *can* be affected (where people live and what they try to grow). Some theories (such as "world-systems" theory and some abstract forms of functionalism) are satisfying to intellectuals because they are so comprehensive and sophisticated; but it is exactly these qualities which may make them harder to

9. A. Dansoko and A. Lerumo, "Famine in Africa: Is It Drought Alone?" *World Marxist Review* 17, no. 1 (January 1974): 128. For other radical analyses, see Nicole Ball, "Understanding the Causes of African Famine," *Journal of Modern African Studies* 14, no. 3 (September 1976): 517–22; and Claude Meillassoux, "Development or Exploitation: Is the Sahel Famine Good Business?" *Review of African Political Economy* 1 (August–November 1974): 27–33.

translate into immediate, limited programs and policies. And once we are faced with two or more "relevant" theories, we still have to decide which is most applicable and we still have to decide what actions are politically feasible, as well as logical and efficient. The moral of an explanation in terms of climatic change might be that the best solution would be mass evacuation. This might well be impossible; we then have to decide, within the limits indicated by this explanation, what the next most feasible policy would be.

Finally, the belief that "results" can be obtained without some clear, explicit choice between goals and between methods of achieving them is obviously absurd and, in its own terms, self-defeating—a particularly pious kind of whistling in the dark. The fact is, as Keohane and Nye point out, that at some level,

> theory is inescapable; all empirical or practical analysis rests on it. Pragmatic policymakers [they continue] might think that they need pay no more heed to theoretical disputes over the nature of world politics than they pay to medieval scholastic disputes over how many angels can dance on the head of a pin. Academic pens, however, leave marks in the minds of statesmen with profound results for policy.[10]

Politicians, then, are likely to be the prisoners of old theories, as Lord Keynes remarked. But they still have to choose, and what they choose to do is a moral or political rather than a logical, intellectual matter. Ideas have consequences, but consequences are the products of moralities and ideologies as well as of ideas. Most theories have both an ideological and a specifically intellectual, logical content. To provide the basis for a successful development strategy, they have to be ideologically appealing as well as intellectually sound. They have to incorporate an objective that is politically or culturally attractive as well as a strategy that is technically and politically workable. Does sovereignty matter more than growth in personal incomes? If personal income comes first, it would make sense to ship all the populations of Mali, Niger, Upper Volta, and Chad down to the Atlantic

10. Robert O. Keohane and Joseph S. Nye, *Power and Interdependence: World Politics in Transition* (Boston: Little, Brown, 1977), 4.

coast, or better still, off to North America or Europe. But this would deal the final blow to the sovereignty of states whose viability has always been rather doubtful. The governments concerned certainly would not want such an outcome; it is even possible that their inhabitants would not.

"POLITICAL ECONOMY" AND CULTURE

As long as there is a variety of cultures, there is likely to be a variety of theories about important social issues, and there will be no strictly logical or intellectual way of choosing between them. For this reason, there is clearly no such thing as "*the* theory of political economy," and there never will be, in the sense of a single, universally accepted complex of assumptions and methodology. There are various ways of conceptualizing political economy—by which I mean not just any theory bearing the label, but rather a set of theories concerned with depicting relationships between political processes and economic processes. The term *political economy*, used generically, refers to a continuing intellectual enterprise, a particular agenda, a specific object of theoretical ambition.

Because "political economy" is an agenda rather than a method, there will always be a variety of theories of political economy. And because a variety of assumptions and values underlies such variety of theory, it may be possible (indeed, it is very desirable) to criticize each theory; but it will never be possible to decide between them, to end the debate, and to remove the variety by purely logical means.

This point is reinforced if we examine the two main deterministic forms of political economy theory identified in this book —"economism" and "politicism." One posits the actual and the explanatory primacy of economic forces; the other, the same primacy of political forces. As Cropsey has pointed out, a careful scrutiny of both formulas shows them to be incomplete and question-begging. Take first the "economistic" approach, adopted by liberal pluralist ("interest group") and Marxist theory. In both, the substance of political life is held to be competition or conflict between predominantly economic interests: "to that extent, the relation between politics and economic life seems to be that political activity grows out of economic activity."[11] But, then, such competition is carried on within a certain structure of laws and institutions that imposes distinct advantages and disadvantages on the various competitors. Politics thus regains its primacy—until we ask what the origins of this structure of laws and institutions are.

The conundrum is not resolved by resort to historical argument about man's ascent from the state of nature. On the one hand, it is argued that economic needs are fundamental, that production and survival are in every way prior to political organization. On the other hand, it is argued that beyond a very rudimentary point of development, economic production and distribution depend on a structure of laws that, most importantly, converts matter into property and regulate its transfer. But here we face not only the question of how this structure came about, but also the further question of how the consequent control of property (or lack of it) affects a person's ability to assert the rights he or she enjoys, including the right (if granted) to take part in making the laws.[12] As Cropsey remarks, the posing of *this* question seems again to make economics the foundation of politics and the determinant of power, and the conundrum remains unsolved: "we seem unable to break out of the endless alternation of the political and economic at what appear to be the foundations, each incontrovertibly determining the other and dependent on the other."[13] Cropsey's point is that the conundrum cannot be "solved" at this level. The two processes are ultimately indistinguishable from each other, and to the extent that they can be distinguished (as separate sets of institutions), they are related in a continual, interactive fashion. Empirically, therefore, one cannot be assigned primacy over the other.

The only primacy possible is a normative one—that is, a return to the subordination of economic processes to morality (and the return of economics to the bosom of normative political

11. Joseph Cropsey, "On the Relation of Political Science and Economics," *American Political Science Review* 54, no. 1 (March 1960): 3.

12. Ibid., 7.

13. Ibid., 8.

theory). In short, we are back with the idea that economics cannot be regarded as morally neutral or self-sufficient any more than politics can. "Values" come first and last. A theory may be—intellectually—a bad theory, even though its creator is "committed" and idealistic. But without some explicit commitment to a value outside of the mere accumulation and circulation of power and wealth it is disingenuous, incomplete, and probably dangerous.

To understand social theory—and to appreciate its impact—we need therefore to examine not only its specific intellectual content but also the moral and political universe in which it was formed. This point is especially pertinent to attempts to forge "global theories" and to apply the concepts of a particular theoretical tradition to societies culturally and historically different from the society or societies in which the tradition developed. Such attempts have often provoked the charge of "ethnocentrism" against Western social science, including theories of political economy. If we accept that we live in a world characterized by a multiplicity of cultures more in contact with each other than ever before, and that political inequality makes it possible for some cultures to overpower others, we can quickly understand why complaints of ethnocentrism occur. Yet if intellectual imperialism has its costs, so does intellectual nationalism. Can only a Cameroonian say anything perceptive or knowledgeable about Cameroonian politics? Was what de Tocqueville or Bryce said about American politics—or Marx about India, France, or Ireland—worthless or second-rate because they were foreigners?

The problem is that, just as countries seek independence while living in dependence or interdependence, so the realm of theories is both global and plural. Intellectual nationalism expresses an understandable resistance to outside domination and wholesale assimilation into a superficially global culture, but it also denies the reality of intellectual dependence and interdependence. The articulate anti-Westernism of Harvard, Oxford, and Michigan trained Third World intellectuals is bound to provoke quizzical glances. On the other hand, it is easy to sympathize with the outrage such intellectuals feel at the arrogance of foreign scholars who insist on the "correctness" of their categories and prescriptions for societies that have distinctive concepts of social organization and different moral and political priorities. In this respect, Wilfred Beckerman's sarcasm was appropriate when he wrote that "the best way to define underdeveloped areas, or rather peoples, is as people who do not think that their mission in life is to show other people how to develop."[14]

What are the implications of all this for "political economy" and for social science in general?

First, I suggest that an interest in culture and context is helpful to understanding the apparent paradox mentioned in chapter 5—namely, that theories which are intellectually unsophisticated, even crude, may nevertheless be more popular and, *in their basic conception*, more relevant than theories that are complex, elegant, and rigorous. Societies that are raw and polarized tend to be depicted analytically in suitably raw terms, connected by suitably simple and unequivocal logic. Crudity begets —indeed, requires—crudity: semantic complexity, like sophisticated weaponry, hinders rather than helps in the struggle to seize or hold power. What, for instance, would the leader of a Third World liberation movement extract in the way of rallying cries from the delectably complex analysis typical of European "university Marxism?" What slogans and tactical guidance could he glean, for example, from the following:

> The State is not "above civil society" even as an objective form channelling and structuring a fluid content of which it will be the objective reflection. To retain the approximating terms form and content, we will say that they do not correspond to each other simply in a reciprocal way which renders them interchangeable, but they are related within a "mediated" reciprocity through which the "form" marries its "content" and internally produces an active co-presence of "form" and "content." However, this active co-presence is at the same time a non-dialectic distance of the two terms only on the level of reality which forbids the identification of one with the other. What can be identified as form without substance is only the implicit tension of a negative latticework through which the exteriority of a process affects the content, stamping its positivity with a negative co-efficient

14. Wilfred Beckerman, "The Economist as a Modern Missionary," *The Economic Journal* 66 (March 1956): 108.

> affecting its structure and maintaining an apparent distance between itself and reality.[15]

In terms of types of political economy theory, there seem to be rough correlations, on the one hand, between a fairly advanced level of development and a preference for complex, usually interactive theory (of which the above is an extreme, even incomprehensible, example) and, on the other, between situations of underdevelopment and a preference for "stripped-down," deterministic theory of an instrumental kind. Such correlations confirm the value of examining the environments in which theorizing takes place, as well as the content of the theories.

Second, a recognition of the impact of cultural diversity implies skepticism toward theories that are closed and dogmatic. In particular, it suggests the need to resist claims to authority on the basis of superior "scientific" or "technical" credentials. Social theorists, especially those intoxicated by visions of global systems, have a tendency to assume the mantle of authority which, as Cropsey laments, rationalism removed from the moralists of pre-Enlightenment Europe. Explanation and an interest in social engineering have been intimately linked in the development of social science. Marxism represents an extreme case of the belief that possession of the tools of social science gives a superior right to judge what is in the interests of a society. Third World societies seem especially prone to revere the edicts of science and the judgments of the educated and in this way to enshrine explanation. To a great extent—as Saul Bellow's Mr. Sammler complained—being right has come to mean having the "correct explanation":

> You had to be a crank to insist on being right. Being right was a matter of explanations. Intellectual man had become an explaining creature. Fathers to children, wives to husbands, lecturers to listeners, experts to laymen, colleagues to colleagues, doctors to patients, man to his own soul, explained. The root of this, the causes of the other, the source of events, the history, the structure, the reasons why. For the

15. Jean-Claude Girardin, "On the Marxist Theory of the State," *Politics and Society* 4, no. 2 (Winter 1974): 211.

> most part, in one ear and out of the other. The soul wanted what it wanted. It had its own natural knowledge. It sat unhappily on superstructures of explanation, poor bird, not knowing which way to fly.[16]

Social science has advanced itself by suggesting ways in which explanatory power can be geared to changing the social environment. Like any other aspiring technology, it presents (limited) opportunities for ending misery and for increasing it. The particular danger is that of scientism, whether in the form of a Leninist elitism or technocratic developmentalism.

The point of this study is not to suggest an anti-intellectual or anti-theoretical conclusion. On the contrary, theories are important, and especially important when their influence is least acknowledged. But the importance of social theories (such as theories of political economy) arises from their function of crystallizing and articulating problems of general interest. Because such problems are perennial, claims to have "the" theory are invariably false, certainly arrogant, and possibly dangerous. In the present case, I set out to question a fad, and I have concluded that a real and perennial problem, that of the relationship between politics and economics, lies behind it. The point of the study, then, is to assert both the inevitability of theories and the consequent, imperative need for criticism that evaluates them, if necessary dethrones them, and in general keeps theorists honest, modest, and intellectually accountable.

16. Saul Bellow, *Mr. Sammler's Planet* (Harmondsworth: Penguin, 1971), 5.

|| REFERENCES

Ake, Claude. "Explanatory Notes on the Political Economy of Africa." *Journal of Modern African Studies* 14, no. 1 (March 1976): 1–23.

Alavi, Hamza. "India and the Colonial Mode of Production." In *The Socialist Register 1975*, edited by Ralph Miliband and John Saville, pp. 160–97. London: Merlin Press, 1975.

Albert, H. "The Neglect of Sociology in Economic Science." In *Power in Economics*, edited by K. W. Rothschild, pp. 21–35. Harmondsworth: Penguin, 1971.

Almond, Gabriel. "Political Theory and Political Science." *American Political Science Review* 60, no. 4 (December 1966): 869–79.

Amin, Samir. *Le Développement du capitalisme en Côte-d'Ivoire.* Paris: Editions de Minuit, 1967.

Amsden, Alice H. "Taiwan's Economic History: A Case of Etatisme and a Challenge to Dependency Theory." *Modern China* 5, no. 3 (July 1979): 341–80.

———. "The State and Taiwan's Economic Development." Unpublished paper.

Anderson, William. "Political Science, Economics and Public Policy." *American Economic Association. Papers and Proceedings* 34, no. 1 (March 1944): 77–85.

Ayres, Robert L. "Economic Stagnation and the Emergence of the Political Ideology of Chilean Underdevelopment." *World Politics* 25, no. 1 (January 1972): 34–61.

Ball, Nicole. "Understanding the Causes of African Famine." *Journal of Modern African Studies* 14, no. 3 (September 1976): 517–22.

Baran, Paul, and Sweezy, Paul. *Monopoly Capital: An Essay on the American Economic and Social Order.* New York: Monthly Review Press, 1966.

Barratt Brown, Michael. *The Economics of Imperialism.* Harmondsworth: Penguin, 1974.

Barrett, R. E., and Whyte, M. K. "Dependency Theory and Taiwan: Analysis of a Deviant Case." *American Journal of Sociology* 87, no. 5 (March 1982): 1064–89.

Barry, Brian. *Sociologists, Economists and Democracy.* Chicago: University of Chicago Press, 1978.

Bates, Robert H. *Markets and States in Tropical Africa: The Political Basis of Agricultural Policies.* Berkeley: University of California Press, 1981.

Bath, C. Richard, and James, Dilmus D. "Dependency Analysis of Latin America: Some Criticisms, Some Suggestions." *Latin American Research Review* 11, no. 3 (1976): 3–54.

Baumgartner, T., and Burns, T. R. "The Structuring of International Economic Relations." *International Studies Quarterly* 19 (June 1975): 126–59.

Bayart, J.-F. "Régime de parti unique et systèmes d'inégalité et de domination au Cameroun: Esquisse." *Cahiers d'Etudes Africaines* 18, nos. 69–72 (1978): 5–35.

———. *L'Etat au Cameroun.* Paris: Presses de la Fondation Nationale des Sciences Politiques, 1979.

Beckerman, Wilfred. "The Economist as a Modern Missionary." *The Economic Journal* 66 (March 1956): 108–15.

Beckman, Björn. "Imperialism and the 'National Bourgeoisie.'" *Review of African Political Economy* 22 (October-December 1981): 5–19.

Bellow, Saul. *Mr. Sammler's Planet.* Harmondsworth: Penguin, 1971.

Bennett, Douglas C., and Sharpe, Kenneth E. "Capitalism, Bureaucratic Authoritarianism, and Prospects for Democracy in the United States." *International Organization* 36, no. 3 (Summer 1982): 633–63.

Bentley, Arthur F. *The Process of Government.* Edited by Peter H. Odegard. Cambridge, Mass.: The Belknap Press of Harvard University Press, 1967.

Biersteker, Thomas J. *Distortion or Development? Contending Perspectives on the Multinational Corporation.* Cambridge, Mass.: MIT Press, 1978.

Black, Duncan. "The Unity of Political and Economic Science." *Economic Journal* 60 (September 1950): 506–14.

Blaug, Mark. "Kuhn versus Lakatos, or Paradigms versus Research Programmes in the History of Economics." *History of Political Economy* 7, no. 7 (Winter 1975): 399–433.

Blumer, Herbert. "Industrialization and Race Relations." In *Industrialization and Race Relations: A Symposium*, edited by Guy Hunter, pp.

220–253. London: Institute of Race Relations/Oxford University Press, 1965.

Bornschier, Volker; Chase-Dunn, Christopher; and Rubinson, Richard. "Cross-national Evidence of the Effects of Foreign Investment and Aid on Economic Growth and Inequality: A Survey of Findings and a Re-analysis." *American Journal of Sociology* 84, no. 3 (November 1978): 651–83.

Boulding, Kenneth. "The Legitimacy of Economics." In *The Political Economy of Development: Theoretical and Empirical Contributions*, edited by Norman T. Uphoff and Warren F. Ilchman, pp. 24–30. Berkeley: University of California Press, 1972.

Brenner, Robert. "The Origins of Capitalist Development: A Critique of Neo-Smithian Marxism." *New Left Review* 104 (July 1977): 25–92.

Bridges, Amy Beth. "Nicos Poulantzas and the Marxist Theory of the State." *Politics and Society* 4 (Winter 1974): 161–90.

Browett, John. "Out of the Dependency Perspectives." *Journal of Contemporary Asia* 12, no. 2 (1982): 145–57.

Brown, Christopher. "International Political Economy: Some Problems of an Inter-Disciplinary Enterprise." *International Affairs* 49, no. 1 (January 1973): 51–60.

Buchanan, James M. *What Should Economists Do?* Indianapolis: Liberty Press, 1979.

———, and Tullock, Gordon. *The Calculus of Consent: Logical Foundations of Constitutional Democracy*. Ann Arbor: University of Michigan Press, 1962.

Campbell, Bonnie. "The Ivory Coast." In *West African States: Failure and Promise*, edited by John Dunn, pp. 66–116. Cambridge: Cambridge University Press, 1978.

Caporaso, James A. "Pathways between Economics and Politics: Possible Foundations for the Study of Global Political Economy." Paper presented at the annual meeting of the American Political Science Association, Chicago, 1–4 September 1983.

Cardoso, Fernando H. "Dependency and Development in Latin America." *New Left Review* 74 (July/August 1972): 83–95.

———. "Associated-Dependent Development: Theoretical and Practical Implications." In *Authoritarian Brazil*, edited by Alfred Stepan, pp. 142–76. New Haven: Yale University Press, 1973.

———. "The Consumption of Dependency Theory in the United States." *Latin American Research Review* 12, no. 3 (1977): 7–24.

———. "The Originality of the Copy: The Economic Commission for

Latin America and the Idea of Development." In *Toward a New Strategy for Development*, pp. 53–72. A Rothko Chapel Colloquium. New York: Pergamon Press, 1979.

———, and Faletto, Enzo. *Dependency and Development in Latin America.* Berkeley: University of California Press, 1979.

Carr, E. H. *The Twenty Years Crisis, 1919–1939*. New York: Harper & Row, 1964.

Cawson, Alan. "Pluralism, Corporatism and the Role of the State." *Government and Opposition* 13, no. 2 (Spring 1978): 178–98.

Chalmers, Douglas. "The Politicized State in Latin America." In *Authoritarianism and Corporatism in Latin America*, edited by James M. Malloy, pp. 23–45. Pittsburgh: University of Pittsburgh Press, 1977.

Chase-Dunn, Christopher. "The Effects of International Economic Dependence on Development and Inequality: A Cross-National Study." *American Sociological Review* 40, no. 6 (December 1975): 720–38.

———. "Socialist States in the Capitalist World-Economy." *Social Problems* 27, no. 5 (June 1980): 505–25.

———. "A World-System Perspective on *Dependency and Development in Latin America*." *Latin American Research Review* 17, no. 1 (1982): 166–71.

Chattopadhyay, Paresh. "Political Economy: What's in a Name?" *Monthly Review* 25 (April 1974): 23–33.

Chenery, Hollis. "Economic Development." In *Economics*, edited by Nancy D. Ruggles, pp. 152–62. Englewood Cliffs, N.J.: Prentice-Hall, 1970.

Chilcote, Ronald H., ed. *Dependency and Marxism: Toward a Resolution of the Debate*. Latin American Perspectives Series no. 1. Boulder, Colo.: Westview Press, 1982.

Choucri, Nazli. "International Political Economy: A Theoretical Perspective." In *Change in the International System*, edited by Ole R. Holsti, Randolph Siverson, and Alexander L. George, pp. 103–29. Boulder, Colo.: Westview Press, 1980.

Clark, J. M. "Educational Functions of Economics after the War." *American Economic Association. Papers and Proceedings* 34, no. 1 (March 1944): 58–67.

———. *Economic Institutions and Human Welfare.* New York: Alfred A. Knopf, 1957.

Coats, A. W. "The Politics of Political Economists: Comment." *Quarterly Journal of Economics* 7, no. 4 (November 1960): 666–69.

Cohen, Dennis L. "Class and the Analysis of African Politics: Problems and Prospects." In *The Political Economy of Africa: Selected Readings*, edited by Dennis L. Cohen and John Daniel, pp. 85–111. London: Longman, 1981.

Cohen, Michael A. *Urban Policy and Political Conflict in Africa: A Study of the Ivory Coast.* Chicago: University of Chicago Press, 1974.

Cohen, Robin. "Class in Africa: Analytical Problems and Perspectives." In *The Socialist Register 1972.*, edited by Ralph Miliband and John Saville, pp. 231–55. London: Merlin Press, 1972.

Cohn, Helen Desfosses. *Soviet Policy toward Black Africa: The Focus on National Integration.* New York: Praeger, 1972.

Collier, David, ed. *The New Authoritarianism in Latin America.* Princeton, N.J.: Princeton University Press, 1979.

Cropsey, Joseph. "On the Relation of Political Science and Economics." *American Political Science Review* 54, no. 1 (March 1960): 3–14.

Dalby, David. "Drought in Sudanic Africa: The Implications for the Future." *Round Table* 253 (January 1974): 57–64.

Dalton, George. "History, Politics and Economic Development in Liberia." *Journal of Economic History* 25, no. 4 (December 1965): 569–91.

Dansoko, A., and Lerumo, A. "Famine in Africa: Is It Drought Alone?" *World Marxist Review* 17, no. 1 (January 1974): 127–30.

deVroey, Michel. "The Transition from Classical to Neoclassical Economics: A Scientific Revolution." *Journal of Economic Issues* 9, no. 3 (September 1975): 415–40.

Diesing, Paul. *Science and Ideology in the Social Sciences.* New York: Aldine Publishing Co., 1982.

Dos Santos, Theotonio. "The Structure of Dependence." In *The Political Economy of Development and Underdevelopment,* edited by C. K. Wilber, pp. 109–17. New York: Random House, 1973.

Downs, Anthony. *An Economic Theory of Democracy.* New York: Harper & Row, 1957.

Drucker, Peter F. "Multinationals and Developing Countries: Myths and Realities." *Foreign Policy* 53, no. 1 (October 1974): 121–34.

East, Maurice A. "The Organizational Impact of Interdependence on Foreign Policy-Making: The Case of Norway." In *The Political Economy of Foreign Policy Behavior,* edited by Charles W. Kegley, Jr., and Pat McGowan, pp. 137–61. Sage International Yearbook of Foreign Policy Studies, vol. 6. Beverly Hills, Calif.: Sage Publications, 1981.

Elliott, John E. "Institutionalism as an Approach to Political Economy." *Journal of Economic Issues* 12, no. 1 (March 1978): 91–114.

Engels, Friedrich. *Herr Eugen Dühring's Revolution in Science.* New York: International Publishers, 1939.

———. *The Role of Force in History: A Study of Bismarck's Policy of Blood and Iron.* Edited by Ernst Wangermann. New York: International Publishers, 1968.

Euben, J. Peter. "Political Science and Political Silence." In *Power and Community*, edited by Philip Green and Sanford Levinson, pp. 3–58. New York: Random House, 1969.

Eulau, Heinz. *The Behavioral Persuasion in Politics.* New York: Random House, 1963.

Evans, Peter. *Dependent Development: The Alliance of Multinational, State, and Local Development in Brazil.* Princeton, N.J.: Princeton University Press, 1979.

Fauré, Y.-A., and Médard, J.-F., eds. *Etat et Bourgeoisie en Côte-d'Ivoire.* Paris: Editions Karthala, 1982.

Fei, John C. H.; Ranis, Gustav; and Kuo, Shirley W. Y. *Growth with Equity: The Taiwan Case.* New York: Oxford University Press for the World Bank, 1979.

Fitch, Bob, and Oppenheimer, Mary. *Ghana: End of an Illusion.* New York: Monthly Review Press, 1966.

Fitzgerald, Frank T. "Sociologies of Development." *Journal of Contemporary Asia* 11, no. 1 (1981): 5–18.

Foster-Carter, Aidan. "Neo-Marxist Approaches to Development and Underdevelopment." In *Sociology and Development*, pp. 67–105, edited by Emanuel de Kadt and Gavin Williams. London: Tavistock, 1974.

Frank, André Gunder. *Capitalism and Underdevelopment in Latin America: Historical Studies of Chile and Brazil.* New York: Monthly Review Press, 1967.

Freund, Julien. *The Sociology of Max Weber.* New York: Pantheon Books, 1968.

von Freyhold, Michaela. "The Post-Colonial State and Its Tanzanian Version." *Review of African Political Economy* 8 (January-April 1977): 75–89.

Friedman, Milton. *Essays in Positive Economics.* Chicago: University of Chicago Press, 1953.

Galbraith, John Kenneth. "Power and the Useful Economist." *American Economic Review* 63, no. 1 (March 1973): 1–11.

Gastellu, J.-M., and Affou Yabi, S. "Un Mythe à décomposer: La 'bourgeoisie de planteurs.'" In *Etat et Bourgeoisie en Côte-d'Ivoire*, edited by Y.-A. Fauré and J.-F. Médard, pp. 144–79. Paris: Editions Karthala, 1982.

Giddens, Anthony. *Politics and Sociology in the Thought of Max Weber.* London: Macmillan, 1972.

———. *The Class Structure of the Advanced Societies.* London: Hutchinson, 1973.

Gilpin, Robert. *U.S. Power and the Multinational Corporation: The Political Economy of Foreign Direct Investment.* New York: Basic Books, 1975.

———. *War and Change in International Politics.* Cambridge: Cambridge University Press, 1981.

Girardin, Jean-Claude. "On the Marxist Theory of the State." *Politics and Society* 4, no. 2 (Winter 1974): 193–223.

Glantz, Michael H. "The Sahelian Drought: No Victory for Anyone." *Africa Today* 22, no. 2 (April–June 1975): 57–61.

Gold, David A.; Lo, Clarence Y. H.; and Wright, Erik Olin. "Recent Developments in Marxist Theories of the Capitalist State." *Monthly Review* 27, no. 5 (October 1975): 29–43; and no. 6 (November 1975): 36–51.

Gourevitch, Peter. "The International System and Regime Formation: A Critical Review of Anderson and Wallerstein." *Comparative Politics* 10, no. 3 (April 1978): 419–38.

———. "The Second Image Reversed: The International Sources of Domestic Politics." *International Organization* 32, no. 4 (Autumn 1978): 881–911.

Graham, Frank D. "Discussion." *American Economic Association. Papers and Proceedings* 34, no. 1 (March 1944): 55–57.

Grieco, Joseph M. "Between Dependency and Autonomy: India's Experience with the International Computer Industry." *International Organization* 36, no. 3 (Summer 1982): 609–32.

Grove, A. T. "Desertification in the African Environment." *African Affairs* 73, no. 291 (April 1974): 137–51.

Gruchy, Allan G. "Law, Politics, and Institutional Economics." *Journal of Economic Issues* 7, no. 4 (December 1973): 623–43.

Gurley, John. "The State of Political Economics." *American Economic Review* 61, no. 2 (May 1971): 53–62.

Haas, Ernst B. "Why Collaborate? Issue-Linkage and International Regimes." *World Politics* 32, no. 3 (April 1980): 357–405.

Hagen, Everett E. "Turning Parameters into Variables in the Theory of Economic Growth." *American Economic Review. Papers and Proceedings* 50, no. 2 (May 1960): 623–28, 654–56.

Haggard, Stephan, and Cheng, Tun-jen. "State Strategies: Local and Foreign Capital in the Gang of Four." Paper presented at the annual meeting of the American Political Science Association, Chicago, 1–4 September 1983.

Hecht, Robert M. "The Ivory Coast Economic 'Miracle': What Benefits for Peasant Farmers?" *Journal of Modern African Studies* 21, no. 1 (March 1983): 25–53.

Heckscher, Eli F. *Mercantilism.*. 2d ed. 2 vols. London: George Allen and Unwin, 1955.

Heilbroner, Robert. "On the Possibility of a Political Economics." *Journal of Economic Issues* 4, no. 4 (December 1970): 1–22.

Hirschman, Albert O. *A Bias for Hope: Essays on Development and Latin America.* New Haven: Yale University Press, 1971.

Holsti, K. J. "Change in the International System: Interdependence, Integration, and Fragmentation." In *Change in the International System,* edited by Ole R. Holsti, Randolph Siverson, and Alexander L. George, pp. 23–53. Boulder, Colo.: Westview Press, 1980.

Huntington, Samuel P. "Political Development and Political Decay." *World Politics* 17 (April 1965): 386–430.

———. *Political Order in Changing Societies.* New Haven: Yale University Press, 1968.

Hyden, Goran. *Beyond Ujamaa: Underdevelopment and an Uncaptured Peasantry.* Berkeley: University of California Press, 1980.

Jackson, Steven; Russett, Bruce; Snidal, Duncan; and Sylvan, David. "An Assessment of Empirical Research on *Dependencia.*" *Latin American Research Review* 14, no. 3 (1979): 7–29.

Jalladeau, Joel. "Restrained or Enlarged Scope of Political Economy? A Few Observations." *Journal of Economic Issues* 9, no. 1 (March 1975): 1–13.

Jeffries, Richard. "Political Radicalism in Africa: 'The Second Independence.'" *African Affairs* 77, no. 308 (July 1978): 335–46.

Johnson, Harry G. *International Economic Questions Facing Britain, the United States and Canada in the Seventies.* London: British-North American Research Association, June 1970.

Johnstone, Frederick A. "White Prosperity and White Supremacy in South Africa." *African Affairs* 69, no. 274 (April 1970): 124–40.

Jones, R. Barry. "International Political Economy: Perspectives and Prospects—Part II." *Review of International Studies* 8, no. 1 (January 1982): 39–52.

Kaufman, R. R.; Geller, D. S.; and Chernotsky, H. I. "A Preliminary Test of the Theory of Dependency." *Comparative Politics* 7, no. 3 (April 1975): 303–30.

Keohane, Robert O., and Nye, Joseph S., Jr. *Power and Interdependence: World Politics in Transition.* Boston: Little, Brown, 1977.

Keynes, John Maynard. *Essays in Persuasion.* London: Rupert Hart-Davis, 1952.

Kindleberger, Charles P. *Power and Money: The Politics of International Economics and the Economics of International Politics.* New York: Basic Books, 1970.

Klein, Philip A. "Confronting Power in Economics: A Pragmatic Evaluation." *Journal of Economic Issues* 14, no. 4 (December 1980): 871–96.

Knight, Frank. "Economics, Political Science, and Education." *American Economic Association. Papers and Proceedings* 34, no. 1 (March 1944): 68–76.

Krasner, Stephen D. "The Great Oil Sheikdown." *Froeign Policy* 13 (Winter 1973–74): 123–38.

———. *Defending the National Interest: Raw Materials, Investment and U.S. Foreign Policy.* Princeton, N.J.: Princeton University Press, 1978.

———. "Transforming International Regimes: What the Third World Wants and Why." *International Studies Quarterly* 25, no. 1 (March 1981): 119–48.

Laclau, Ernesto. "Feudalism and Capitalism in Latin America." *New Left Review* 67 (May-June 1971): 19–38.

Lall, Sanjaya. "Is 'Dependence' a Useful Concept in Analysing Underdevelopment?" *World Development* 3, nos. 11–12 (November/December 1975): 799–810.

Langdon, Steven. "The State and Capitalism in Kenya." *Review of African Political Economy* 8 (January-April 1977): 90–98.

Leaver, Richard. "The Debate on Underdevelopment: On Situating Gunder Frank." *Journal of Contemporary Asia* 7, no. 1 (1977): 108–15.

Leca, Jean. "Postface à J.-F. Bayart: Nuances." *Cahiers d'Etudes Africaines* 18: nos. 69–72 (1978): 38–44.

Legassick, Martin, and Innes, Duncan. "Capital Restructuring and Apartheid: A Critique of Constructive Engagement." *African Affairs* 76, no. 305 (October 1977): 437–82.

Lewis, W. Arthur. *The Evolution of the International Economic Order.* Princeton, N.J.: Princeton University Press, 1978.

Leys, Colin. *Underdevelopment in Kenya: The Political Economy of Neo-Colonialism.* London: Heinemann, 1975.

———. "Underdevelopment and Dependency: Critical Notes." *Journal of Contemporary Asia* 7, no. 1 (1977): 92–107.

———. "African Economic Development in Theory and Practice." *Daedalus* 3 (Spring 1982): 99–124.

Lieberson, Jonathan. "The Silent Majority." *New York Review of Books* 22 (October 1981): 34–37.

Lipton, Michael. "Interdisciplinary Studies in Less Developed Countries." *Journal of Development Studies* 7, no. 1 (October 1970): 5–18.

Lofchie, Michael F. "Political and Economic Origins of African Hunger." *Journal of Modern African Studies* 13, no. 4 (December 1975): 554–65.

Lonsdale, John. "The State and Social Processes in Africa." Paper presented to the Twenty-Fourth Annual Meeting of the African Studies Association, Bloomington, Ind., 21 October 1981.

McGowan, Patrick J. "Economic Dependence and Economic Performance in Black Africa." *Journal of Modern African Studies* 14, no. 1 (March 1976): 25–40.

MacRae, Duncan, Jr. "Normative Assumptions in the Study of Public Choice." *Public Choice* 16 (Fall 1973): 27–41.

Magubane, Bernard. "The Evolution of the Class Structure in Africa." In *The Political Economy of Contemporary Africa,* edited by Peter C. W. Gutkind and Immanuel Wallerstein, pp. 169–97. Beverly Hills, Calif.: Sage Publications, 1976.

Malloy, James M. "Authoritarianism and Corporatism in Latin America: The Modal Pattern." In *Authoritarianism and Corporatism in Latin America,* edited by James M. Malloy, pp. 3–19. Pittsburgh: University of Pittsburgh Press, 1977.

Martin, Robert. "The Use of State Power to Overcome Underdevelopment." *Journal of Modern African Studies* 18, no. 2 (June 1980): 315–25.

Marx, Karl. *Capital.* Edited by Friedrich Engels. New York: International Publishers, 1967.

———, and Engels, Friedrich. *Selected Works.* New York: International Publishers, 1968.

Meillassoux, Claude. "Development or Exploitation: Is the Sahel Famine Good Business?" *Review of African Political Economy* 1 (August-November 1974): 27–33.

Miliband, Ralph. *The State in Capitalist Society.* New York: Basic Books, 1969.

———. "Political Forms and Historical Materialism." In *The Socialist Register 1975,* edited by Ralph Miliband and John Saville, pp. 308–18. London: Merlin Press, 1975.

Mitchell, William C. "The Shape of Political Theory to Come: From Political Sociology to Political Economy." *American Behavioral Scientist* 11, no. 2 (November/December 1967): 8–20.

———. "The New Political Economy." *Social Research* 35, no. 1 (Spring 1968): 76–110.

Monson, Robert A. "Perspectives on Corporatist Approaches to Political Change in Latin America." *Plural Societies* 10, nos. 3–4 (Autumn/Winter 1974): 21–38.

Moore, Barrington, Jr. *Social Origins of Dictatorship and Democracy: Lord and Peasant in the Making of the Modern World.* Boston: Beacon Press, 1966.

Moran, Theodore. "Multinational Corporations and Dependency: A Dialogue for Dependentistas and Non-Dependentistas." *International Organization* 32, no. 1 (Winter 1978): 170–200.

Morse, Edward L. "Interdependence in World Affairs." In *World Politics: An Introduction,* edited by James N. Rosenau, Kenneth W. Thompson, and Gavin Boyd, pp. 660–81. New York: The Free Press, 1976.

Mueller, Dennis C. *Public Choice.* Cambridge: Cambridge University Press, 1979.

Murray, Roger. "Second Thoughts on Ghana." *New Left Review* 42 (March-April 1967): 25–39.

Myrdal, Gunnar. *The Political Element in the Development of Economic Theory.* New York: Simon and Schuster, 1954.

Nettl, J. P. "The State as a Conceptual Variable." *World Politics* 20, no. 4 (July 1968): 559–92.

Nordlinger, Eric A. *On the Autonomy of the Democratic State.* Cambridge, Mass.: Harvard University Press, 1981.

North, Douglass C. *Structure and Change in Economic History.* Cambridge: Cambridge University Press, 1981.

O'Brien, Philip. "A Critique of Latin American Theories of Dependency." In *Beyond the Sociology of Development: Economy and Society in Latin America and Africa,* edited by Ivar Oxaal, Tony Barnett, and David Booth, pp. 7–27. London: Routledge and Kegan Paul, 1975.

Odell, John S. *U.S. International Monetary Policy: Markets, Power and Ideas as Sources of Change.* Princeton, N.J.: Princeton University Press, 1982.

O'Donnell, Guillermo. *Modernization and Bureaucratic Authoritarianism: Studies in South American Politics.* Berkeley: Institute of International Studies, University of California, 1973.

———. "Corporatism and the Question of the State." In *Authoritarian-*

ism and Corporatism in Latin America, edited by James M. Malloy, pp. 47–87. Pittsburgh: University of Pittsburgh Press, 1977.

———. "Reflections on the Patterns of Change in the Bureaucratic Authoritarian State." *Latin American Research Review* 12 (Winter 1978): 3–38.

Ojha, Ishwer C. "The Kremlin and Third World Leadership: Closing the Circle." In *Soviet Policy in Developing Countries,* edited by W. Raymond Duncan, pp. 9–28. Waltham, Mass.: Ginn-Blaisdell, 1970.

Oliver, Henry. "Study of the Relationships between Economic and Political Systems." *Journal of Economic Issues* 7, no. 4 (December 1973): 543–51.

Olson, Mancur, Jr. *The Logic of Collective Action: Public Goods and the Theory of Groups.* Cambridge, Mass.: Harvard University Press, 1965.

———. "The Relationship between Economics and the Other Social Sciences: The Province of a 'Social Report.'" In *Politics and the Social Sciences,* edited by Seymour Martin Lipset, pp. 137–62. New York: Oxford University Press, 1969.

———. *The Rise and Decline of Nations: Economic Growth, Stagflation, and Social Rigidities.* New Haven: Yale University Press, 1982.

Oppenheimer, Joe A. "Small Steps Forward for Political Economy." *World Politics* 33, no. 1 (1980): 121–51.

Palma, Gabriel. "Dependency: A Formal Theory of Underdevelopment or a Methodology for the Analysis of Concrete Situations of Underdevelopment?" *World Development* 6, nos. 7–8 (July-August 1978): 881–924.

Papandreou, A. G. "Economics and the Social Sciences." *Economic Journal* 60 (December 1950): 715–23.

Parkin, Frank. *Marxism and Class Theory: A Bourgeois Critique.* London: Tavistock, 1979.

Popkin, Samuel L. *The Rational Peasant: The Political Economy of Rural Society in Vietnam.* Berkeley: University of California Press, 1979.

Poulantzas, Nicos. "The Problem of the Capitalist State." *New Left Review* 58 (November-December 1969): 67–78.

Prothero, R. Mansell. "Some Perspectives on Drought in North-West Nigeria." *African Affairs* 73, no. 291 (April 1974): 162–69.

Ray, David. "The Dependency Model of Latin American Underdevelopment: Three Basic Fallacies." *Journal of Interamerican Studies* 15, no. 1 (February 1973): 4–20.

Ray, James Lee. "Dependence, Political Compliance, and Economic Performance: Latin America and Eastern Europe." In *The Political Economy of Foreign Policy Behavior,* edited by Charles W. Kegley, Jr., and Pat McGowan, pp. 111–36. Sage International Yearbook of Foreign Policy Studies, vol. 6. Beverly Hills, Calif.: Sage Publications, 1981.

Rimmer, Douglas. "The Abstraction from Politics. A Critique of Economic Theory and Design with Reference to West Africa." *Journal of Development Studies* 5, no. 3 (April 1969): 190–204.

Robbins, Lionel. *An Essay on the Nature and Significance of Economic Science.* London: Macmillan, 1946. Reprint.

———. "Economics and Political Economy." *American Economic Review. Papers and Proceedings* 71, no. 2 (1981): 1–10.

Rogowski, Ronald. *Rational Legitimacy: A Theory of Political Support.* Princeton, N.J.: Princeton University Press, 1974.

———. "Rationalist Theories of Politics: A Midterm Report." *World Politics* 30, no. 2 (January 1978): 296–323.

———. "Structure, Growth, and Power: Three Rationalist Accounts." *International Organization* 37, no. 4 (Autumn 1983): 713–38.

Rothchild, Donald, and Curry, Robert L., Jr. *Scarcity, Choice, and Public Policy in Middle Africa.* Berkeley: University of California Press, 1978.

Rothschild, K. W., ed. *Power in Economics.* Harmondsworth: Penguin, 1971.

Roxborough, Ian. *Theories of Underdevelopment.* London: Macmillan Press, 1979.

Rubinson, Richard. "The World Economy and the Distribution of Income within States: A Cross-National Study." *American Sociological Review* 41, no. 4 (August 1976): 638–59.

Saul, John S. "The State in Post-Colonial Societies: Tanzania." In *The Socialist Register 1974,* edited by Ralph Miliband and John Saville, pp. 349–72. London: Merlin Press, 1974.

Schatten, Fritz. *Communism in Africa.* London: George Allen and Unwin, 1966.

Schatzberg, Michael. *Politics and Class in Zaire: Bureaucracy, Business and Beer in Lisala.* New York: Africana Publishing Co., 1980.

———. "The Emerging Trialectic: State, Class, and Ethnicity in Africa." Paper presented to the African State Colloquium, Institute of International Studies, University of California, Berkeley, 25 May 1982.

Schelling, Thomas. *The Strategy of Conflict.* Cambridge, Mass.: Harvard University Press, 1960.

Schmitter, Philippe. "Still the Century of Corporatism?" *Review of Politics* 36, no. 1 (January 1974): 85–131.

Schumpeter, Joseph A. *Capitalism, Socialism and Democracy.* London: George Allen and Unwin, 1954.

Schwartzman, Simon. "Back to Weber: Corporatism and Patrimonialism in the Seventies." In *Authoritarianism and Corporatism in Latin America,* edited by James M. Malloy, pp. 89–106. Pittsburgh: University of Pittsburgh Press, 1977.

Scott, James C. *The Moral Economy of the Peasant: Rebellion and Subsistence in Southeast Asia.* New Haven: Yale University Press, 1976.

Seers, Dudley. "A Step towards a Political Economy of Development: Illustrated by the Case of Trinidad/Tobago." *Social and Economic Studies* 18, no. 3 (September 1969): 217–53.

———. "Income Distribution and Employment. A Note on Some Issues Raised by the Colombia Report." *Bulletin of the Institute of Development Studies* (Brighton, England) 2, no. 4 (July 1970): 4–10.

Shivji, Issa G. "Peasants and Class Alliances." *Review of African Political Economy* 3 (May-October 1975): 10–18.

———. *Class Struggles in Tanzania.* New York: Monthly Review Press, 1976.

Sklar, Richard L. *Corporate Power in an African State: The Political Impact of Multinational Mining Companies in Zambia.* Berkeley: University of California Press, 1975.

———. "The Nature of Class Domination in Africa." *Journal of Modern African Studies* 17, no. 4 (December 1979): 531–52.

———. "On the Concept of Power in Political Economy." In *Toward a Humanistic Science of Politics: Essays in Honor of Francis Dunham Wormuth,* edited by Dalmas H. Nelson and Richard L. Sklar, pp. 179–206. Lanham, Md.: University Press of America, 1983.

Skocpol, Theda. "Wallerstein's World Capitalist System: A Theoretical and Historical Critique." *American Journal of Sociology* 82, no. 5 (March 1977): 1075–90.

———. *States and Revolutions.* Cambridge: Cambridge University Press, 1979.

Smith, Adam. *An Inquiry into the Nature and Causes of the Wealth of Nations.* Edited by Edwin Cannan. New York: The Modern Library, 1937.

Smith, Sheila. "Economic Dependence and Economic Empiricism in Black Africa." *Journal of Modern African Studies* 15, no. 1 (March 1977): 116–18.

———. "The Ideas of Samir Amin: Theory or Tautology?" *Journal of Development Studies* 17, no. 1 (October 1980): 5–21.

———. "Class Analysis versus World Systems: Critique of Samir Amin's Typology of Under-development." *Journal of Contemporary Asia* 12, no. 1 (1982): 7–18.

Smith, Tony. "The Underdevelopment of Development Literature:

The Case of Dependency Theory." *World Politics* 31, no. 2 (January 1979): 247–88.

Smith, Trevor. "Trends and Tendencies in Re-Ordering the Representation of Interests." Paper presented to the annual conference of the Political Studies Association, Nottingham, England, 22–24 March 1976.

Solo, Robert. "The Need for a Theory of the State." *Journal of Economic Issues* 11, no. 2 (June 1977): 379–85.

Spero, Joan E. *The Politics of International Economic Relations.* London: St. Martin's Press, 1977.

Stauffer, Robert B. "Philippine Corporatism: A Note on the 'New Society.'" *Asian Survey* 17, no. 4 (April 1977): 393–407.

Steele, Bruce. "ITOD's Expansion Covers Campus." *University Times* (University of Pittsburgh) 15, no. 10 (27 January 1983): 9.

Stehr, Uwe. "Unequal Development and Dependency Structures in Comecon." *Journal of Peace Research* 14, no. 2 (1977): 115–28.

Stepan, Alfred. *The State and Society: Peru in Comparative Perspective.* Princeton, N.J.: Princeton University Press, 1976.

Steuart, James. *An Inquiry into the Principles of Political Economy.* London, 1761. Reprint. New York: Augustus M. Kelley, 1967.

Stigler, George J. "The Politics of Political Economists." *Quarterly Journal of Economics* 73, no. 4 (November 1959): 522–32.

Strange, Susan. "International Economics and International Relations: A Case of Mutual Neglect." *International Affairs* 46, no. 2 (April 1970): 304–15.

———. "*Cave! hic dragones*: A Critique of Regime Analysis." *International Organization* 36, no. 2 (Spring 1982): 479–96.

Street, James H. "The Latin American 'Structuralists' and the Institutionalists: Convergence in Development Theory." *Journal of Economic Issues* 1, nos. 1–2 (June 1967): 44–62.

Sweezy, Paul M. *The Theory of Capitalist Development.* New York: Monthly Review Press, 1968.

Tabiso, Nga. "Revolution and Class Alliances." *Maji Maji* (Dar es Salaam) 12 (September 1973).

Taylor, John. "Neo-Marxism and Underdevelopment—A Sociological Phantasy." *Journal of Contemporary Asia* 4, no. 1 (1973): 5–23.

Taylor, O. H. "Economic Science Only—Or Political Economy?" *Quarterly Journal of Economics* 71, no. 1 (February 1957): 1–18.

Travis, Tom. "A Comparison of the Global Economic Imperialism of Five Metropoles." In *The Political Economy of Foreign Policy Behavior*, edited by Charles W. Kegley, Jr., and Pat McGowan, pp. 165–89.

Sage International Yearbook of Foreign Policy Studies, vol. 6. Beverly Hills, Calif.: Sage Publications, 1981.

Truman, David B. "Disillusion and Regeneration: The Quest for a Discipline." *American Political Science Review* 59, no. 4 (December 1965): 865–73.

Valenzuela, J. Samuel, and Valenzuela, Arturo. "Modernization and Dependency: Alternative Perspectives in the Study of Latin American Politics." *Comparative Politics* 10, no. 4 (July 1978): 535–57.

Vengroff, Richard. "Dependency, Development, and Inequality in Black Africa." *African Studies Review* 20, no. 2 (September 1977): 17–26.

———. "Dependency and Underdevelopment in Black Africa: An Empirical Test." *Journal of Modern African Studies* 15, no. 4 (December 1977): 613–30.

Vernon, Raymond. "The Power of Multinational Enterprises in Developing Countries." In *The Case for the Multinational Corporation,* edited by Carl Madden, pp. 151–83. New York: Praeger, 1975.

Wade, Nicholas. "The Sahelian Drought: No Victory for Western Aid." *Science* 185, no. 4147 (19 July 1974): 234–37.

Wallerstein, Immanuel. *The Modern World-System: Capitalist Agriculture and the Origins of the European World-Economy in the Sixteenth Century.* New York: Academic Press, 1974.

———. *The Capitalist World-Economy.* Cambridge and Paris: Cambridge University Press and Editions de la Maison des Sciences de l'Homme, 1979.

Warren, Bill. "Imperialism and Capitalist Industrialization." *New Left Review* 81 (September/October 1973): 3–44.

Weinstein, Franklin B. "Multinational Corporations and the Third World: The Case of Japan and Southeast Asia." *International Organization* 30, no. 3 (Summer 1976): 373–404.

Whitaker, C. S., Jr. "A Dysrhythmic Process of Political Change." *World Politics* 19, no. 2 (January 1967): 183–214.

Winch, D. M. "Political Economy and the Economic Polity." *Canadian Journal of Economics* 10, no. 4 (November 1977): 547–64.

Yoffie, David. "The Newly Industrializing Countries and the Political Economy of Protectionism." *International Studies Quarterly* 25, no. 4 (December 1981): 569–99.

———. *Power and Protectionism: Strategies of the Newly Industrializing Countries.* New York: Columbia University Press, 1983.

Young, Oran R. "International Regimes: Problems of Concept Formation." *World Politics* 32 (April 1980): 331–56.

Yudelman, David. "Industrialization, Race Relations and Change in South Africa." *African Affairs* 74, no. 294 (January 1975): 82–96.

Zimmerman, William. *Soviet Perspectives on International Relations, 1956–1967*. Princeton, N.J.: Princeton University Press, 1969.

———. "Dependency Theory and the Soviet–East European Hierarchical Regional System." In *The Foreign Policies of Eastern Europe: New Approaches*, edited by Ronald Linden, pp. 159–85. New York: Praeger, 1982.

Zweig, Michael. "New Left Critique of Economics." *Review of Radical Political Economics* 3, no. 2 (July 1971): 67–74.

INDEX